Missing, believed killed

Margaret Hayes

Editor: John Petley

Day One

© Day One Publications 2002
First printed 2002

Scripture quotations are from The Authorized Version unless otherwise stated

British Library Cataloguing in Publication Data available
ISBN 1 903087 32 5

Published by Day One Publications
3 Epsom Business Park, Kiln Lane, Epsom, Surrey KT17 1JF
☎ 01372 728 300 FAX 01372 722 400
email—sales@dayone.co.uk
www.dayone.co.uk

Day One wishes to thank David Simm and John Petley for their invaluable assistance
during the preparation of this revised edition

Designed by Steve Devane and printed by CPD

Contents

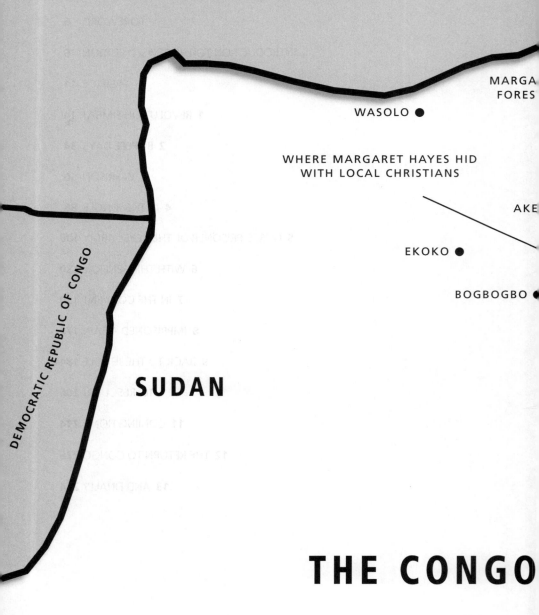

CENTRAL AFRICAN REPUBLIC

MARGA
FORES

WASOLO ●

WHERE MARGARET HAYES HID
WITH LOCAL CHRISTIANS

AKE

EKOKO ●

BOGBOGBO ●

DEMOCRATIC REPUBLIC OF CONGO

SUDAN

THE CONGO

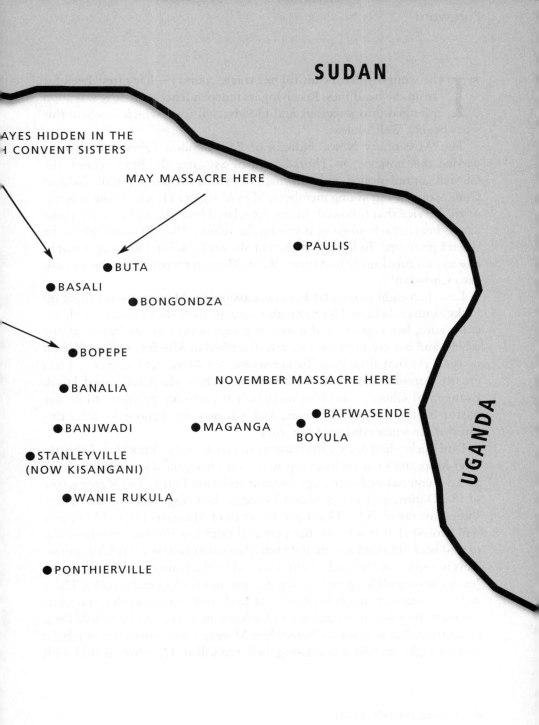

SUDAN

AYES HIDDEN IN THE
H CONVENT SISTERS

MAY MASSACRE HERE

●PAULIS

●BUTA

●BASALI

●BONGONDZA

●BOPEPE

NOVEMBER MASSACRE HERE

●BANALIA

●BAFWASENDE

●BANJWADI   ●MAGANGA   ●
                         BOYULA

●STANLEYVILLE
(NOW KISANGANI)

UGANDA

●WANIE RUKULA

●PONTHIERVILLE

The Congo—that beautiful but tragic country—has rarely been far from the headlines. Receiving its independence in 1960 it was soon plunged into a vicious and bloody civil war. Which is where this story begins. Well, almost.

The 'Missionary News' bulletin of East London Tabernacle in 1957 carried this notice: 'On Thursday, April 25, after the Bible school, the Church commissioned and sent forth to preach the Gospel in the Belgian Congo, one of our young members, Miss Margaret Hayes.' In the account of the service that followed, Margaret related how she had recently come across her first school essay. It was on the subject, 'What I would like to be when I grow up.' To her astonishment she read, 'When I grow up I would like to be a missionary in Africa'. When Margaret wrote that, she was not yet a Christian!

Less than eight years after her commissioning, Margaret was caught up in the Simba rebellion. Her miraculous escape from the massacre of all her colleagues, her capture and harrowing experiences at the hands of the rebels, and her eventual release, was described in *Missing, Believed Killed* in 1966. At that time Paul Tucker wrote, 'As Margaret's pastor... I feel greatly honoured to write the foreword.' When Margaret joined Hook Evangelical Church, Surbiton in 1975 it became my privilege to be her pastor for the next twenty years, and it is now *my* honour to write this foreword to a new edition of her story.

Paul Tucker had drawn attention to an article in the *Daily Sketch* shortly after Margaret's release from captivity which had linked her with 'the truly great'—comparing her to Captain Scott and Anne Frank. The *Sketch* wrote of the 'Darkness of savagery and hatred in the Congo' and added, 'There shines one ray of light. That ray is the faith of Margaret Hayes.' Margaret will protest that it was not her personal faith but the One in whom she placed her faith that brought light into the cruelty of those terrible months. This is a story of the God of miracles and of the reality of the presence of Jesus Christ with his people in the darkest nights of human cruelty. There were, of course, many other stories of faith and courage at that time, but her own story was outstanding, and it has long needed to be re-told for a generation that was not yet born when Margaret was a prisoner of rebels, and for eight months was missing, believed killed. Her story is told with

Above: Margaret Hayes MBE

simple sincerity and with honesty and humour. Few will read it without both tears and smiles.

Margaret's closing chapter is called 'And Finally'. But it wasn't. Her unquenchable love for Africa and its people, and her readiness to serve the Lord anywhere, meant that she was soon back on that great continent. Margaret not only returned to work in the country of her captivity, but later served her Lord in Niger as a Sister Midwife in a remote hospital on the edge of the Sahara Desert. She well deserved the Queen's honour in 1987 by the award of the Member of the Order of the British Empire 'for nursing and welfare service in Niger'.

But Her Majesty knew only a little of Margaret's true service, character and strengths. Her warm-hearted and straightforward faith in Christ, her sound and practical common sense, her mischievous sense of humour, her ability to face hardship and danger, and her humble and devoted service for all who needed her help, are only a few of the reasons why a new generation should know her story.

To her local church in England and to the wider church in Africa Margaret has always been – and still is – much more than her childhood wish, just 'a missionary'. She is an example of Christian character and selfless service, and she is a true friend. There is so much more that Margaret could tell us. Her long service in the Congo and in Niger has provided her with rich experiences that would be of inestimable value for today's new soldiers of the cross. So, Margaret, we wait impatiently for the sequel!

Brian H Edwards
Surbiton, June 2002

Introduction to the revised edition

When I first wrote my story in the 1960s the background to the events described was very topical and frequently in the news, but now forty years on, many readers will know little of the radical change that was taking place throughout much of the continent of Africa at that time.

The late 1950s was the period when many of the colonial governments were preparing to grant independence to the countries they had governed for many years. In some countries, nationals were being trained to take over the reins of Government, but in the Belgian Congo little changed. It remained a white-dominated colonial country. However, as the people heard news from other parts of the continent, they became restless, and demanded independence too. Riots occurred in the capital Leopoldville, and the government began to lose control over two important areas, namely the economy and the military.

In January 1960, Belgium finally agreed to the demand for independence, but gave no opportunity for any nationals to gain the necessary experience to rule the country; in fact there were only twelve university graduates in the whole land!

In the rural areas where I worked, there was much talk about 'Independence', although few people really knew what it meant. Their concept of independence simply meant money, power and no need to work.

National and provincial elections were held in the spring of 1960; but no single party gained an overall majority in the national assembly. The largest number of seats, 47 out of a total of 137, was won by a party headed by Patrice Lumumba, a man who had formerly been convicted on a charge of embezzlement.

A provisional constitution was drawn up, with both a president and a prime minister. Joseph Kasavubu became president, with Lumumba as prime minister. This uneasy alliance came to an abrupt end when Lumumba was assassinated.   ▷

Independence Day finally dawned on June 30th 1960, but only five days later the army mutinied, which led to the immediate departure of the top European civil servants who had stayed behind to help with the transition of power. Then two provinces seceded and thereby deprived the new government of most of its revenue.

In many areas there were ugly scenes in some of the plantations and many of the planters went home. The embassies ordered all their nationals to return home, and this order was ratified by our field leaders. We therefore immediately had to leave our bewildered national friends, colleagues and employees to carry on the work by themselves. During our journey to the airport our car was stoned, and generally the population was very hostile as we travelled.

When we returned, we came back to a shattered economy, rapidly deteriorating dirt roads and neglected plantations. The schools were staffed with unqualified teachers while the colleges and universities were told they were not allowed to fail any student even though the pass mark was set at 70%, much to the despair of the expatriate professors.

Between April and August 1964 a rebel army was formed, which then seized power in the North East of the country where my mission, the Unevangelised Fields Mission, or UFM for short, was based. On September 5th 1964 Christophe Gbenye proclaimed himself head of a revolutionary government in Stanleyville.

Moïse Tshombe, who had replaced the assassinated Lumumba as Prime-Minister, recruited about a hundred white mercenaries to help the Congolese National Army regain control of the area. It was to be a long and difficult campaign, even though the rebels were untrained and poorly organised. They were still holding out in some areas when I was flown home the following June.

Such, then, is the background to the events recorded in this book.

Margaret Hayes
Surbiton, Surrey, June 2002

Preface to the revised edition

Writing such a book as this has not been easy, as I have had to re-live the trauma of my experiences during the terrible days of the Congolese Simba revolution of 1964. However, many years on— not only from the events described, but also from my first attempt to give an account of them, I can see how God sustained me in a remarkable way and even cushioned me emotionally through it all. I remain more convinced than ever that our sovereign God is in control of events and though we do not, may not, indeed cannot understand why he allows such things to happen, ultimately all things do indeed work out for his own good purposes.

In the opening chapter, which covers the first month of the revolution, I have tried to set the scene by focussing on events in the particular corner of the UFM field in Congo in which I worked alongside other missionary colleagues. The rest of the book consists essentially of my own memories. With normal channels of communication broken down, I was unable to find out much about my colleagues apart from a few letters smuggled in by friends. For a while, I was imprisoned with others who were able to give me their account of events up to the point of their arrest, but these too came to an abrupt end as you will read.

Many people have asked how I felt being the only person to escape the massacre at Banalia. The answer is that for years I felt very guilty, and carried that guilt with me, but now that pain has gone, and I can only marvel with humility at the grace and mercy God has shown me over these years.

In 1969, I returned to Congo for another term on the mission field and, together with Miss Olive McCarten and other missionaries who had been caught up in the rebellion, we travelled over our old mission area. Olive kept a record of these early weeks in letter form, and I am so grateful to her for selecting items from these letters and with the permission of her late mother Mrs Eleanor Ward and her friend Miss Sheila Murby, I have been able to piece together the events of those first six or seven weeks.

Preface

My thanks also to Mrs Helen Brett for typing the manuscript and putting it all on disc; to Rev. Brian Edwards for consenting to write the foreword; to Mr John Roberts for his persistent encouragement; and finally to the many who have upheld me with loving prayer support at this time.

The problems in the Congo are ongoing, and we need to be much in prayer for the suffering church in that land.

Yours in sacred bonds,

Margaret Hayes

Revolution Simba!

Bopepe was a unique place to live, as all the adults who lived there were committed Christians. Situated in the jungle of northeast Congo, not far from the equator, it was hot and steamy with lush vegetation and trees. It was also very peaceful. In the village we had a small boarding school, a very busy dispensary and maternity unit and a large brick-built church.

July 1964 was a busy month for us at Bopepe, for in addition to our normal activities, we were preparing for a conference of our church leaders—both nationals and missionaries. At the time none of us envisaged that our corner of Congo would be plunged into a bloody revolution within three weeks.

Having said this, Pastor Asani—one of identical twin brothers who were both pastors—did have a premonition of a terrible time coming. He often talked to us about the unrest in Congo, and said he had dreamt that a time was approaching in which we would witness terrible things and much bloodshed. In fact, he did not really want the conference to be held at all, as it would mean a large number of people being together in one place. Although he was the senior pastor of Unevangelised Fields Mission and president of the Congo Protestant Council, his objections were overruled.

All the travel permits came through in time, and we were even promised a goat to eat by the local chief—although he later changed his mind. The first day of the conference duly dawned, and a good number both of Congolese and missionaries made their way to Bopepe from every one of our stations. It was a wonderful time of fellowship and making new friends. Our little house was packed; in fact I think most homes in Bopepe were bursting at the seams.

Each station was equipped with a transceiver—a radio on which we could contact each other on a fixed wavelength at a pre-arranged time each day. It was amusing to watch the behaviour of our men folk. On the one hand, they were trying to appear so terribly independent away from their wives, but on the other, they crowded into our little office so they could talk to them at their respective stations, and there would be a gleam of

Pictured above left
Margaret Hayes aged 34

Above right
Mary Baker

Pictured left
*Pastor Asani—one of
identical twin brothers who
were both pastors—often
talked to us about the unrest
in Congo, and said he had
dreamt that a time was
approaching in which we
would witness terrible things*

satisfaction and relief on their faces when all was reported well. It was a happy week; we ate together for every meal, mostly African food prepared by the ladies of Bopepe and nearby villages.

Looking back, it stands out to me as a very precious time spent with others of like faith. It was to be the last time we would all meet in that way again, and for some it was the last conference they were ever to attend.

The week culminated in a very solemn but challenging service. Bob McAllister from Northern Ireland preached on 'If it be possible let this cup pass from me, nevertheless not as I will but as Thou wilt.' I do not think any of us came away from that service without being moved by the stirring and soul-searching message we had heard.

The aim of the conference had been to plan the way forward for various aspects of the work, both in the immediate future and longer term. Once the week was over, everyone left and went their various ways, some on vacation, others back to their stations, hoping to put these ideas into practise. God, however, had other plans.

At Bopepe our stores were understandably depleted and a trip to Stanleyville (now called Kisangani) ninety-two miles away, would be needed very soon. Owing to the pressure of work over the previous two years I was very tired, and reluctantly agreed with Mary Baker, my senior missionary co-worker, that I needed to get right away for a rest. So we decided that I should leave on August 1st for a month at our mission station of Banjwade, which was on the road to Stanleyville about forty miles from the city. While there I could go into town at some stage and stock up with supplies.

It was further arranged that Mary would come down during the third week, pick up her new Volkswagen Camionette, which was due from Belgium in August, and then drive me and the shopping back to Bopepe on August 30th.

As a mission with a medical ministry, we were perpetually short of nurses, and with vacation time many stations were having to close down their dispensaries and maternity units. Although this decision caused much soul-searching, there was no alternative as there were simply no spare nurses to relieve us. I often thought of the many Christian nurses at home and wished that some would come out and help us. Surely they too would find it a rich and satisfying ministry.

In such circumstances, I was naturally reluctant to be away from Bopepe for a whole month. However, the day for my departure soon arrived, and I completed the final preparation to hand over to Mary, leaving her with a well-equipped first-aid box and instructions on how and when to give various pills. We knew patients would still come hoping to find someone to meet their needs. We also arranged to be in radio contact every day in case anything alarming happened.

I had hoped to have a lift to Banjwade by car, but this fell through, so it was decided I should go on the bus, which passed our village twice a week. As usual, it was late, and I decided that if it did not turn up by 5.30pm, it would be a sign that the Lord did not want me to go. The bus had to take the ferry across the river at Banalia, thirty minutes away, which closed down every evening at 6.30pm when it got dark. Anyway, it came at 5.25pm precisely and practically the entire village came to see me off. The bus was a boneshaker if ever there was one, and the driver, who was well known to us, must have thought he was a pilot flying a jet aircraft judging by the way he drove! We covered the fifteen miles to Banalia in twenty minutes; very fast for a large bus full with a laden trailer behind, especially considering that the roads in Congo are full of large pot-holes.

There were other vehicles there when we arrived so we had to take our place in the queue. The ferry took them over one at a time, but when it was our turn darkness had fallen and they refused to come back for us. They said it was 6.30pm and work was through for the day. The Africans travelling with me accepted the overnight delay with patient resignation. I was not so patient, and eventually found two men who were willing to take me over in their canoe—for a fee of course. On landing I made my way to the Government doctor's house. He was a Belgian and a friend of ours who frequently visited us with his delightful wife and children, so we always called in whenever we found ourselves that side of the river in Banalia.

They were very hospitable and housed me that night. The nine o'clock news from France did not mention Congo at all, but the BBC at ten o'clock told of various trouble spots, which were springing up throughout our North East Province. We talked about the possibility of any trouble coming our way, but could only speculate as to what might happen.

On Sunday morning the bus eventually crossed the river on the ferry and

Pictured above and right
The Sharpe family.
Ian Sharpe and his wife
Audrey had been friends of
Margaret's since their days
at the same hospital and
church in London. They had
also studied together in
Belgium

once more I was on my way. The driver sang excerpts from the Requiem Mass all the way. He had a beautiful tenor voice but in view of my conversation with the doctor the previous evening, it was hardly a comforting theme song as the bus and trailer bounced along at an incredibly hair-raising speed. It was impossible to hear anyone speak above the singing of the driver and din of the rattling bus, so I was more than glad when we arrived at my destination at midday. Most of my fellow travellers were well-dressed young men carrying briefcases. I often wondered what happened to them subsequently, as they were all bound for Stanleyville.

On arrival at Banjwade, I made my way past the church which was not only packed inside but had a crowd standing outside each window and doorway. Had I arrived the evening before I would have been part of the congregation but, although I felt rather guilty, I soothed my nagging conscience firstly by blaming the ferry and secondly by reflecting I had arrived at midday hot, sticky and dusty.

It was wonderful to meet up again with Doctor Ian Sharpe and his wife Audrey, with whom I had been friends since our days in the same hospital and church in London. We had also studied together in Belgium. With them was Ruby Gray, an Irish nurse who worked with the Sharpes at Bongondza station, and a missionary family, Chuck and Muriel Davis with their two children who had only arrived a week ago. Chuck was going to teach in the Seminary at Banjwade. They had come to Congo three months ago from the United States.

The only permanent residents of Banjwade at this time were David Grant and his nurse-wife Sonia from Canada. They had only arrived back from furlough (now called Home Assignment) the month before and were living in the house of our American seminary director, Marshall Southard, who was in Leopoldville (now Kinshasa) attending a conference. His wife Thelma and five year old son Larry were, we hoped, en route to Banjwade after a vacation in Kenya. They were due on August 5th. Also absent were the Muchmore family, who had just gone home to America on furlough the previous Friday, the Artons from England, who were away up country to meet their daughter Heather, a teenager who was coming out for her summer vacation from school, and finally, the Morris family, who were home in England on a month's vacation paid for by the Congolese government's education department.

This was the situation when I arrived on what seemed to us a perfectly normal Sunday morning. War was far from our minds; yet although we were unaware of it at the time, it had already affected two of our mission stations.

The Grants extended the already large table, and somehow in the evening, we all managed to sit round it—the five Sharpes, four Davis's, two Grants, Ruby Gray and myself. Four nationalities were represented: American, Canadian, English and Irish.

After the meal, we gathered for a service. Ian Sharpe played the little organ, and Chuck Davis gave us a message from the Word of God. It seemed a perfectly normal, happy Congo Sunday, but it was the last we were to experience.

The following morning, the Sharpes and Ruby Gray left for Bongondza, which was a medical station with a hospital and about two or three hours' drive further on from Bopepe. Arrangements were made to follow their progress over the radio, as we expected them to be at Bopepe by midday. All stations made radio contact with each other every day at noon, except on Sundays.

Midday came, and when we tuned into our Headquarters at Stanleyville, we heard our field-leader, Al Larson, say that our station at Wanie Rukula, forty miles the other side of Stanleyville, had been off the air since Saturday, and they were very worried by news of rebel advances in that area. It was decided to call all the stations again at 4pm. In the meantime we would pray. At 4pm there was still no news, and reports coming in to Stanleyville were not very reassuring. We were told to have a bag packed in case we had to be evacuated out of the area.

That night as we met for prayer before going to bed, David read the *Daily Light* portion for the evening of August 3rd, 'Fear none of these things which thou shalt suffer. Be thou faithful unto death...' It was with heavy hearts that we separated, though not to sleep. We thought and prayed for the folks at Wanie Rukula—the Gscheidles, a German couple in their first term. We also remembered all our Congolese friends there too and wondered...

Above:
The Arton Family. John Arton, aged 55, and Betty Arton (55), with Heather Arton (13).
John was brought up in Blackpool, Lancashire, and first worked in the Congo in 1945 as
a village evangelist. Betty Arton trained for missionary service at Mount Hermon
College, and had a great burden for the neglected and ostracised leprosy patients.
Both the Arton family and Jean Sweet were massacred on the river bank at Bafwasende
on 27 November 1964

Right:
Jean Sweet, aged 38. Prior to flying to the
Congo in 1962, Jean quoted the apostle
Paul on a prayer card, 'For I am
persuaded that neither death, nor life,
nor angels, nor principalities, nor
powers, nor things to come...shall
separate us from the love of God which is
in Christ Jesus Our Lord' (Romans 8:38).
Jean was converted while at teacher
training college in London before
answering the call to service with UFM

Chapter 1

By next morning, several Congolese were standing in little worried groups outside the house. The BBC had announced that the rebels were making rapid advances in all the areas around Stanleyville and we could hardly wait for midday and radio contact with headquarters. Apparently there was still no news from Wanie Rukula, but gunfire was reported to be audible very near Stanleyville, about ten miles from the city. Al Larson then said that those of us who wished to leave the country were to do so immediately; those near to Stanleyville were to come immediately as there were planes at the disposal of evacuees. Women and children were to leave first. Al said that he himself would not leave the country while there was one of us still there, unless he was forced to.

Quite frankly, we did not know what to expect, but we remembered 1960 when Congo became independent. Due to the general panic at the time we were evacuated, but nothing much happened. We felt bad about this, for we had been criticised by outsiders who stayed put in areas far removed from political activity. We were therefore not too worried at this stage. It would probably turn out like 1960, we thought, so we all decided to stay and carry on our work. Even Mary Baker who was alone in Bopepe just as she was in 1960 shared our feelings.

However, as a precaution it was decided that we should all call headquarters on the radio every hour. It is surprising how quickly an hour goes by when you are busy; it seemed as though we had hardly put the microphone down when it was time to listen again. By now, little groups of worried Congolese would be either in the sitting room or outside the windows, waiting for us to interpret the latest bulletin. It was far from encouraging. Curfew in Stanleyville from 3.30pm to 7am. All roads closed. Rebels advancing around Stanleyville. The big airport captured. Then the national radio went off the air, only to come back again a day later in rebel hands.

We felt right from the start that we should lay aside all unnecessary work and concentrate on prayer, so we met to pray together five or six times a day. These were times of great encouragement to us, and as we read the Word of God it brought new peace to our troubled thoughts.

Al Larson then gave orders that nobody was to leave their stations, as the national army was in flight and the rebels were right on their heels.

Above:
Bongondza—a medical station with a hospital which was about
two or three hours' drive from Bopepe. Nurse Ruby Gray
(pictured) had planned to travel there by road, together with the
Sharpe family

Knowing how we felt at Banjwade where there were seven of us, I began to wonder about Mary Baker alone in Bopepe. The whole scenario was becoming a nightmare and I did not think it fair to stay on at Banjwade while Mary was alone. After all, Bopepe was my station. Finally Al granted me permission to go back provided safe transport could be guaranteed.

By this time, various folk were stranded. Thelma and Larry Southard had arrived at our Boyulu station, unable to get any nearer home. The resident staff (Olive McCarten and Louie Rimmer, both teachers from England, and Chester and Dolena Burke, evangelists from Canada) had several other guests who were also stranded—Hector McMillan of Canada with four of his six boys (he normally worked at Bongondza with the Sharpes), the Arton family, Jean Sweet, a teacher from England, and Laurel McCullum, an Australian evangelist.

Days went by, but still no news from Wanie Rukula, and Al Larson's news was not very encouraging. A cablegram was sent out to both the American and British headquarters of the mission via a radio link to the Africa Inland Mission (A.I.M) station, which was at that time unaffected by all this. They received an answer and radioed it back to us. We were very grateful to A.I.M. for their help in this matter. At least we knew that folk at home would be alerted to our predicament and would be praying for us. Eventually the time came when Al Larson advised the A.I.M. to get out while they could, as the rebel movement was definitely anti-American, and most of the A.I.M. missionaries were Americans. They were all able to escape over the border without loss of life.

In order to keep a certain amount of secrecy about our conversations on air, we called the rebel army 'Robert' and the National army 'Louis'. During those early days the rebels were an unknown quantity as far as we were concerned. We hadn't seen a single rebel yet, let alone a whole group of them, but all the uncertainty made us tend to fear the worst. I can remember the day when Al told us that if he went off the air suddenly it was because the rebels were either in the house or the grounds. If this happened all the other mission stations were to stay tuned in, but to stay silent. One day, right in the middle of a sentence, he suddenly announced 'Robert has arrived.' A weighty silence fell and we all held our breath at Banjwade, imagining all sorts of terrible things happening to Al, his wife and their little daughter. We were praying silently for all we were worth.

The great value of the Word of God is one of the memories I have of those days. It seemed that every reading was written for the specific needs of the moment. Even the devotional readings from F.B. Meyer and Charles Spurgeon, which David would read to us after a meal, were so relevant to our particular situation, yet both men had lived a full one hundred years earlier. Then there was that little book *Daily Light*. I wonder how many others who read it regularly have ever noticed, just as we did, how much there is in it about trouble, and how the Lord promises he will undertake for us in such times. Best of all of course, were our regular personal Bible readings. We all had different ways of Bible study and were all looking at different portions, yet when we compared notes and thoughts, it was amazing how they all somehow seemed to coincide.

One day at the regular time to contact each other by radio we failed to get a response from Mary Baker at Bopepe. Then we heard Mary calling us and asking us to call her back as she had ten Simbas with her in the office. (The rebels called themselves Simbas, which is a Swahili word for lion.) They wanted to know why she had the radio transmitter. Ian Sharpe and Hector McMillan both spoke to the Simbas, who were finally convinced it was not a broadcast to America (Mary after all was an American), but all the same they said they would have to take the set. After this episode, one by one our stations went off the air. We did hear calls from Marshall Southard in Leopoldville and on one occasion we were able to answer, but the next day we had to promise the Simbas not to speak to Leopoldville. Being the seat of the legitimate government it was a sensitive area, but it was painful to hear the Southards' call when we did not dare to answer. All these radio broadcasts could be picked up on an ordinary short-wave radio. After almost three weeks, the Simbas came one evening and took the Banjwade radio too.

Our first encounter with the Simbas occurred during our second weekend. We were still on air at this time and were able to warn Mary when they were on their way to her. A Land Rover pulled in and stopped outside the house where I was staying and out jumped Dr John Saether of the Norwegian Baptist Mission. We had known each other since spending six months in the same boarding-house in Antwerp where we were both taking a course in tropical medicine. John had three other colleagues from his mission with him but also two fierce-looking Simbas, who would not enter the house, so we studied them from the shelter of the doorway. They looked perfectly ordinary people except they would not smile, only scowl. They were fully clothed (some later were half-naked), and also had the accoutrements of their 'military' status, in other words, pieces of fur on their hats and around their wrists, which were apparently their charms against death. They also carried rifles. It is our custom to offer hospitality to all travellers, so we asked them if they would like some tea or coffee. One refused to answer or even to turn around. We found out later that he was a local boy and probably a little ashamed. The other Simba agreed to a cup of coffee 'if Bwana made it.' So dear obliging David made it. I took it out to him. By this time a crowd had gathered, probably as much apprehensive as curious. We were all astonished when the men curtly ordered me to put the cup and saucer on the ground. Having been trained in the school of 'obey first and question later', I promptly obeyed, and placed a beautiful and decorative bone china cup and saucer on the muddy ground. (Remember, this was long before the advent of mugs!) The second Simba then picked it up, drank the coffee, and returned the cup to the ground, from where I later recovered it. This was in direct contrast to the traditional courtesy of the nationals. We were puzzled. Apparently in those early days the Simbas were not allowed to eat anything made by a woman, nor receive anything from one. This order persisted right up to the end of November. Everything had to be put down on the ground, in order that they could pick it up without any physical contact.

Dr Saether told us they had 'baptized' his car, in order to make it invulnerable to bullets if ambushed on the journey. It must have been a peculiar sensation for Baptists to watch the 'baptism' of their car by Simbas! We asked the doctor if he would take me through with him to Bopepe, especially as he was planning to stay there overnight, but there was no room, so I had to content myself with writing a hurried note to Mary.

The National Army was hopelessly outnumbered in Stanleyville, and the many who were captured were brutally murdered, so we could hardly blame those who survived for getting out while they could. They would come into Banjwade, tired, hungry and desperate and we would give them something to eat such as a banana, or gasoline for their cars. We would then pray with them and wave them off. Most had their wives and children with them. They knew what would happen if they were caught by the Simbas. A quick despatch would be the order of the day. Simbas didn't take or keep prisoners.

One day we had a note from a local Roman Catholic Priest, asking us to get help for an expatriate family about twenty miles away who were stranded on their coffee plantation. Sadly the request came too late. The Simbas got there first. The priests kindly sent us fresh vegetables and salad from their gardens, knowing we usually bought ours from town and would therefore be in short supply now.

Another time a question arose about buying party political cards. We had heard that the young peoples' movement (Jeunesse) was operating in the area, forcing people to buy these cards. Al Larson advised us against buying such a card, unless our lives were threatened. However, although we were later approached about buying them when I was back in Bopepe—and warned about the consequences if we did not—we were never forced to submit. The local population had to have them, however. If anyone did not possess one or belonged to a different political party, it meant almost certain death.

One day we noticed that the village folk were in a state of excitement and were walking about with bunches of flowers. The reason, we were told, was that the 'Big Man' (mutu mukubwa) was coming and would pass us by en route to Banalia and Buta. It was typical of the rebels that he turned up four days late, by which time the flowers were very wilted. We heard his approach by the sound of rifles being fired into the air, every mile or so. The village folk asked if we would go down the road to meet him, but we decided against it, on the grounds that we were foreigners, and he was not really our 'big man'; but if he stopped and came in we would give him a cup of tea. He stopped at the station entrance and gave the usual party political talk: 'The people for the people; no more tribes; soon we will all be equal' and so on. He also ordered that missionaries were to be protected and helped.

By this time the Simbas had taken cars and lorries from most of our stations. Perhaps I should not say 'taken', rather 'borrowed for the duration' with a duly signed receipt in triplicate so that we could get them back later.

It was not surprising that during this first month we did not enjoy our food as before; Sonia Grant was a wonderful cook, but we just could not find an appetite. It helped even less if a lorry-load of Simbas would drive in when we were having a meal. Somehow it seemed as though our stomachs just contracted down.

One night, as we were praying together, we heard somebody coughing outside the door. (Houses had no bells or door-knockers in Congo.) It proved to be two or three men from the village who had come to tell us to flee across the river as the Jeunesse were on their way, and we would be in for big trouble. I shall always remember the baffled look on the faces of these men as Sonia Grant said serenely, 'We will not run away, if we have to die we will die here.' About half an hour later, another man came; evidently he too had been urged to come by the others who were so afraid for us. We gave him the same answer. We did not feel particularly brave, but happily our faith in the Lord does not depend on our feelings. We prayed together again and went to bed. In comparing notes in the morning, we were amused to find that we had all only half-undressed, so that we could be up in a minute if the rebels came, and also, none of us had really slept. We had been straining our ears all night to listen for people who didn't come! We laughed about it in the morning, but we all still felt ashamed of the fear we had in our hearts. 'Perfect loves casts out fear,' says the Bible, but how much our love to the Lord needs perfecting.

A lovely respite from the constant demands of the Simbas was the day a young Simba asked for a Bible. We told him to come back the next day for it, as it had to be brought out from the stores, and we did not particularly want the Simbas inspecting everything in the station. The next morning he was back, and as Sonia walked out of the house with the Bible in her hand, it was wonderful to see the look of joy in the face of the Simba. In fact he was so overjoyed he took it directly from Sonia's hand, instead of her having to place it on the ground. Our prayers followed the boy and the Book. I wonder if he survived. We will never know.

One quiet Saturday afternoon, our peace was shattered by the arrival of a car, and the officer-in-charge asked David the nationalities of the missionaries. Only the Davis's were American, and though I am very much British, I felt so proud of Chuck, for when the officer asked him his nationality, he almost stood to attention and said loudly and clearly with obvious pride in his country, 'I am an American.' He then showed his papers. The officer said he would have to take him and his family to Stanleyville as the American Consul had asked for them to go to the consulate. He showed us a paper on which were written the names of several American missionaries. The first names on the list were those of Al Larson and his family, giving his Stanleyville address.

How easily we were fooled, though there was nothing we could do. These men only knew two words—obey or else. Sonia and David took the officer into the house for a cup of coffee and I went down to the Davis's house. The two children were asleep as it was siesta time. They hurriedly packed a few belongings into a case, left the house and dog to us, and got into the car.

As the officer entered the car, they gave the usual Simba greeting, 'Simba! Simba! Simba! Mayi! Mayi! Lumumba Mayi!' and then the officer asked if there was any 'mateka'. The answer was 'yes!' We did not know then what it meant in Simba-code.

As the car drove off, we were very apprehensive, more so when the Africans who had been standing around explained to us the meaning of 'mateka'. It is a Swahili and Lingala word for butter, but used in Simba-code it meant death. The reason was that if they found an African able to afford butter, it was immediately assumed he had obtained the money illegally and must therefore die. We prayed and prayed; yet the awful presentiment of danger did not leave us. The officer had promised that they would return next day, but we were beginning to find out what good liars they were.

The Davis's had a nightmare journey to town; especially as they had two children with them, a boy of four and a tiny girl of eighteen months. They were made to witness a man being shot, while rifles were pointing at them in the car. When they finally arrived, not at the Consulate, but the Airport Hotel, they were told to get out of the car, helped by rifle-butts, and made to enter the men's toilet. There they found, to everyone's amazement, the American Consul and four of his staff. After a little while they were taken outside and lined up against the wall as if they were going to be shot. Muriel prayed that they would all die together. However the Simbas changed their minds and decided to let Muriel and the children go, keeping Chuck and the other men imprisoned.

A car appeared to take Muriel to the military camp, but happily, in the Lord's providential care, it did not have enough petrol to get there. Muriel quickly remembered that Mr and Mrs Jenkinson, our most senior missionaries from England, lived in the centre of town, right opposite the prison. She persuaded the chauffeur to go there, and they arrived just as dusk was falling, about 6.30pm. Chuck was later moved to the general prison and was cruelly beaten, and made to undergo great privations along with the other men. Eventually he was released after seventeen days, though the other men were imprisoned until November 24th.

Meanwhile, at Bodela, ninety miles from Stanleyville and eighteen miles from Banalia, on a Sunday afternoon, Dennis Parry, an English evangelist, was in church taking the afternoon meeting. His wife Nora was in the house with their two younger children, teaching them. A car with six Simbas in it pulled up outside and the men went into the house. They verbally abused Nora, and then hit her, knocking her across the room and sending her spectacles flying. The children were afraid, though Andrew, almost eleven, did not show it, but eight-year-old Grace was naturally very upset and frightened. The men next went and found Dennis, pulled him out of the church and physically abused him. They demanded to have his Jeep. Dennis explained that the battery was dead and that there was another fault. They surrounded him and insisted he repair it, saying they would return in two hours. Leaving two Simbas to guard him, they went off, returning four hours later, very drunk. Dennis finally proved his point, but they accused him of deliberately putting the car out of action so that they could not have it. They then locked the car and went off with the keys. As they departed, their car overturned and the man who had struck Nora had an arm and a leg broken. 'Vengeance is mine, says the Lord, I will repay.'

At Bongondza station, a hundred and twenty miles from Stanleyville, Ian and Audrey Sharpe were in their house with their three children when a carload of Simbas arrived. They had arrested Pastor Masini Phillipe, senior pastor of Bongondza church and, calling Ian and Audrey out of the house, beat Masini unmercifully in front of them. Audrey defended Masini, and was struck across her face for her pains. The Simbas then 'inspected the house', took all they wanted, including the radio-set (an ordinary radio), and went away.

At Bopepe, Mary Baker was alone and resting during siesta time. A car with eight Simbas came and sneaked up to the house pointing their rifles. Mary let them in—though she had no option. They verbally abused her for sleeping 'when there was a war on', then proceeded to search the house from top to bottom. Pastor Bo Martin, twin brother of Pastor Asani, heard they had come, and demanded to be in the house with her. They said some terrible things to Mary but did not touch her. At one point they took her outside on to the veranda and pointed a rifle to her cheek, asking if she wanted to die. Mary said later to me, 'I wasn't afraid anymore, and told them to go ahead and shoot me as I was quite ready to die.' They put the rifle down and said they admired her courage. They took her transistor short-wave radio, and after threatening to come back and marry her, left after one and a half hours. The villagers, who had witnessed what had happened, were very impressed and said, 'Why, she looked at the gun and didn't even cry or show sign of fear. Truly she practices what she preaches!'

These three episodes all happened on the same day. Bodela, Bopepe and Bongondza were all apparently targeted because they were mission stations with expatriate staff.

Back at Banjwade, I was very burdened for Mary, and the last week in August the Lord gave me the assurance that he would get me back to Bopepe. Poor David and Sonia must have been really fed up with me. It was not that I did not appreciate their hospitality, but Mary was alone and Sonia *did* have David. The Lord gave me real peace about it all, and the following Saturday afternoon at four o'clock precisely, the Belgian doctor from Banalia arrived with a special request from the British Consul to take me back to Bopepe. 'Quick, quick' he said, 'I cannot wait.' He did not have to, I was prepared! Five minutes later we were on our way, and I rejoiced and praised the Lord all the way.

The journey was very interesting in that we had Simba escorts in the car, and each time we came to a village that had chickens or goats, we had to stop to bargain with them for their livestock. The people were obviously terrified of the Simbas, so fearful that their answers to questions the Simbas asked were at times quite incoherent. The Simbas for their part enjoyed wielding such power and would add empty threats to their commands, just to see what the results would be. On several occasions the doctor pleaded with them to have pity on the poor folk.

I had been shocked when I first saw the doctor. It was four weeks since I had left him at Banalia, and he told me that two weeks later, the Simbas took him to Stanleyville to work there as chief surgeon of the area. In those two weeks he had lost over sixteen pounds in weight. He looked lined, haggard and was obviously under great strain.

He had an emergency operation awaiting him at Banalia, so as we could not cross on the ferry once again I stayed the night at Banalia. I could not but notice the difference compared with four weeks ago—the house was full of Simbas, the houseboy had two black eyes from being beaten, and most of the doctor's property had been stolen, including all his sheets and blankets.

This time it was advisable to make sure my bedroom door was locked as it did not really look too promising for a good night's rest with Simbas all around the house. However, when I opened *Daily Light* that night, August 29th, I read, 'I will both lay me down in peace and sleep, for Thou Lord only makest me dwell in safety. Thou shalt not be afraid of the terror by night', and the last text 'I will trust and not be afraid'. I praised the Lord for his promises, laid down and slept all night.

Morning came and the doctor greeted me with the news that the ferry was out of order and we would therefore be returning to Banjwade. This did not fit in with what I thought was the Lord's plan; I felt so sure he would not have allowed me to come within fifteen miles of Bopepe and then let me down. After all, he was not the kind of God whose plans would be thwarted by a mere ferry. The doctor went to the hospital and I was left on my own. I spent the time in prayer, stating my case quite simply, and telling the Lord I knew he could get me across that river by ten o'clock in accordance with the doctor's programme.

At 9.30, the doctor returned, almost falling out of his jeep in his haste. He grabbed my case and said the ferry would be able to cross right now. I will always be grateful to him for his kindness in taking me right through to

Bopepe, as apparently his orders were only to go as far as Banalia. I praised the Lord all the way there. We had to pull up at one roadblock but, having Simbas in the car, we were allowed to continue unmolested.

It was 10.45 when we arrived at Bopepe. Everyone was in church, but Mary came out and was so overjoyed and relieved to see me she burst into tears. Obviously it was hopeless to carry on the service, so the poor preacher had to close the service hurriedly with a hymn. As it finished, Mary asked me to pop my head into the church to greet the folks. I was overwhelmed with their welcome! You would have thought I had been away for years instead of just one month, but these were not ordinary times.

Chapter 2

Bopepe days

My return to Bopepe was like a homecoming. It was so good to see Mary and other familiar faces again. As the folk from the village and the surrounding area came to greet me, they asked for news of relatives and friends who lived near to Banjwade or Stanleyville. Unfortunately I didn't know very much about any of them.

As it was vacation time for schools, all six of our schoolteachers had been in Stanleyville when the revolution began, and they too had been through a harrowing time. It was with much praise to God that all returned safely to Bopepe, though two of them came quite close to death.

One teacher named Bwanachui, a father of five small children, was accused by the rebels of being a 'reactionary'. Part of their reasoning was simply that he knew how to read and write, but his main crime was wearing a white shirt and tie. He was savagely beaten and condemned to die in a 'kangaroo court' situation, with no way of defending himself. The people had voted and that was final. He was imprisoned forthwith in a room with nineteen other men. Later on three Simbas came in with machine guns who tied the prisoners' hands together behind their backs, stood them all in line and shot them. They all fell of course, Bwanachui with them, but in the mercy and mysterious wisdom of God, he was not even hurt. Almost immediately he heard the noise of people running, and in came a Simba officer to enquire as to the cause of the shooting. Looking at all the bodies lying on the floor, he asked, 'What is going on here?' The Simbas explained that the men had all been condemned to death by the people's court. The officer then called out, 'is anyone still alive?' Bwanachui lifted his head. They helped him to stand up, dazed, frightened and bloodstained from those who had fallen each side of him. He was the only man who had survived that massacre.

On questioning him, the officer could not find any reason for him to have been condemned to death, and berated the Simbas for killing people who were intelligent and highly trained. They untied Bwanachui's hands, gave him a stick and asked him to point out who had accused him. When he had done this, he was told to go and beat them. However, he had temporarily

lost the use of his hands and arms as they had been tied up so tightly, so he was only able to look helplessly at his accusers. At this point, the officer took the law into his own hands and promptly shot them all.

As if that was not enough, poor Bwanachui arrived back at Bopepe just half an hour after his daughter of two and a half had died of leukaemia. In spite of everything, his faith in the Lord never wavered. Up to our arrest in November, he frequently gave the message on Sunday mornings, and he was always both challenging and a great blessing to us all.

Our school director Paul Ponea, who had recently married, had also gone to Stanleyville with the other teachers. In two separate incidents, he was severely beaten and then thrown on to the death truck to be taken down to the river where they threw in those who were unconscious or had died from their beatings. On both occasions he was taken off the lorry at the last minute. He was a man of great potential, an excellent school director and a keen Christian, who was maturing in the school of prayer. He was incidentally a nephew of the twin pastors Bo and Asani, but he was not a 'yes-man'; he liked to think things through logically for himself.

At Bopepe, the confiscation of our radio-transceiver meant that we were cut off from the outside world. Fortunately I still had my small transistor radio which we kept tuned to the BBC World Service. That little radio kept us in touch with what was going on in the rest of the world, although news about the Congo was often several days out of date.

Both Mary and I established a new routine so that we could meet several times during the day to pray together. As it was vacation time for the school—with little chance of it resuming in the foreseeable future—and my own dispensary and maternity work reduced because people were scared to travel any distance, we were able to set a large part of the day specifically to pray. Needless to say these times became increasingly precious to us as the weeks went by.

At this stage, let me tell you more about Mary Baker. She was a warm-hearted American from Richmond, Virginia, who looked much younger than her fifty years, heavily built and getting heavier. Congo life obviously suited her! An incurable optimist (and at such a time who would want to cure her?), she just refused to see the dark side of anything. Not that she buried her head in the sand—she was very much a realist—but somehow she could always find something positive about every situation. She was a great talker and very interested in people. She loved having visitors and would always find time to sit down and chat over tea or coffee.

She loved animals too; dogs being her favourites, but she also came to love my cats. Her dog was called Simba, which was a combination of her two family names, but at this particular time not a very appropriate name. He followed Mary everywhere.

Mary loved the Congolese, and they in turn both loved and respected her to a degree rarely found among the Kibua tribe among whom we lived. During the turmoil which followed independence in 1960, when most of us were evacuated home, Mary stayed on alone at Bopepe, and not once was she arrested or questioned; such was the esteem in which she was held by the population.

One interesting feature of an American and an Englishwoman living so closely together was how we adopted each other's habits. The early morning cup of tea became as much part of her daily routine as it had been mine, and she would go through this ritual even when I was away.

Such, then, was my senior missionary and companion, with whom I lived, ate, prayed and worked from 1962 to November 1964.

The Simbas would call into Bopepe at any time, day or night, usually for medicines, and though Mary had a natural fear of them, she never showed it. Usually when they arrived, Mary's dog would rush out barking furiously, followed by Mary yelling 'Simba! Simba!' to the dog; and to our amusement the Simbas would answer 'Simba! Simba! Simba!' Then we would have to explain that Mary was only calling the dog who was named Simba. One man complained about the dog's name and told Mary to change it, but she answered that the dog had had that name for the last seven years and that it was the rebels who had taken his name rather then he who had taken theirs.

During this time we were having prayer meetings with the villagers three times a week; until one night Pastor Bo Martin came to tell us that they would be holding the meeting in another house, and regretfully we were not to go. Apparently the people from outlying villages were saying that we were holding political meetings, and Mary, being American, was the proof. It was then that we realised that we could be a liability to our friends, as their continued friendship and contact with us could be counted against them later, so reluctantly and sorrowfully we had to acquiesce.

Later that night, as we prayed together, we read 2 Chronicles 20:12, 'O our God, wilt thou not judge them? For we have no might against this great company against us, neither know we what to do, but our eyes are upon thee.' The glorious answer comes in verse 15, 'The battle is not yours, but God's', and then in verse 17, 'Ye shall not need to fight in this battle: set yourselves, stand ye still, and see the salvation of the Lord with you.' We quietly committed the situation into our Father's hands.

Food began to be short, as we had been unable to buy supplies during my stay in Banjwade. Amazingly, just when we were on the last tin, a parcel would arrive from headquarters in Stanleyville, usually brought by a faithful friend who travelled regularly on the mail bus, which still passed our village even though it had no mail. We had asked the Lord to supply our need, of course, but we certainly never expected European foods. God so frequently does over and above what we ask or think.

Happily we were both well used to Congolese food and liked it. In fact, we had one dish every day even before all the troubles. Manioc (a root vegetable rather like a potato when cooked) and rice took the place of potatoes, and African spinach was a favourite food anyway, spiced with capsicum peppers and cooked in palm oil. We enjoyed our food even though it eventually became monotonous.

One of my hobbies was to raise chickens, and it certainly paid off in these times as they provided us with eggs and meat, though frequently a Simba would come and demand two or three chickens at a time. When November came we had just two chickens and ten baby chicks left. Sometimes we felt we had eaten so much chicken we ought to have grown our own wings and flown away from the problems!

One day in September, the Simbas took all our diesel oil, which ran our small generator, so we were without electricity and had to resort to kerosene lanterns. This was no great hardship but a bit inconvenient. Then they came and relieved us of all but ten litres of our kerosene. It meant a strict economy with lights and the refrigerator, which also ran on kerosene. Occasionally we were able to buy some from the local plantations.

We had small hurricane lanterns and one large pressure lamp; although this used too much kerosene and also needed precious methylated spirits, so we decided only to use it in a dire emergency in the dispensary or maternity. Frequently it meant a patient would have to wait till daylight, when I could put in stitches or open an abscess or probe a wound. God was gracious even in this situation and only once did I have a really serious maternity case at night which necessitated using the big lamp.

By the end of September, we needed to cut down even more, so we stopped work when it got dark and instead we would light a log fire on the veranda and sit near it until bedtime. This enabled us to identify even more closely with our Congolese neighbours. We would then watch the cars go by at the end of the village and, of course, pray together, as we could not read until we lit the lamps to go to bed. When it was moonlight, Mary would get out her accordion and play. The two dogs—ours and a neighbour's—would sit and howl with noses pointed upward to the moon. The last time we did this was a few days before our arrest in November. Mary, true American as she was, played 'The Star Spangled Banner' and 'America the Beautiful'. We both sang lustily accompanied by the dogs, hoping there were no Simbas around, or if there were, that they would not know the tunes were American.

Our houseboy, Fidèle, was rather a problem. He had worked for Mary for many years, and then later for both of us. He was not naturally brave, and whenever a lorryload of Simbas came into the village, Fidèle would be out of the back door and into the jungle like a flash of lightening. It was not until later that we learned that everyone in his village was a member of the rebels' political party, the MNC (Mouvement National Congolais.) This meant that he had divided loyalties. Every day when he returned home he would be harangued for working for foreigners, especially the hated whites, but he loved Mary, having been her houseboy for seven years. He knew we were not planning anything, but was still forced to listen to all the grisly details of what they claimed they were going to do to us. They enjoyed his apparent fear. It was hardly surprising therefore that whenever the lorries arrived he thought our time had come, and rather than stay to watch, he took to his heels. We got used to this behaviour from him, and waited patiently for him to return, relieved but ashamed. We understood.

The third week in September, we had news via our trusted friend on the mail bus that our colleague Bill Scholten from America, who had worked in our furthermost station Ekoko, had died in prison. We were all naturally very upset, especially Bo Martin, who said he would go on his bicycle to Ekoko to see what had happened. We did our best to talk him out of going, as the journey would have taken several days and we knew it would only mean trouble for him, but he was adamant. 'Don't you realise that one of my brothers in the Lord has died, and that it was my countrymen who killed him?' He was so ashamed. However, the village elders told him he could not go and leave us two women, as he had vowed to protect us. He finally agreed to stay home, but it was evident Bill's death had a depressing effect not only on Bo, but on all the villagers who became even more nervous about having two foreigners living with them. Bo prayed hard for Mrs Scholten and her four very young children. Many prayed too for those responsible for Bill's death. We redoubled our prayers for the workers in the Aketi-Ekoko area who were stranded there, as we had heard various ugly reports on the grapevine of trouble in those parts.

Our tribal chief, Mulaba Fidèle, was the one who had promised us a goat for our conference but subsequently let us down. We heard later that he had wanted a fantastic price for it, but our local Africans had refused to allow him to exploit the missionaries. Now the Simbas were coming in every day taking away three or four animals and not paying him anything.

Chief Fidèle, as we called him, was an uncle of the twins and therefore technically a relative of ours as we had been made members of the tribe and family. He had been a nominal Catholic, and though he had gone to mass whenever the priest came round, he was not averse to coming to Bopepe church for our services on a Sunday, especially if either of the twins were preaching, so we had come to know him fairly well. Frequent threats from the Simbas made him realise it was time to take a good look at his spiritual state. It was time to get his soul right with the Lord. He sent for Bo Martin, as by this time Asani was away up country—and talked long and earnestly with him. Bo eventually had the joy of leading him to the Lord for salvation. The transformation in him was remarkable. He changed from a weak and frightened man to a brave and decisive chief. He had been very convicted about the animal business and said to us, 'I had refused to give God's people an animal, and now he has taken them all away.'

Pictured above:
Pastor Bo Martin on the left with his twin brother, Asani,
together with a Pigmy convert

One night, shortly after his conversion, he had a very late visit from several lorry-loads of Simbas, who commanded him to go out and call in the women to dance for them. It was about 2.30am. As he was on his way home, he met a messenger from his village who warned him not to return as they had overheard the Simbas saying they were planning to beat him. The poor chief did not know what to do or where to go. He knew that if anyone was caught hiding him in their house, they would almost certainly be killed. So he put his new-found faith to the test, and prayed there and then in the middle of the road, halfway between his village and ours, a distance of about 1½ miles. The Lord sent an immediate answer in the form of a snake which bit him in the ankle. Now there was only one course of action. He would have to go to Bopepe dispensary for treatment, even though it would be agony for him to walk.

At 3.15am we were wakened by a very sick man calling out to us from our veranda. I only had one ampoule of anti-snake venom serum left, so I administered it to him with much prayer that this would be sufficient, and Bo Martin said he would lodge him in his house and take the consequences if found out. The chief became seriously ill, his glands swelled up all over his body and he was in much pain. Bo nursed him faithfully in his sickness, and all the church prayed earnestly that God would spare his life. Our prayers were answered and he recovered.

While he was in Bo's house, he would spend many hours reading his Bible, saying he did not realise how much he had missed all these years by not reading it. He stayed with us at Bopepe for two weeks in all and Bo was able to teach him many spiritual truths. How Bo found the time I do not know for he had a wife and six children, the eldest just a young teenager.

Chief Fidèle became one of our strongest friends when the days became more and more difficult, visiting us whenever he could—always with a gift of food from his own diminishing supplies.

Often the Simbas would call into Bopepe for food or medicines. They arrived one day in the middle of a real tropical downpour—a frequent occurrence during Congo's nine-month wet season. Three Simbas came on to our veranda, one just a young boy of perhaps nine or ten years old. He was shirtless and soaking wet but was wearing his 'magic medicine' (a fur armband) and carried a rifle. I asked him if he really was a Simba or their mascot. How naïve can I be? He drew himself up to his full height—about up to my shoulders—and informed me he was actually an officer—an adjutant, and what was more, a doctor to the rebel army! I was just incredulous. As he talked, he was shivering like someone with malarial chills. His magic medicine obviously did not stop him feeling the cold. Poor kids, so very young. We felt sorry for them when they climbed back into their open lorry, for it was still raining heavily. They were probably hungry and tired, though not yet disillusioned at this time. A gun in their hands must have made them feel very powerful, no matter how young they were.

As the People's Army is fed by the people, the villages surrounding their encampment were commanded to take it in turns to take food to them twice a week, and then the women were made to sing and dance all day.

As Bopepe was a Christian village, we provided the requisite foods, but it was always a sore point that the women would not stay to dance. In addition, not one man from Bopepe had joined the People's Army. Consequently, whenever the Simbas passed our village, we often suffered verbal abuse and threats. We were all reactionaries: Bo Martin was preaching against the rebels; the schoolteachers were 'eating' all the money which should be shared between the people; and Mary and I were spies for Tshombe (the leader of the legitimate government). Understandably this did not make for a happy environment. We still found, in spite of all the stress, that we could find real peace in the Lord, and it seemed that the harsher and more personal the threats, the deeper the peace.

Mary taught religious instruction in the school for a while, but finally was forced to give it up due to pressure from parents, especially those from MNC villages. Mary was terribly upset by this, but all we could do was to pray for the little ones, that their minds would not be poisoned by all this.

Each week, the school director Paul Ponea would come to us with a new list of names of boys who had joined up with the Simbas. Paul was in despair over this, as several of the boys were only nine or ten-year-olds. One of these boys later became one of our guards while we were in prison, and later essentially my personal bodyguard. Strangely enough the big Simbas respected and at times feared the 'petit Simbas' as they were always called.

Frequently lorries full of Simbas would go past our village on their way to battle. Usually they would be singing their songs of hate, terrible words,

Above:
Bopepe church where Margaret worked during her second term

but sung to beautiful melodies. As we watched them go by we felt sad. These were young boys, indeed many of them still children, going to fight against modern weaponry only armed with machetes, spears and clubs. What chance would they have? Our hearts just ached for them, going to a virtual suicide for a dying cause. Mary would pray that the wheel of their lorry would come off, or they would run out of gasoline—a far more likely occurrence—but 'Anything, Lord, to stop them arriving at the place of battle.'

Sometimes when they called into Bopepe, they would ask us to pray for them, and we would honestly assure them that we prayed for them every day, but we did not tell them *how* we prayed.

One day in October, a captain arrived on one of the lorries. He was a believer, who had been forced to join the rebel army because he was an ex-soldier. He had called in to ask if he could be baptized as he felt sure he would die in battle. He had left Buta with twenty-five wounded men on his lorry, and by the time he arrived at Bopepe ninety-five miles further on, all but four had died during the journey, and one of the remaining four was almost dead.

We arranged that he would be baptized whenever he could come back, which turned out to be a week later. Bo baptised him in the river, and we all gathered in the church afterwards for communion with him. He did not return from the war.

One evening as we sat on the veranda, two men appeared on bicycles and stopped outside our house. We had stood to greet them, but after approaching us they then sat down in our chairs, leaving us standing! They were civilian members of the MNC, the rebel political party, who had cycled in from Banalia about 15 miles away, no mean feat in the dark on bad roads. One of them had been sent along by his father to sell Mary and I the latest version of their party political card. We politely refused the offer, explaining that we were missionaries and foreigners, and not interested in politics of any party. The man whose father had sent him leaned over and said very quickly, 'There is a bad time coming for you foreigners; it would be wise to buy one as it may be the means of saving your life.'

We knew that the rebel 'President' Gbenye was pursuing a scorched earth policy, and was making threats against expatriates, but we wondered just what was behind the words of our visitor. However we insisted that we had no intention of buying a card, and they eventually left us, no doubt to report unfavourably about our attitude. I don't think we even offered them a drink.

Later, when Bo Martin came over to tell us the news bulletin he had heard from Leopoldville, and to hear if we had any news from the BBC, he said we had done the right thing, but it was obvious that he was very disturbed by the visit. He was also missing his twin brother during these tense days. Pastor Asani was up country in AIM territory with his wife and two of our catechists. We heard later that he had crossed the border into Uganda and flown from there to Leopoldville, but at this time we did not know if he was alive or dead. Strangely, Bo had dreamed that he saw his twin in another country. In a way we were glad Asani was not with us, as he would certainly have run into serious trouble with the rebels, being well-educated—more so than Bo and because as the senior twin he was the one who had all the authority.

Both Bo Martin and Asani were suspected of being reactionaries and belonging to another political party. This was hardly surprising; they both lived at Bopepe and had close associations with missionaries, they were always neatly dressed, spoke French fluently, and in Asani's case had received training in Europe. We heard on the grapevine that the administrator at Banalia was searching through the lists of members of the other party in the hope of finding either of the twins' names, but Bo said that it would be a fruitless task—they had never joined any political party.

As tension mounted, feelings ran high against the twins, and all sorts of false accusations were made. Bo was fearless in his preaching, so much so that we felt we should warn him not to preach against the movement, but to keep to the pure Word of God. Even though he agreed to do so, at times he would still get carried away in his righteous denouncements.

Our worst fears were realised when one day he was called to the administration in Banalia to answer a charge that he had preached against Lumumba, the dead Prime Minister, saying he was a devil. Bo had preached on 'Thou shalt have no other gods besides Me' (Exodus 20) and Lumumba was regarded as a god by the rebels. Bo had wisely not mentioned Lumumba by name, but they still thought Bo was preaching at them. In a sense he was—but not in the way they thought.

One Sunday morning during a church service, we heard a truck stop right outside and within minutes Simbas were rushing into the church, with their rifles at the ready. The church had many doorways and they poured in through them all, looking very menacing. Whoever was preaching had stopped speaking, and several women began to weep. Apparently they were looking for the missionary nurse, as one of their members had toothache and wanted some aspirins! I was only too happy to comply with this request, and having identified the suffering Simba took him out with me to the dispensary, accompanied, as always, by several others. Mary whispered to another Simba that she would make a drink for anyone who would like one, but they would need to come to the house. Anything to get them out of the church. They liked this idea and left with her. Once outside, a Simba of about fourteen emptied his rifle into a tree, which also had the effect of emptying the church of women who thought they were killing Mary. The delight of frightening people knew no bounds, as I was to discover time and time again.

The Simbas were given drinks in our sitting room, and Mary later told me that as one of them received his, he took off his hat and returned thanks to God. Another crossed himself. They were for the most part young boys, between the ages of fourteen and eighteen. One of them had been educated at our UFM School in Wanie Rukula and asked if he might sit in on the rest of the service. Several came back with him and sat with us, sharing our Bibles and hymnbooks, and obviously quite at home in the church. The Simbas really were a strange mixture.

Another evening as we were talking together on the veranda, the subject of death came up, as it frequently did during those days, especially as the death toll mounted within Simba ranks. Mary said that we had died to self years ago, or else we would never have come to Congo in the first place. If we regarded ourselves as dead, it did not matter what happened to our bodies, as our souls were assured of eternal life with the Lord, which was far better. She quoted Paul's reference—2 Corinthians 1:9 'But we had the sentence of death in ourselves...'

One evening during the last week in October, we saw a plane flying over, very high in the sky. This sparked off rumours in nearby villages that it was the foreigners who were calling the planes. It was also the time that

Christophe Gbenye, the 'President' of the rebels, decided to collect hostages.

On Thursday October 29th, we saw several lorries pass Bopepe on their way to the various plantations, in order to arrest all the foreign planters. Missionaries were exempt from arrest, but for how long we wondered?

The following day we heard the lorries returning along the road. I was at the dispensary and ran out to watch them. We recognised a number of neighbours and friends who had been herded into these vehicles with their wives and children. We waved to each other as they went by. It was very disturbing and we both found it difficult to concentrate on our work after that. We wondered if we would ever meet them again. Unknown to us, the revolution was entering a new phase.

To be practical we packed our evacuation cases with things we might need for a long stay in prison, though at the same time hoping it would not come to that.

We continued in this state of tension for several days. We would pray, but even our prayers did not seem to ease our anxiety. Judging by radio reports put out by the rebels, we had to face up to the possibility not only of imprisonment, but also a violent death.

On Sunday November 1st, Bo Martin preached fearlessly on Ephesians 6 'Put on the whole armour of God.' We had the presentiment that this would be our last Sunday at Bopepe, and we were not alone in thinking this, for the attitude of the people made it obvious that they felt it too. They were even more loving than usual, many bringing us gifts of food. Some were quite tearful. All day long we had visits from various church members who just wanted to shake our hands, and having done this they would then sit in bleak silence on the veranda, looking at us with sadness and cracking their finger-joints, always a sign that they were uneasy. Occasionally they would cry out 'Omaou', a tribal word indicating acute distress.

That evening Mary played her accordion for a long time. Neither of us spoke although somehow it eased our pent-up feelings to hear the well-known hymns again. Neither of us sang either, and strangely enough neither did the dogs; did they know something too? Before we separated to go to bed, we prayed together. Mary had a hard time controlling her tears, but I let mine flow.

Monday and Tuesday passed in the same state of heightened tension. Traffic on the road was heavier; several lorryloads of singing Simbas went by—presumably off to battle. In the other direction some came back, usually with a blood-stained spear tied to the front. These carried the wounded and dead and were not a pretty sight.

On Tuesday night, November 3rd, we went to bed as usual after hearing the ten o'clock news from the BBC. Once again, there was nothing about events in Congo. The mail lorry had failed to come that day, though that was not particularly unusual. At 11.30pm Mary heard a lorry coming along the road. It stopped outside Bopepe village, and thinking it might be the mail lorry, she got up and went hoping to meet the friend who always travelled on it. Instead she was confronted by six half-naked Simbas on the veranda, all carrying spears, and with their bodies decorated with palm leaves and magic medicines. 'Get back into the house, white lady, you are under arrest.' Mary hastily complied with the order, and called out to me to get up as we had visitors.

Chapter 3

In prison

When I heard Mary call out that we had visitors, I knew immediately who they were, as I could hear their demands from my room. Hastily putting on my housecoat and lighting a hurricane lamp, I went out to meet them, praying for guidance and wisdom.

They were standing half-naked with palm branches on their heads and chest, menacingly grasping their spears, and leering at us. Their spokesman said he had come to inspect the house—yet again—and then to take us both to Banalia.

Then he saw young Julienne, a child from the village, who was in bed in our lounge. They demanded to know who she was and insisted that she get up. She had slept through all the noise, in fact even then she was still sound asleep. I shook her violently, and when she saw the Simbas she almost fell out of the bed. The Simbas were impressed that we had given her a real bed with sheets and a blanket, just as we would have had. Poor Julienne was even wearing one of my nightdresses and was acutely embarrassed to be standing in front of all these men so inadequately dressed. Sensing her embarrassment, I quickly found her cloth and she hastily wound it round herself.

Julienne was a brave fifteen-year-old who was not afraid to correct the Simbas in no uncertain terms when they accused her of having lived an immoral life. After all, who were they to talk?

The Simbas were tired and hungry, so Mary, with true Virginian hospitality, offered to feed them. As we only had two tins of sardines and some rice left, Mary explained our poverty. To our amazement they understood and told her only to open one of the tins, and to keep the other one for ourselves. We ushered Julienne into the kitchen out of sight of the men and Mary asked if the girl could go home to her mother, only three houses away, as she had done nothing wrong. She was only sleeping in our house to ease the overcrowding in her own, as many visitors had arrived and every house was full. To our relief and Julienne's too they agreed to let her go, and we watched her walking calmly down the hill and into her own home as though this kind of thing happened every day.

'Many were crying quite openly, many also turned their backs on us as we passed—this was not a sign of disrespect but a tribal tradition expressing sorrow'

After about an hour we heard Bo Martin at the door, though it was not until then that we realised that two of the Simbas had gone to his house to arrest him as well. They had searched his house from top to bottom looking for the inevitable transmitter radio they thought we all possessed.

When Mary had finished preparing the food, she placed it on the table with some coffee. The Simbas ate hungrily, though there was only one sardine each for them. We were allowed to cook their food as they said we were 'good women' and did not live immoral lives, but 'good' or not we were still under arrest.

After they had eaten, they wanted to search the house. They went to my room, and the first thing they saw was my little transistor short wave radio with its aerial up. As radios were regarded as great status symbols, they took it immediately, and demanded that I showed them how it worked. Very quickly I moved the dial from BBC to the local Stanleyville station. It would have made matters worse if they had heard a foreign station. I had marked the radio with a pencil for ease of finding BBC or Leopoldville, so while pretending I could not see very well in the poor light, I ran my finger over it, which erased the marks.

The Simbas were tired, and as it was past 2am by now, they decided to postpone the inspection until morning. They gave us permission to go back to bed. As Mary's room was off the living room, she did not fancy sleeping there, so she asked and was given permission to put Julienne's bed, a folding roll-away type, into my room. Bo Martin sat in a chair with them all night. We could hear the conversation clearly. Bo tried on several occasions to preach the gospel, but they always refused to listen and told him to shut up.

It is hardly surprising that we did not sleep in such circumstances. We lay on our beds whispering to each other, though I cannot remember what we whispered about. At some point we prayed. The night seemed endless. Eventually at 5.30am we hastily washed and dressed and put some last minute things into our evacuation cases.

We made a cup of tea, both for ourselves and the Simbas. Bo Martin was allowed to go back to his house with an escort, as he had a wife and five children at home, but was made to return after fifteen minutes.

We asked the Simbas about the proposed programme for the day. The house would be inspected from top to bottom, then we could eat, and finally depart for Banalia. If a lorry came we would go by lorry; if not we would go on foot. Our hearts sank. 'This is it,' we said.

At 6.30am they surprised us by asking why we had not gone to church. They then dispatched all three of us to go—with escort. Bo took that last service. I cannot remember what he spoke about at all, but I can vividly remember the last hymn was the Bangala version of 'Fight the good fight', and how difficult it was to sing with a lump in my throat and tears in my eyes. Mary experienced the same problem. After that service, nobody came to shake hands or to greet us; they were all too upset.

Back at the house they began our 'inspection', starting with Mary's room. All six Simbas crowded in, and they made Bo Martin stay with them. Even the mattress was lifted, but not damaged. Of course we had nothing to hide. Next came my room. Every item had to be explained, and any medical equipment in particular was examined over and over again, especially my auroscope (for use in examining ears) which I had brought from the dispensary in case I needed it for the odd caller who would come to the house for treatment after the dispensary was closed. They were amazed by how many books I had. Due to lack of space, I kept most of them in a trunk or a case. They carefully studied all the titles, but as they were either in English or French, the Simbas were none the wiser. They were all medical or theological books anyway. Next, we went as a group through the rest of the house—the office, bathroom, living room, dining room and kitchen. Nothing escaped the scrutiny of six pairs of inquisitive brown eyes. In the attic they found the remains of an old broken tape recorder and also an old transformer. They were quite excited by the transformer, being convinced that it was a transmitter we had hidden there. When we explained what it was used for they were none the wiser, never having heard of a transformer before. Like all transformers, it was very heavy, and if they wanted to carry it all the fifteen miles to Banalia, that was up to them.

By this time our houseboy Fidèle had arrived, and was told by the Simbas to feed us. The Simbas then left the house to supervise a meal which the schoolgirls who lived in the village were preparing for them.

We sat down to a breakfast of coffee and bread and marmalade which Fidèle had prepared. Neither of us had any appetite and even half a slice was a struggle. It seemed to taste like sawdust because of the state we were in. The leader of 'our' Simbas was concerned about our lack of appetite and quite genuinely could not understand why we ate so little, so he pleaded with us to eat more as he knew we had a long day ahead of us. We tried again but it was no use.

Having obtained permission to go to my little hospital, I went, fully intending to give some last minute treatment to all the inpatients. (I knew there would not be any outpatients.) I need not have bothered—the hospital was empty; everyone had fled. Sadly and tearfully I locked the doors. Somehow we felt so apart from our people. They were too scared to come near us, though I was sure they were watching our every movement.

On the way back to the house, I met one of the schoolteachers. He had often helped me with my chickens, and I gave him permission to eat them or keep them as he felt best. There were not that many left by now as the Simbas had taken so many. He was so sure we would only be gone for a few days that he refused to take them but said he would keep an eye on them.

The villagers were standing about in little groups; some women had their hands on their heads, one of the tribal signs of grief. We were unable to speak to them or even go near to them, so we could not comfort them.

Daily Light that morning had been very topical for us as we read it at the breakfast table: November 4th, morning reading 'Now for a season, if need be, ye are in heaviness through manifold temptations'; 'Beloved think it not strange concerning the fiery trial which is to try you.' It continued down the page in the same vein. As we prayed together that morning, those words brought real peace and comfort to our heart. We knew that everything was in the permissive will of our God, so it was not our responsibility what would happen, but his.

The Simbas wanted to take my radio, of course, but under their laws it had to be given, so I had to sign a piece of paper stating they had my full permission to take it 'for the duration'. In many ways we were glad to see it go, for it had been quite a liability. Whenever we had listened to Radio Leopoldville, one of us had always sat outside on the veranda to watch for Simbas or any other visitors who might have reported us.

By 10am there was no sign of any lorries calling by. It was obvious that we were going to have to walk the fifteen miles to Banalia, and as it was the middle of the dry season, we both knew it would be a hot cloudless day. We looked at our suitcases. How could two very helpless white women unused to carrying heavy loads even a short distance manage such a journey in these conditions? We should not have worried; the Lord had it all planned out for us. Paul Ponea, our school director and another teacher Ndama Gregoire, both volunteered to carry our cases on the back of their bicycles all the way to Banalia. We were embarrassed but relieved to say the least. Other friends wanted to carry our handbags and lamps for us, in order to identify with us, even at the cost of danger to themselves. As a result, we started out virtually empty-handed.

Our hearts were heavy as we set out on that long walk. The folk from Bopepe lined the pathway from the village via the dispensary. Many were crying quite openly, many also turned their backs on us as we passed—this was not a sign of disrespect but a tribal tradition expressing sorrow. A few took our hands in both of theirs and whispered, 'God bless' or 'God go with you'. Mary was able to find the composure to say a few words, but I dared not trust myself to speak at all; my heart was too full. Once we reached the main road our pace was brisk. We could hear the drums sending messages ahead. Consequently as we neared each village large groups would be gathered by the roadside to greet us or to weep as we passed through. The womenfolk in particular astonished me by the vehement way they rounded upon the Simbas for taking away their two 'Mamas'. Before the day was through we were even feeling sorry for the Simbas!

The Simbas honoured us inasmuch as they allowed us to head the procession, made up of the various people who were carrying our things and those who walked with us simply to identify themselves with us— including many young mothers with babies tied to their backs. Occasionally we would hear an argument behind us and on looking back, we discovered it was because other folk wanted to have the opportunity to carry our belongings. Such a display of love was very moving.

Towards the back of the crowd was Bo Martin; the Simbas kept him close to them all the time as he was indeed a prize catch.

As we passed the Chief's village, the Chief was there to meet us. With a face like thunder he took our proffered hands in his, and without a word, but with tears in his eyes, he bowed low. We did not then know how much this man was to put his life in danger while fighting for our release.

We stopped every two or three miles at the order of the leading Simba so that Mary could rest. After all, she was 50 years old and had arthritis in both her feet. He commanded chairs and refreshment to be brought. We drank the water but did not have any appetite for food.

As we walked ahead of and apart from the nationals, we felt free to talk to one another in English, and our conversation turned to the sufferings of the Lord. We reminded each other of various promises in the Bible. It was rather like the Emmaus Road experience for us, for it really felt like Jesus was walking with us. Certainly our hearts burned within us. Was it like this for him we wondered—the heat, the fatigue, the tension and the ever-present crowds with him?

The two men with our cases on their bicycles had gone on ahead and left them with Christians at Banalia. They then cycled back, leaving their bicycles with us and the Simbas gave us permission to ride ahead and wait for them at Banalia. I was so grateful as Mary's feet were beginning to be very painful and we were needing to stop more and more frequently. We cycled until I nearly fell off my bicycle with faintness, and had to take a rest. At the village where we stopped, the people gave us sugar cane, baked corn, some bananas and a long drink of lovely cool water.

Suitably strengthened, we were able to cycle to within one mile of Banalia, where we waited for the rest of the party to catch us up. The villagers all along that interminable road were incensed at our arrest, but they were also very frightened, though there were women in each place who spoke their minds freely to the Simbas.

Looking back I realise how courteous and thoughtful our Simbas were. They really went out of their way to cushion the effect of our arrest.

By 4.30pm the remainder of the group caught up with us, and to our astonishment the Simbas said we would wait until 5.30pm for the ferry. They then explained that by that time most of the Simbas would be 'in camp' and there was less chance of our being molested. We were very grateful for this thoughtfulness and had cause to praise God even more when, four days later, the Sharpe family arrived in Banalia during the morning and we saw the terrible way they were treated.

Top: A group of Simba soldiers

Above: The Parry family. Hazel and Stephen, in the centre, were in England at the time of the uprising, and so escaped the massacre

At 5.30pm we finally crossed the river. We were beautifully sunburned, especially my nose, which had turned a brilliant red and was the butt of jokes for days to come.

As we were crossing we could see that a crowd was gathering on and near the landing stage and it was obvious that it was Mary and I who were the focus of interest. As we stepped off the ferry, a mob of young Simbas came and surrounded us, brandishing their spears and threatening terrible things. It was a very tense moment until suddenly we heard 'our' Simba leader say something in his own tribal language and as one man all the young Simbas stepped back away from us, and our own original six surrounded us, two in front, two behind and one each side. The leader said very gently to us, 'Do not be afraid; we are responsible for you, and we will not let these people touch you; only stay within our guard.' We didn't have any option anyway but we obeyed.

We marched off to an accompaniment of catcalls and threats. Our destination was the local Simba headquarters; a house that had formerly belonged to a European before being plundered and then commandeered for its present use. Our leader stood smartly to attention and gave his report, which was apparently very much in our favour. Then we were taken into a room which had probably once been a beautiful lounge, but was now filthy after being wrecked by the Simbas. Bo Martin joined us there. The orange-coloured dust on the road had made us filthy too, and we felt absolutely exhausted both physically and mentally. It had been a long, tiring and stressful day, and it was still only 6pm.

Bo Martin was told he was free to go. He had only been made to come with us as a chaperone, as we did not have husbands. However, he continued to sit with us as our papers were examined. None of us spoke; we were too busy with our own thoughts.

As we sat there wondering what would happen next, we overheard reports that a similar escort party had been sent to Bodela for the Parry family, and another to Bongondza for the Sharpes. We immediately brightened up at the thought of seeing our friends and colleagues again. We did not feel quite so isolated now.

The Simba administration kept our identity cards, but returned our passports. The commander of the base apologised to us before reading out the orders from Stanleyville to arrest us all. He stressed that we were not to be beaten or killed.

Perhaps I should mention that when I refer to these men by rank (commander, captain, general or whatever), these were their own self-styled positions. None of them were real military personnel.

We were eventually taken to a house we had often noticed when in Banalia. It was right on the main road with a commanding view of the river and the ferry. It was also devoid of furniture except for a wooden settee and a small round coffee table. We decided to do a tour of inspection. It was filthy. There was no water in the bathroom and as for the toilet, not only did it have no water, but it seemed as though the entire Simba army had used it. The stench was nauseating even to me, and I pride myself that as a trained nurse I can stand anything.

Bo Martin was with us as we toured round the house, and he too was appalled at this state of affairs and immediately set off to see if he could do anything for us.

While Bo was away on his errand of mercy, eight or nine Belgian plantation owners and their wives were brought in, followed by Simbas bringing in chairs for us all. They all sat around in glum silence. I asked one woman how long she had been a prisoner. 'Three days,' she said. She rightly guessed by my sunburnt nose that we had only just arrived, and they were all appalled that no transport had been laid on for us.

Shortly afterwards Bo came back with several officers and also the poor civilian who was supposedly responsible for the upkeep of the house. They produced a single-size bedstead and a very hard lumpy mattress from another house. The mattress only covered one third of the bed. This was hardly suitable for eighteen to twenty adults, and Bo was so incensed at this that he insisted on something better for his two demoiselles. The arguments became very heated, and Mary pleaded with him not to antagonise the Simbas any further. He remained dauntless, and went on and on until the senior officers ordered the young Simbas who were supposedly guarding us, to arrest him and put him in the 'calshot' (solitary confinement) all night. He was chased out of the house, and later we heard they had made him run all round Banalia at spear-point, before finally shutting him up in the real prison block, which was even filthier. The 'calshot' Simba-style meant standing to attention over an open privy for hours on end without a light. The poor victim usually had to take his shoes off, if he was wearing any, and as the ground around the privy was not very sanitary and the stench overpowering, it was not a pleasant experience. At some stage during the night they relented and pushed him into a damp dark single cell. Bo then took his coat off, made a pillow of it, then after a long time in prayer, lay down on the cold damp cement floor and went to sleep. Poor Bo! All because of us.

Mary pleaded with the senior officer to have mercy on him, explaining that he was only trying to look after us. They were adamant, accusing Bo of being a reactionary. The fact that he was trying to shield the white people was proof. We were very distressed, and all we could do was silently to commit our brother to the care and keeping of the Lord.

About an hour after Bo's arrest, the Parry family arrived. They were all absolutely exhausted, but obviously overjoyed to meet with us again. They had not been so well-treated as us, their Simbas being very unsympathetic to their plight.

The ordeal had begun at 6am that morning, when the Simbas arrived and gave them exactly five minutes to leave. Their two children, Andrew, who was ten, and eight-year-old Grace, were still in pyjamas, but Dennis and Nora were dressed. The coffee had been made and was on the table, and Nora was in the process of mixing the milk (we used powdered milk in Congo), but they were not even allowed to drink their coffee. Permission was granted for the children to dress. Dennis grabbed everything he could and packed it all into two small suitcases. By 6.40am they were on the road.

The Simbas would not allow anyone to carry their luggage, in fact they had to carry the Simbas' baggage as well as their own. As if this was not enough, throughout the entire eighteen-mile journey they suffered all manner of torments, especially the children, who were hit on the head with their spears just for the Simbas' amusement. Nora warned them not to cry, as it would only aggravate the situation.

They tried to make Grace carry things on her head as Congolese girls do, but of course, she had not been taught how to, so everything fell off and for this they hit her again. In spite of such abuse, this brave little eight-year-old girl still did not cry.

The Simbas would race on ahead and drink the very potent palm-wine which was made locally, and they soon became very drunk. Whenever they stopped for a break, the Parrys were made to stand in the hot sunshine. They were not offered any food or drink, and the local people were too afraid to help them.

Once Grace wanted to go to the toilet. Permission was grudgingly given, but a Simba insisted on going along with her. There were no toilet facilities anywhere but the jungle is very dense and would have given a degree of privacy. The Simba was half way there, when the other Simbas called him back, reminding him that Congolese men do not go with womenfolk under such conditions. He sheepishly returned.

After about seven miles, Nora collapsed into a deep faint. The Simbas were very frightened about this, so they carried her into a house and left her with the women of the village. Someone was sent ahead to Banalia to arrange transport, but they had to wait almost six hours before a tractor and trailer finally appeared.

In the meantime, the children were made to prepare food for the Simbas, and were humiliated when they made mistakes. Grace was also made to dance. When the food was finally ready, all the family were allowed was one plantain (cooked banana) each. The children ate ravenously, hardly surprising as they hadn't had anything to eat or drink all day. Dennis and Nora were not hungry and gave their portion to Andrew.

They finally arrived in Banalia at 6.30pm and came to our place of imprisonment an hour or so later. Nora, never robust at the best of times, looked terrible, and the children were too tired physically and emotionally to talk. I took off their coats and Grace's shoes. Her feet were badly blistered, but even then she didn't make a fuss.

We made some sandwiches from the loaf of bread and our last tin of sardines which we had managed to pack before leaving Bopepe. The children ate well, but the rest of us had little appetite, although we all ate something, as it was obviously a wise thing to do. Someone brought us some water, which we drank up very quickly.

By this time young Grace had started to whimper. We whispered to her to try and be brave, as otherwise the Simbas would get angry with us. The amount of suffering, both physical and emotional, that this poor little bewildered girl had been through that day would have been enough to send an adult mad. She sat by me, clutched my hand and whispered that she had asked Jesus to make her brave.

The two hurricane lamps we had brought with us were lit, and the Simbas arranged themselves by the doors and windows to mock us. We tried not to listen, but it was very hard. We were all very tired and also very uncomfortable, as there were still no toilet facilities. The Simbas enjoyed themselves singing their hate-filled war songs and generally being very offensive.

As the evening wore on, various pieces of furniture were brought in, and a large African-type bed-frame was laid on the floor in one corner, and a bedstead with no mattress in another. We put Nora on the bedstead, which was raised about one foot from the floor. Though its springs were intact, they were also exposed. Mary, Grace and I lay on the other wooden bed in the opposite corner. Dennis and Andrew stretched out on the wooden settee, but because it was near the door, they were constantly badgered by the Simbas.

Little Grace whimpered, and would sit up every half an hour or so, saying, 'Where is Daddy?' or, 'What are they saying to Daddy?' I prayed with her very quietly almost in her ear. She clutched my hand all night.

The night was cold and we had no blankets. Mercifully one of the planters had some bed-linen and he lent a blanket to us and a sheet to Nora. The men stretched out where they could on the floor. Some of them must have gone to sleep, because I can remember hearing the sound of snoring.

During that long, cold, uncomfortable night, a young Simba—maybe in his late teens—came to me, and kneeling at my head, (I was practically at floor level) whispered to me in Bangala. He asked if I was really a Protestant missionary, and when I told him I was, he then asked if I could show him how to accept Christ as his own personal Saviour. Although he spoke in Bangala, he had a Swahili version of the gospel of John. I could not move from my position, and he did not want me to speak out loud, so while lying flat on my back with little Grace stretched out beside me, I showed him the way of salvation through the Scriptures. Finally he prayed very simply and sincerely, handing over his life and soul to Christ, and with great joy in my heart I then prayed with him. We did not realise then how much help he would be in the difficult days that lay ahead of us.

In the morning we rose very stiffly and shook ourselves. All eighteen of us had no alternative but to use the nauseating toilet facilities. There was no water either. We read and prayed together, though I cannot recall what we read.

There was still no news of the Sharpe family or Ruby Gray, the Irish nurse who worked with them, and we kept wondering what was happening to them, especially considering how the Parrys had been treated. We knew that neither Audrey nor their son Andy could walk very far. Audrey had broken a bone in her foot, and had only had the plaster removed a week ago. Andy had very bad motor co-ordination of his legs, due to spasticity, though he could walk with a brace. However I knew that he was a plucky child, and incredibly although only four years old, besides speaking English and some French he was already fluent in two African languages.

We heard that Bo Martin was still in prison. The commandant came and Mary pleaded with him to release him, and to our astonishment he said he would and kept his word. We found this out from the two teachers who had carried our belongings on their bicycles. They came later and told us that Bo had been released and was actually in the commandant's office.

The plantation men and their wives were sent off to a different place, leaving us in that awful house. We mentioned the problem with sanitation to the Simbas, who promised help and actually sorted it out before the day was through by making the poor national prisoners do the work. They even filled the bath with water from the river, but the plug didn't fit very well, and in two hours the bath was empty again. We were also given a bucket. Unfortunately, it had a number of holes, but if you were quick enough you could just about manage to carry water to the toilet from the bath, although it meant getting your feet wet all the way.

Now we had water and Bo was out of prison, our main problem was food. We adults still had little appetite, but not so the children, especially Andrew who would announce to us all at half-hourly intervals, 'Say, but I'm real hungry' and would clutch his abdomen to emphasise the point. An active, growing boy of ten was bound to be hungry even under normal circumstances. Our Simba guards were unsympathetic. The village men who had come with us to Banalia realised our problem and went to a village about a mile away where UFM had a district church with a resident evangelist and his wife. They returned in the late afternoon with a steaming bowl of rice, some chicken, some bananas and a pineapple. Congolese women cook over open fires and probably had to catch the chicken first, cut the pineapple from their garden, and ask someone to climb a banana palm to get the fruit. It was therefore hardly surprising that the food took so long to arrive. They would also have had to cook for themselves at the same time, as there was a curfew at sundown.

We then realised just how hungry we all were. There were no plates or cutlery—in fact none of the refinements of our western society—so after we had given thanks for the food, we all dipped our fingers into the communal bowl, and it was literally finger-licking good! We laughed hysterically at the sight we must have presented to the continuous stream of onlookers who were always at the windows and doors. With hindsight, I realise that the majority of the Africans who were watching us always ate like that, so they would not have understood why we were laughing. Actually I think it was a release of tension, but it also cured Andrew's hunger pangs.

There was still no news of the Sharpes or Ruby. When the commandant came to check up on us, we asked him for information. He said he was worried too, and if they had not come by morning he would personally go to find them, although I think he said that just to keep us quiet.

We only had one lamp between us now, as the Simbas had taken the second and the Parrys had not brought one. Sadly no sooner had we lit it than the Simbas insisted on taking it too, so there was only one thing to do at sundown—go to bed.

When the plantation folk left, we explored the house, and found another room with two single beds and one very lumpy mattress, and yet another room with a three-quarter-size bedstead and a tiny mattress stuffed with leaves. The Parrys decided to take the two-bedded room, and Mary and I the other. We then all had a time of reading and prayer in the semi-darkness together before separating to go to our rooms.

We pushed our 'mattress' into the middle of the springs, and decided to 'top and tail'—no doubt it would have been amusing under different circumstances, but by this time we were too tired to care. Mercifully, we slept through most of the night, though we woke up very early in the morning because we were freezing. Even though we hadn't undressed, it was still very cold without bedclothes. In the tropics, especially in places on the Equator like Congo, when the sun goes down the temperature can fall 15°C (or 27°F). We lay there whispering in the dark until at long last daylight came and we were able to get up. We washed in a cupful of water and combed our hair, feeling much better for the night's sleep. Dennis led us in family worship.

We ate the bananas which we had saved from the day before. We had also saved the pineapple, but did not eat it in case we might be hungry later.

Bo Martin was allowed to come to see us, and he said he would go back to Bopepe to arrange for blankets and eating utensils to be sent to us. He also made arrangements with the local evangelist and his wife to feed us twice a day, and we gave him some money so they could buy some food from the market. We watched as he and the two teachers cycled away. While he had been in Banalia, we felt we had somebody who could help us; now we felt very much alone—at least from a human point of view.

During that morning we were thrilled to see several of the Bopepe women, each carrying a bundle on her head. They had met Bo who told them where we were. Mercifully, they had no problems getting permission from the Simbas to see us. I feel very humbled when I recall that they had taken a collection among themselves which raised enough money to buy rice and peanuts (the staple diet for that tribe) and four chickens! They had brought along enough for two or three days and promised to come every other day. We were very moved by this lovely gesture on their part, for we knew their lives were hard and most lived at poverty level. Their willingness to do this was an outward witness of the indwelling Christ. We sat and talked, and when the women left we all wept together. They took the food to the evangelist's wife and then proceeded to cross on the ferry before cycling the 15 miles back to Bopepe. They had set out from Bopepe at 5am, a whole hour before daybreak. It had been a long and tiring day for them— and all for us.

Later that same day we were to experience the ugliness of mob violence at first hand. It was about 2.30 in the afternoon and we had nothing to do, so we were just sitting talking quietly, and Andrew was teasing Grace as only boys can tease their little sisters. Suddenly a lorry full of singing

Simbas turned into Banalia past our 'prison-house'. We heard it screech to a stop, then we heard their cry, 'Where are the foreigners?'—indicating the colour of our skin. Our stomachs contracted and our mouths went dry. We could only pray an emergency prayer for help.

They surrounded the house, seemingly very, very angry with us. A youngster of about eleven or twelve years old stood in the doorway. Our guards had fled in fear of these angry Simbas and the little ones in particular. The boy at the door turned his back on us, and addressed the now rapidly growing crowd. He told them how the white people were fighting for the National Army, how the white women were joining the National Army and how he personally had seen lots of Simbas shot down and killed by the white women. We heard the rumble of agreement and astonishment from the crowd. We knew it was untrue, but by this time, the crowd were in an ugly mood and ready to believe anything. We later discovered that the rebels had just lost another town to the National Army. We were ordered out of the house—'Get your things and go to Stanleyville!' they yelled at us.

In looking back I often have wondered if it was like this for Jesus when he was arrested and taken from pillar to post with the screaming mob behind him all the way. We rushed to grab the belongings which we had kept in our cases, for in a way we had anticipated a sudden move like this. We were separated from each other by the mob, and I was surrounded by angry Simbas digging their spears into my ribs. The others were in exactly the same predicament. I was forced to run with my heavy suitcase. 'Mateka, that's what you are Mateka, Mateka, Mateka,' they kept repeating, all the time making gestures clearly intended to represent the cutting of throats. Strangely enough all fear left me and I was able to answer them, if rather breathlessly, 'Oh, that is fine, I'm ready to die, but what about you? Are you ready?' This only made them angrier. I expect we were all shooting off arrow prayers, but how does one pray in such a situation? Mostly 'Help, Lord!' I caught a glimpse of Nora in the crowd ahead of me, but could not see Dennis, the children or Mary, but supposed they were behind me somewhere among the ever-increasing crowd.

Suddenly in the middle of all the noise and confusion, a loud voice was heard yelling, 'Not the missionaries, they're Protestants, send them back!'

What being Protestant meant to them we weren't sure but we were duly turned around and allowed to return at our own pace. After that, most of the crowd left us in order to harass the plantation owners instead, who presumably had the same treatment meted out to them. Even so, we still had several Simbas around us, one of whom was a boy of about ten years of age. He was dressed in a monkey-skin hat and had fur pieces on his wrists, and of course the usual medicine charms around his neck, and he carried a spear, the handle of which was cut down to size. He smiled at me, and I noticed that not all his upper molars were through. Isn't it strange the things one notices under such conditions? He then asked, 'Aren't you Mademoiselle Margarita from Bopepe?' and when I nodded, he added, 'You delivered my mother last time—you're good.' Then, pointing to Mary he added, 'And that woman over there—isn't she Beka?' (Beka was how they pronounced Baker. Mary was seldom referred to as 'Mademoiselle'.) Again I nodded, hardly believing the gentle way he spoke. 'She once took my mother in her car to the Banalia Hospital before you had a place at Bopepe. She's a good woman too. Why are you here? You've not done anything wrong.'

We reached the house absolutely exhausted. The little Simba immediately made himself our guard, and very effective he was too. Why the little Simbas were feared by their older colleagues we never found out, but somehow they had an authoritative air despite their lack of years or size. The house was surrounded by Simbas peering in at the windows. Some were gesturing obscenely, while others mimicked a throat being cut. All of them were brandishing spears.

None of us felt very brave at that time, but our main concern was for Grace. She was ashen and on the verge of hysteria. Dennis suggested we prayed with our eyes open, literally 'praying and watching'. As he prayed, so we calmed down, and eventually even Grace settled down quietly too.

Our self-appointed ten-year-old guard found another youngster of about fourteen and a youth of maybe nineteen or twenty to stand with him, and thanks to his authoritative attitude the crowd dispersed.

We heard a shout and saw the lorry go past the window again, packed tightly with chanting Simbas as before, but also carrying the plantation owners and their wives who had left us the day before. The women looked terribly pale. We wondered what fate awaited them at their journey's end. To this day I do not know if any of them survived.

Amazingly we actually felt quite hungry at this point and regretted sending all the peanuts to the village to be cooked. We had not eaten since 9.30am and it was now 4.30pm. We knew that if nothing came by 5pm when the curfew began we would have to wait until at least 7am the next morning when it was lifted. The curfew arrived but the food did not—hardly surprising in view of the events of the afternoon. Time to tighten our belts again—literally. How hard this would be for the children, especially Andrew with his healthy boy's appetite. However he did not utter a word of complaint. Eventually, at 6.30pm with no light and nothing to eat, we prayed together, then went to our rooms, ostensibly to sleep.

Mary and I were still getting ourselves into the top and tail position on the miniscule mattress when the door suddenly flew open. One of the Simbas who had originally arrested us at Bopepe burst in saying that a VIP had arrived who would probably demand to see the white prisoners. He warned us in a loud voice that this man was very hard and might even shout and scream at us. However, if we were polite, he, the Simba would speak well on our behalf. Then, lowering his voice to almost a whisper, he added that the Sharpes were just the other side of Bopepe, and would arrive in Banalia in the morning.

We quietly thanked God for positive news of Ian and Audrey, and committed them yet again to God's care and protection. We wondered who the VIP could be, as the Simba had spoken of him with such awe. While we lay there on our mattress, top to tail, balancing precariously, we heard the outside doors of the house being opened and the Simba on guard being interrogated by somebody evidently in authority. The VIP had obviously arrived. We heard footsteps going into the Parrys' room, and Grace's scream of terror as she awoke from sleep to see the room full of men.

How do you pray in a situation like this? It is so difficult to voice thoughts when your heart is pounding and seemingly racing at an incredible speed, and your ears are strained for sound. I started to pray, 'This is an SOS, Father; we need your help,' and found myself saying it over and over again. Mary was repeating quietly, 'We're in your hands Lord, we're in your hands.'

The door of our small room was thrust open and in marched a group of men carrying lamps. I struggled to sit up, being blinded by the sudden light. For some unknown reason I have always felt it degrading to lie in bed when people are in the room. What a sorry sight we must have looked—Mary lying with her feet by my head, and me with my feet by hers, both of us clutching the mattress to stop ourselves rolling off. It may sound funny in retrospect but it was not at the time.

It turned out that there were two VIPs. One held a radio in his arms which was blaring out the cha-cha-cha, so beloved of these Simbas. He didn't bother to turn it down, but spoke above the noise. I wondered whose it had been originally. He listened politely while 'our' Simba made his report on us, then asked us several questions about our work and nationality. He told us not to worry and said that he would try and find us more suitable accommodation. Then they all filed out, closing the door as they went, and taking the lights and noisy radio with them. They then left the house, and eventually everything quietened down. Not to worry! What did he think we were worried about?

The VIP turned out to be the civil administrator and he kept his promise, for the next day we were allowed to use his house during the day, although we had to return to the dirty house in the evening. He had a clean home, well furnished and with a real bathroom with real water. We were so grateful for this respite from our squalid conditions.

The Sharpe family and Ruby Gray still had not arrived so the commandant and the civil administrator went by lorry to look for them.

The day passed quietly enough. Our guard was kept to a minimum and the mob was kept at bay. Food was brought at 10am—bananas fried in palm-oil. They tasted delicious, and were still hot even though the village was a mile away. We were promised some more at 2pm.

We had several visits from Simbas who wanted to tell us personally what they thought of the white race and Protestant missionaries in particular, but when they became too abusive even by Simba standards, our guards would make them leave.

Mary had a chain attached to her reading glasses which she wore round her neck. It meant she could have them with her all the time, even when she did not need to wear them. The clips which fastened the chain to her glasses were large and ornate. One day we heard the guards discussing them and saying they were a secret radio, so Mary very wisely decided to remove the chain and left it in the administrator's house tucked down between two of his cushions.

The long periods of inactivity while keeping an eye on us soon led to our guards becoming bored. They decided one day that we had drugs and weapons with us which were capable of being used to take our own lives with. Even though we explained that this was against all our Christian teaching, they insisted on searching our baggage. Personally, I think they did this out of sheer curiosity. They relieved us of anything that had a sharp point—pins, needles, nail scissors, two small kitchen knives and even the tin-opener. They also wanted Mary's hairpins, and made her remove them. She had long hair, which she usually wore either in a bun or plaited round her head. As it fell down her back she asked what was she expected to do with it. They suggested tying it round her neck. We laughed so much at this ridiculous idea, especially when Mary demonstrated how impossible it was, that they gave her pins back—realising that they had made fools of themselves. It never occurred to any of them to cut it off, probably because they had never seen long straight hair before. They also took our aspirins and anti-malarial drugs, but said we could have them if we needed them provided we asked. This turned out to be an empty promise, as we found out later.

On Sunday November 8th at about 9am our colleagues from Bongondza finally arrived. We were greatly relieved and naturally thrilled to see them, but appalled at the state they were in. They were filthy, covered in the thick red dust from the road, sunburned, tired and hungry, but pleased to see our friendly faces again.

They had been arrested on November 4th and forced to go on foot to Kole, fifteen miles away. As neither Audrey nor Andrew were able to walk very far, the local Christians loaned them their bicycles, pushing them all the way. As a reward for such kindness, when they reached Kole they were struck across the face for helping the white people.

The stay at the small administrative outpost of Kole lasted rather longer than planned. Dr Ian Sharpe was supposed to have brought all his equipment with him, as well as any food they would need. As these details had been overlooked, poor Ian and Ruby Gray were sent back—with the inevitable Simba escort—to do the necessary packing. A lorry followed them to pick up all the goods.

Meanwhile, Audrey and the three children, Jillian, aged eight, Alison, seven and four-year-old Andrew all had to wait at Kole. They were not given anywhere to lie down or rest. There was a bench for them to sit on, but it had no back to it. Nobody gave them any food, which is totally contrary to African culture, but probably the local people had either fled into the jungle or were too afraid to befriend them. They were there for twenty-four hours. Audrey told us that the children slept most of the night on the ground.

The Bongondza Pastor, Masini Phillippe, was also arrested. His son Mbongo Samuel, should have been arrested too, but he was away in Stanleyville. They took his wife and baby as hostages until he returned, although they were not even sure if he would be able to come back. With them also was another Christian, Tele Gaston, who refused to leave the party. Both Tele and Masini were cruelly tied up and then beaten, unable to defend themselves.

The next day Ian, Ruby and the lorry arrived at Kole. Ian was ordered to take off his shoes and socks. In that area most Africans walk barefoot and the wearing of shoes, let alone socks, was anathema to the Simbas. They surrounded Ian, dancing, yelling, and brandishing their spears. Suddenly an officer appeared on the scene having been attracted by all the noise. He demanded to know why they were treating the doctor in this way. Ian was allowed to put on his shoes and socks again, and the entire party boarded the lorry and set off on the fifty-mile journey to Banalia.

At one place on their journey they were made to dismount and both Ian and Audrey were struck across the face, but the Simba who struck them was immediately set upon by the other Simbas, tied up and cruelly beaten. It was very distressing and frightening for the three children to have to witness all these events.

They finally arrived at Banalia after taking four days—horrendous ones at that—to cover approximately seventy miles. We were in the administrator's house when they arrived and they were only too pleased to utilise the bathroom facilities and have a thorough clean up.

There was little we could offer them in the way of food, as we only had a few bananas left over from the day before. It was not much when shared among all six of them, but no-one complained, not even the children.

Pastor Masini Phillipe and Tele Gaston were brought in, but placed in another part of the room. They both had rope burns on their arms and wrists where they had been bound. We shared our food and water with them, but they were not allowed to clean themselves up. They were sent straight to the official prison building with all its appalling squalor.

Later on that morning we were informed that we were to be moved to yet another house; and our friends from Bongondza would be separated from us, so that Ian and Ruby could work in the hospital. We would continue to be held prisoner in the house. We quickly repacked our few belongings and transferred to our new quarters.

The Bongondza party were put in another house about five hundred yards from ours. Its windows amazingly still had curtains; we wondered who had left it in such a hurry. They had guards who would protect them from any anti-white demonstrations, so they were told. We found out later that the Simba I had led to Christ that first night was the chief of the military police, and it was he who always chose our guards. The Bongondza house always had ex-Bongondza schoolboys, so everyone was happy with this arrangement. We were told all this by Audrey who was able to send us a note.

Our new house—or rather prison—was almost opposite the ferry landing stage, the first house past the now defunct post office. We had a lovely view across the river but that was all. There was very little in the way of furniture, a dining table and six chairs in one room, a bedstead with a base of the open woven-type made with vines in one bedroom, and nothing except an enormous wardrobe in the second. I realise now that an African would have regarded this amount of furniture as more than ample for our needs.

The 'wardrobe' room led into what we called the 'sun-room', a long narrow room four feet by twelve feet which trapped all the afternoon sun. There was also a filthy stinking bathroom, in much the same state as we had found in the first house.

Our hearts sank as we viewed our new quarters. We had a word with the administrator and he arranged for the bathroom to be cleaned, and water

Pictured: *Pastor Masini Phillipe*

brought, which improved our situation somewhat—at least in the short term. He could not do anything about the lack of beds, but the Lord had it all in hand for later that day the teacher from Bodela, the Parrys' village, brought them some blankets, which they graciously shared with us. I gave them my Bible as they had been forced to leave in such a hurry that they had not been able to take one with them. Mary let me share her Bible with her. I also had *Daily Light*, which is usually a very small book.

So, we had 'beds', blankets, water and Bibles; what more could we want? Just one more thing—something to eat. Even this need was met when the evangelist's wife and son arrived during the afternoon with some food for us.

That first night the four Parrys slept on the bed frame, though I doubt whether Dennis and Nora really slept at all. Mary and I stretched out on the dining-room table—again in top and tail fashion. It made a very hard bed—so much so that in the morning Mary ruefully said that she understood what the Psalmist meant when he said, 'Thou tellest all my bones', she did not realise she had so many until then! We slept there for a second night, after which we discovered that the shelves in the big wardrobe in the inner room were removable, so we took them out and placed them on the cement floor, and slept on them instead. They were just as hard, being solid mahogany, but not quite so much in the public eye as we had been on the table.

Personal hygiene was minimal for all of us; we slept in our clothes and were not as neat and tidy as we would have liked—but what else could we do when our water supply was so restricted?

After a few days, a small trunk arrived from Bopepe with two blankets, two cushions, some basic cutlery and plates. We felt quite civilised! During this time Ian Sharpe and Ruby Gray were assigned to work at Banalia Hospital, about a quarter of a mile away. It was a fairly new, purpose-built hospital, with modern equipment including an x-ray plant and a well-equipped operating theatre.

Our friend the Belgian doctor had been in charge not only of the hospital but all the surrounding dispensaries and maternities, but as he had been taken to Stanleyville as surgeon-in-chief, there was no-one left to run Banalia Hospital except an elderly Catholic nun and the Congolese staff.

'There was still no news of the Sharpe family or Ruby Gray, the Irish nurse who worked with them, and we kept wondering what was happening to them, especially considering how the Parrys had been treated...'

The nun was relieved of her work when Ian and Ruby arrived, though they did allow her two or three days to explain the procedures before handing over to Ruby.

The nearest hospital to Banalia after crossing the river was 170 miles away, so Banalia Hospital was strategically placed to receive the rebel wounded. Ian and Ruby were consequently kept very busy, frequently being called out at night.

About this time, the evangelist and his wife, who had been kind enough to prepare food and bring it to us twice daily, were threatened with reprisals if they came again. They had four young children, and we felt it was not right to ask them to run risks for us, so sorrowfully we bade them farewell. We learned later that their house had been burned to the ground because they had helped us in this way.

So now our food supply was cut off. How would the Lord feed us now, we wondered. Surely he who could feed five thousand at a word could provide for the six of us. Our answer came from a very unexpected quarter.

It was 12.30pm, and we were sitting around the dining table. Mary was knitting and the Parrys were playing Scrabble, which Mary had packed in her suitcase back at Bopepe with her knitting. Suddenly the guards were all changed, and we noticed the new ones were military policemen. They brought their chairs into the house and sat facing us, acute hostility written all over their faces. Although they were talking among themselves their conversation was actually directed at us—how we were going to dance to their music. They would keep glancing out of the window, rubbing their hands together with obvious glee and great anticipation. Somebody whose arrival would bring them great pleasure was coming along the road towards our house.

I should mention here that only Mary and I, as Lingala speakers, could understand what was being said. Most rebels, including our guards, spoke Lingala as their mother tongue. The Parrys only knew Swahili, which I also spoke, although not Mary.

Mary said very quietly, 'Go on playing your game as though nothing has happened, but at the same time pray.' A noisy crowd was gathering all round the house, and the tension became almost unbearable.

A shout announced the arrival of three nuns and a priest carrying their shoes and stockings in their hands. They looked so pitiful. We knew how they were feeling. They had been resting when the rebels arrived and ordered them to walk a mile or so barefoot on the stoniest parts of the road to the house where we were staying, and all this during the hottest time of day when the sun was directly overhead.

They were unceremoniously pushed into the room Mary and I had occupied. The Simbas then ordered us to remove our shoes and to follow the others. We were told to stand to attention, then out they went shutting the door behind them. We had no idea what had caused this new outbreak of open hostility, and even as we whispered among ourselves, we were none the wiser, for neither the nuns nor the priest had heard anything on their radio.

About every ten or fifteen minutes the Simbas came back to taunt us and to make sure we were all still standing. Even though the children were frightened, they co-operated and kept quiet, though Grace tended to cling on to her mother. Then the priest had a mild attack of angina and had to sit on the floor. When the Simbas saw him there, they were furious and one of them kicked him. He remained on the floor. Another time, when they opened the door, Dennis, who had been leaning on the wall, did not stand up in time so he was struck across the face. These men clearly enjoyed their new-found power.

At about 5.30pm the sisters' houseboy came with rice and corned beef for them, but they were not hungry. They offered some to us, but we were not hungry either, not even Andrew. We were not allowed any water.

As darkness fell at 6.30pm we found we had a lamp, although we were not sure where it came from. The priest had some matches and we lit it. Unfortunately, no sooner was it lit when the Simbas came in and removed it, leaving us in the dark.

The Simbas on the veranda sang songs of hate about us, this time in Swahili. I was glad Mary could not understand the words, but all the Parrys did, even Grace.

By 8pm the children were beginning to fidget and Grace was beginning to whimper with tiredness, so Nora asked permission for them to lie down. The request was granted, in fact Nora was even allowed to sit with them in their room and given a light, so we had some cause to praise God even in this situation.

How we all prayed during that long night I do not know, except I know how *I* prayed. Two verses of scripture kept coming to my mind, which Dennis had read to us that morning when we had devotions together: 'I will trust and not be afraid' (Isaiah 12:2) and the counterpart 'What time I am afraid, I will trust in thee' (Psalm 56:3.) It was the latter verse that formed the basis of my prayers. I would pray something like this; 'Lord I am afraid, therefore I am trusting in thee to help us in this special hour of need.' How many times I prayed that prayer I do not know, but I think it was fairly often. No doubt all the others were sending up their own particular prayers.

The Simbas' visits became more and more unpleasant. They said outrageous things and threatened us with all kinds of torture. One Simba came in with a pipe full with hemp (cannabis), and tried to make us smoke it. He started with the sisters, who refused, although the priest, who was a smoker, accepted. Then they moved along the line and came to us. I was first. 'Smoke this or we'll beat you,' they ordered me. I was given the courage to answer, 'You will have to beat me then, for I will not smoke it.' He then filled his mouth with smoke, and putting his nose against mine, blew the smoke over my face. It was a simple measure just to hold my breath. Mary's turn came next, followed by Dennis and Nora, who had been pulled back into the room for this particular ceremony. Each time the same command, each time the same answer. He then came back to me and repeated his little act, after which they all left. Nora went back to the children, slamming the door behind her, and we all began breathing freely again, praising the Lord for his help thus far, and asking for strength to get through the rest of the night.

The Simbas came back to take the priest out of the room. They made him smoke cannabis for several hours, until eventually he kept vomiting, and had to be laid out on the floor in Nora's room.

Just after midnight, we were ordered to lie down on our so-called bed, three in a row with myself in the middle, and the eldest sister at our feet, which by this time were filthy. We had to place our feet on her back, which we tried to do gently, so as not to hurt her and also to avoid making too much mess of her white habit.

Mary was taken to the bathroom, and made to stand to attention for a whole hour in the dark by the side of the stinking toilet, in bare feet. When her hour was up, I had to take her place. During my hour a Simba crept up in the dark and grabbed me by the arms. I threatened to scream if he did not leave me alone, whereupon he abandoned whatever evil intentions he may have had and left me alone. After my hour was up, I was ordered to lie down again with Mary, but the three sisters and Dennis (who was brought back to our room) were made to stand to attention in the dark again. This lasted for a further half an hour after which they were told to lie down again. Dennis was allowed back with Nora and the children, and the sisters lay down again, this time with two at our feet and one next to Mary.

The Simbas went on smoking their cannabis until they were mentally inflamed and totally irrational. At 4.30am they decided that Mary and I would dance to their music. We were ordered to get up and were taken to what had been the dining room. We still had no shoes on our feet. The only light in the room came from a palm-oil lamp—presumably they had run out of kerosene, for the hurricane lamps were out of action. Though the light was poor, we saw a number of Simbas sitting around. One of them was dancing, a sensual dance usually reserved for the villages on moonlit nights. He came over to get me to dance with him, but I refused to move. My feet felt as though they had taken root just where they were. He threatened to beat me, but the Lord gave me courage, and as I argued with him, a Simba who had been in the shadows came into the light and commanded this man to leave us alone, threatening him with punishment if he tormented us anymore. I recognised him as one of the group who had arrested us at Bopepe, and he was apparently a senior military policeman. We were then ordered back to our room and made to lie down again, praising God again for his gracious intervention.

Never had a night seemed so long, but at last daylight came, and we were left alone. The Simbas went to bathe in the river, or perhaps to look for food.

As I had loaned my Bible to Dennis and Nora, and Mary's was shut away in the sun-room, it was good that I still had my little *Daily Light* with me. It was November 14th, and I will quote the verses in full, as they were so relevant for us, and gave us all such comfort. Mary translated each verse for the sisters.

'Thou art my help and my deliverer; make no tarrying, O my God.' Psalm 40:17.

'The steps of a good man are ordered by the Lord: and he delighteth in his way. Though he fall, he shall not be utterly cast down: for the Lord upholdeth him with his hand.' Psalm 37:23–24.

'In the fear of the Lord is strong confidence: and his children shall have a place of refuge.' Proverbs 14:26.

'Who art thou, that thou shouldst be afraid of a man that shall die and of the son of man which shall be made as grass; and forgetteth the Lord thy maker?' Isaiah 51:12–13.

'I am with thee to deliver thee.' Jeremiah 1:8.

'Be strong and of a good courage, fear not, nor be afraid of them; for the Lord thy God, he it is that doth go with thee, he will not fail thee, nor forsake thee.' Deuteronomy 31:6.

'I will sing of thy power; yea I will sing aloud of thy mercy in the morning; for thou has been my defence and refuge in the day of trouble.' Psalm 59:16.

'Thou art my hiding place, thou shalt preserve me from trouble; thou shalt compass me about with songs of deliverance.' Psalm 32:17.

These were precious promises which we could claim for ourselves and as we shared them with the nuns they too were visibly comforted.

Later that same morning the door was thrust open, and in came several senior rebels. The leader said he was the district commissioner, a self-imposed rank of course, but it sounded important. He was a short, stocky man, with an enormous black beard which covered half of his face. He wore a pair of sunglasses—another Simba status symbol—although one lens was cracked and the other still had the price tag stuck to it. He was accompanied by quite a large retinue, some of whom were soldiers and the rest presumably administrative staff. The administrator was standing right at the back of this crowd.

The commissioner proceeded to lecture us for half an hour in rather poor French. He said he was a Protestant and knew his Bible. He quoted how the Jews had been oppressed in Egypt and how Moses was appointed by God to lead them out. He went on to say that Patrice Lumumba was the God-appointed Moses of the present day, and that they, the Congolese, were like the Jews in Moses' time. We, the hated foreigners, were the Egyptians of course and, having reminded us of their fate, he assured us that ours would be similar. He then asked our nationalities. The nuns, who were Belgian, came in for his verbal, almost vitriolic abuse. He made fun of them, and almost spat on the crucifix one of them was wearing before venting his wrath on Mary because she was American. We just had to listen; there was nothing we could say or do. After finishing his long monologue, he marched out very pompously, followed by his faithful retinue. We had to laugh, what he had said was so obviously propaganda and so utterly ridiculous.

No sooner had they gone when the administrator returned and quietly told us not to worry. The commissioner had made his speech simply in order not to lose face in front of his staff. We were grateful for his kind and courteous words, for we had felt pretty battered mentally at the time. The sisters wickedly said the commissioner looked like the devil, and from then on we referred to him as 'Monsieur the Devil'.

At midday the administrator came back, and we were called into his presence. It felt like 'a presence' as he was immaculate, clean and well groomed, while we were dirty, dishevelled, unkempt and still barefoot. We had to stand at attention before him. He then abused us verbally in good French, which surprised us somewhat after his kind words earlier on, but we assumed it must be for the same reason—that he could not be seen to lose face in front of his inferiors. He gave permission for us to put our shoes on and allowed us to sit down again. He said we would not be tormented unless the rebels suffered a further defeat, in which case we would have to be punished for the deeds of our relatives (in other words the foreign mercenaries fighting for the Government). We did not ask him what had happened yesterday and he didn't volunteer the information. However, we would no longer have the freedom of the whole house, only the room we occupied and the bathroom. In addition, our guard would be doubled. We went back to our room grateful for even a small respite, and an hour later were allowed some food.

The following morning Nora Parry collapsed, and was taken to the hospital to be cared for by Ian Sharpe and Ruby Gray. Dennis and the two children went too. The Catholic priest was sent along with them because of his heart condition, and while he was there he kindly shared his food with the Parrys. Where it came from we never knew. Conditions at the hospital were terrible, nowhere to sleep as all the beds had been stolen, no water, no toilet facilities, and everyone under constant supervision with virtually no privacy. The guards were very rude and they had little if any peace.

On Sunday morning and specifically because it was a Sunday, the Simbas made Dennis and Andrew pick up leaves and rubbish in the hospital grounds for about two hours. They hit Dennis several times for no reason at all except to show their power over him. On the Monday evening he and the children were sent back to our prison-house, leaving Nora alone and without help. We wrote several letters to the administrator about this and he eventually allowed Nora to come back too. We were so glad to see her, even though she had only been away three days. She looked so frail and tired, and it was both a joy and a privilege to minister to and comfort her, the sisters vying with us in making a fuss of her.

Our days were spent reading and praying, playing Scrabble or just talking. We made our own amusement, taking it in turns to sit on one of four chairs we had found. As the youngest in our room, I made a seat out of my case. It was rather low down, but better than the cement floor.

The house was situated right by the administration post, and each morning we would watch the Simbas at roll-call. One day, as we watched prisoners from the real prison go marching by, we saw Masini Philippe, his son Mbongo Samuel and Tele Gaston marching with the others, so we knew they were still alive and would watch for them every morning after that. Later we heard that Masini had been made foreman of the working party because of his exemplary conduct. We felt justifiably proud of him. Often we would see the prisoners carrying one of their number who had been beaten unconscious. Frequently such a man would die before the roll-call was finished.

There was one man who was notably different from all the other Simbas, in that he had a military bearing and his clothes were immaculate and in good condition. He spent all his time with the new recruits (mostly young boys), and we rightly guessed he had been a sergeant-major in the National Army. From time to time he would visit us in prison. He would march in, salute, and stand smartly to attention before proceeding to talk to us in disjointed sentences, using several languages and laughing very heartily at his own jokes at the end of each sentence. We all thought he was crazy. He never said anything that made sense. Mary called him 'Mr Jingle' after the Charles Dickens character. One evening when he came to see us he was slightly drunk and as he burst into his usual hearty laughter, he threw his head back and his hat fell off. His escort picked it up and put it back on his head for him without so much as a smile. Obviously the joke was lost on them too.

On November 17th, we were informed that we were technically free, and that Ian Sharpe and the others from Bongondza had been free all the time; Nora aptly described our freedom as 'the freedom of compulsion'. We were still strictly guarded, and not allowed to move about in the house apart from our rooms. Surely if we really had been free one of the group at the hospital would have been allowed over to see us. Nora had told us that Ian and Ruby were always under armed guard whenever they went to work in the hospital.

About this time I was called into the administrator's office and when I entered, Masini Philippe was there. In front of the administrator was a typewriter, which I immediately recognised. He asked if I knew how Masini came to have it and I explained that I had given it to him when I was stationed at Bongondza. So *why* had I given it to him? Because I did not type, I explained, and as Masini was a friend who had need of it I was only too glad to give it to him. I then had to sign a form to that effect.

Looking out of the window we saw our tribal chief Mulaba Fidèle. He saw us at the same time, and was given permission to come in and speak to us. He said they were trying hard to secure our release. Apparently he had come the thirteen miles every day to plead for us, and the local people had even organised a petition and signed it. His life was in danger as the rebels obviously resented his interference on our behalf. He looked thin and tired, but was undaunted in his new-found faith in the Lord.

Towards the end of our third week we heard the sound of a plane overhead. Outside our house panic reigned. We wondered what it was doing. Only after my rescue did I find out that the plantation people had told the authorities that we were in Banalia, and the plane had been sent out to see if we were still there. The rebels said to us that if it had bombed Banalia, they would have shot us immediately, and we believed them, for they were extremely angry.

Chapter 3

During our captivity, I had continued my usual pattern of Bible readings, and at this time I kept coming across many promises of deliverance. I was not especially looking for such verses, simply following the pattern of study I had begun at Bopepe. One day I shared these thoughts with Mary and she said, 'For you Margaret, but not for me; I think I'm going to die here in Banalia.' Another time she said that she felt the sentence of death was on her, but that I would be delivered. A third time she said that of all places in Congo, she was glad it would be Banalia where she was going to die. No matter what I said to the contrary, she was so sure she would die there.

Nora Parry had read the verse, 'Now is your salvation nearer than when ye believed', and she said she felt that this was God's word to her to prepare her for death. In vain did I remonstrate with her; I showed her the promises of deliverance I had received, and like Mary she said, 'For you Margaret, but not for me.' Her main concern was for the children. What would happen to them? They had two other children, Hazel and Stephen, who were in boarding school in England. One of the evangelists from their village had brought their photographs to our house, and both Nora and Dennis would look at the pictures several times a day, doubtless praying for them at the same time.

On November 23rd, a Monday, I was told that there would be a lorry going past Banalia en route to Kole, but going via Bopepe. It was due at 2pm and I was to get on it. A road pass was given to me, showing that I was being sent back to 'resume my activities'. In many ways I was fearful of returning to the village alone, as we were right on the main road. Still, surely if I was to be freed, was this not a sign that the others would surely follow?—after all, had we not been told that we were technically free anyway? Mary made up my mind for me—not that I had any real choice in the matter. I was to go back, put the house in order, and send provisions through, along with a spare bicycle for her to ride in case there was no lorry to take her back when she was released. She could not face the prospect of that long walk again.

So I prepared to leave them, armed with a list of things to send and three weeks' worth of very dirty washing. I was allowed to call in on the Sharpes and Ruby Gray, to tell them I was going back to Bopepe that afternoon. Ian said he expected to go back to Bongondza the next day to get further supplies, and said he would call in to check if I was all right if they allowed

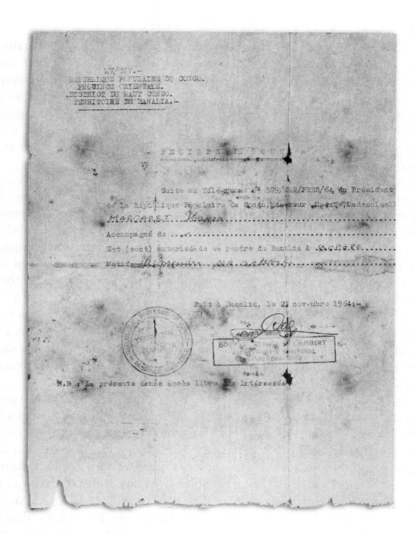

Above:
Margaret Hayes' road pass, giving her permission to take up her work in
Bopepe. It was issued at Banalia on November 23 1964. Pastor Bo Martin
found it much later in the forest

him, as he had to pass Bopepe,

As we had no idea of what was happening in the world outside Banalia, I said that if the mercenaries came to rescue them, please could they remember me at Bopepe, and reserve me a seat on the plane. Ian answered very seriously, 'Very well Margaret, we'll meet either on the plane, or in Glory.' Did he too have a premonition? They had been well cared for, and the children were allowed to play in the grounds. In many ways they were living as near normal a life as was possible in the circumstances, although always under guard.

I said my goodbyes, and then went back to the others. Dennis was permitted to carry my case to the lorry. As we said goodbye to each other, he added, 'We will be much in prayer for you there alone, and if we do not meet down here again, I will see you in Heaven.' So he too had a premonition?

After a short word of prayer together, I was off. The ferry slowly crossed the river, and I could see Mary, Nora and the sisters waving from the window of our house. I waved back until I was too far away to make them out clearly.

When I stepped off on the other side of the river, for the first time in ages I felt very much alone, even though I was surrounded by lots of people. The promise I had received that morning was, 'Whoso hearkeneth unto me shall dwell safely, and shall be quiet from fear of evil' (Proverbs 1:33). The fear of evil seemed to be all around me; it was almost tangible.

At the same time as I was making my way back to Bopepe, the National Government was finalising plans for the rescue of 1,200 hostages in Stanleyville, of whom twenty-eight were from the Unevangelised Fields Mission. The following day, Tuesday November 24th in a well-coordinated move, ground troops advanced on the city while parachutists were dropped in by air. By 3pm the city had been completely retaken. Most of the hostages were rescued, but over thirty-five lost their lives, including Hector McMillan of our mission, who was normally stationed at Bongondza with the Sharpes and Ruby Gray. Two of his six boys were also wounded when machine-gun-fire was directed into the house where they were staying. Once the city had fallen, it was virtually a deathtrap for any rebels who were caught there.

In the other direction west of Banalia and Bopepe another smaller city, Aketi, had also fallen to the National Army that same day after much fighting. No-one there had yet heard about the loss of Stanleyville, so the following day, Wednesday 25th, the rebels loaded their wounded on to lorries, and set off hoping to take them to the hospital there.

They had to pass Bopepe and then Banalia, and it was when they arrived at Banalia that they first heard about the fall of Stanleyville and realised they were effectively trapped, unable to go forward or go back.

Earlier that week their 'Prime Minister', Christophe Gbenye, had told his followers that in the event of an attack on Stanleyville, all foreigners were to be killed. The Simbas who had just arrived at Banalia were beside themselves with rage and fear, and demanded that the white prisoners be brought out. The time was 3.45pm.

Ian Sharpe was operating at the hospital, the patient a wounded Simba. Audrey and the three children, together with Ruby Gray were in the house. The Parry family, Mary Baker and the three sisters were in the prison-house, and the priest was in the hospital as a patient.

The rebels divided into three groups. The hospital group took a jeep and brought back both Ian and the priest—the Rev. Herman Bischoff, a Dutchman. They shot the patient on the table and the Congolese male nurse who had been assisting the doctor.

The doctor and the priest were taken to the ferry landing stage. Without further ado they were made to strip, then their throats were cut and their bodies thrown into the Aruwimi River.

The guards at the two houses were heavily outnumbered by the angry mob and soon overpowered. The missionaries and the children were then led to the same landing stage and made to strip. They were lined up in a row, and the children were killed first by machine-gun fire in front of their parents and each other. Then the adults were called forward one at a time and killed with knives and machetes. Any still alive when thrown in the river were given the 'coup-de-grâce'. The last to be killed was Mary at 4pm.

'In death they were not divided.'

'Be thou faithful unto death and I will give thee a crown of life.'

Thus they entered into the presence of the Lord to receive their crowns.

Their bodies were never recovered, even though the Christians from Bopepe wanted to go and find them. It was simply too dangerous, due to continual enemy activity in the area.

Chapter 4

In the jungle

I completed my journey to Bopepe in a lorry filled with Simbas going to a plantation to find some food. This was to be my first of many journeys in a vehicle commandeered by the rebels, and it was quite an experience. I was wedged into the cabin between two of them. The door on the passenger's side was fastened with wire, the ignition key was missing, and the lorry had been started by manipulating two wires.

We were passing through an area where most of the inhabitants had stayed put in their villages in spite of all the upheavals. As we neared the chief's village I could make out the sound of singing. The reason for this became apparent as we passed through—the Simbas were being entertained, not through any choice on the villagers' part; they had been forced to sing and dance. Consequently, we had to slow down, for the crowd was spilling over into the road. Several people recognised me, and promptly left their dancing to follow us to Bopepe.

My welcome back was very heart-warming, and I felt so glad to see these dear friends again. The Simbas inspected our house, and asked me to report if anything had been taken. Before continuing on their way, they ordered me to ensure I had some food prepared for them when they returned the next day. As soon as they had gone, the villagers swarmed into the house hugging me or shaking my hand till I thought my arm would fall off. Some wept with joy, some danced, all asked for news of the others at Banalia.

Mary's dog came bounding towards me and my black cat rubbed contentedly against my legs. They both looked very thin. I made the inevitable cup of tea but it was almost impossible to drink it due to the constant stream of visitors. Not that it mattered, it just felt good simply to be home again!

Bo Martin had arranged with his wife Yenga that I should eat there that evening, which meant that I had time to start putting the house in order first. We spent a long time talking about the situation we now found ourselves in, and discussed the possibility of sending a bicycle to Banalia for Mary.

Telephones were unknown in this area at that time. The main method of

'The rebels were in full flight with the National Army in hot pursuit. A few minutes later, a runner arrived from the chief's village specifically to order me into the forest with the others'

communication between the villages was by messages played on drums, the jungle making a very effective sounding-board. I had learnt to 'read' some messages and could recognise my own 'drum-name' which was 'the little animal lost in the forest.' The drums came in useful if I needed to send for my maternity aide when she was away in the jungle somewhere. That evening I heard my name being drummed out again. They were telling our houseboy, Fidèle, that I was back and that he was to come to work next day.

In the evening, Julienne, the young girl who used to sleep with us, was sent by her family to spend the night with me. There was no problem now with overcrowding in their home; but they thought it would be good for me to have some company. I moved her bed into my bedroom and we both turned in for the night before 10pm. The villagers had lent me a lamp and some kerosene, so we had some light if we needed it. I found it hard to sleep, and at midnight I got up and washed my hair. I eventually returned to bed at 2.30am and slept until 5.30am.

The day began normally, though there was a feeling of tension. Fidèle came and made bread and when the water arrived from the river he began to tackle the mountain of washing I had brought back from Banalia. I went down to the dispensary and maternity unit and cleaned everything from top to bottom, so that I could reopen it the following day. Several mothers came to show me their lovely babies, and stayed to chat with me. After lunch I started to sort out some of the things Mary had requested, and packed them into cartons convenient for carrying to Banalia.

At 3pm everything went quiet, unnaturally quiet, as though birds, animals and people were all listening for something. You could feel the tension. I was in Bo's house when two of our schoolteachers arrived and started speaking rapidly to him in their tribal language. They were excited, but at the same time apprehensive.

Bo turned to me and said, 'Stanleyville has fallen and the National Army are coming this way. You must go to the forest with the women.' I argued, but he insisted that as a woman I had no place in the war, and being white my very presence was putting them all in danger. I admit to my shame that even then I still hesitated, and Bo became very cross with me. He reiterated that the safety of the village depended on my going into the forest with the women and children.

He had hardly finished speaking when we heard the drums from the chief's village three miles away. He too was ordering that all women and children should flee to the forest, and all men were to defend their villages. The rebels were in full flight with the National Army in hot pursuit. A few minutes later, a runner arrived from the chief's village specifically to order me into the forest with the others.

I felt physically sick. Almost mechanically I took the washing off the line, repacked my case, and collected a small overnight bag and a lantern. My thoughts were racing. I wondered what was happening to my friends in Stanleyville, not to mention the folk at Banalia, Aketi and Bafwasende, who did not have the option of hiding in the jungle. I could only whisper, 'Dear Lord, I don't understand, but I'm trusting you to take care of the situation.'

Suddenly the drums sounded out in a way I had never heard before, heavy and very menacing. The men explained that this was the war cry. It went on for a long time, as each village relayed the message to the next, adding further to the sense of tension and urgency. The very air seemed to be throbbing.

I followed the women into the jungle with a sense of amazement. They were all walking at great speed with heavy loads on their backs, yet without ever tripping up, whilst I was struggling to carry my own suitcase more than a few yards without puffing, panting and constantly changing hands. Mercifully one women who was carrying a load larger than herself plus a baby on her hip grabbed my case and swung it up on top of her own belongings without even slowing down. She then carried on as quickly as before, hardly seeming to notice the extra weight. I felt very humbled and ashamed of being so weak and pampered.

The hideout had been prepared weeks before, and was three miles into the forest. We had to cross a fairly large river by means of a fallen tree trunk. I wanted to close my eyes as I crossed but dare not do so. We scrambled over trees, under trees, through mud and water, and even without my case, I was struggling to keep up with the others, frequently tripping up, stubbing my toes on tree-roots or catching my clothes on the bushes. The sun rarely penetrates into the depths of the jungle, as it is so dense, so you can lose sight of the person in front of you even though they are only a few feet away.

Chapter 4

I have no idea how the women knew the way, for there were no recognisable footpaths. I simply followed them as best I could, hoping that they knew where they were going. I'm sure I must have slowed them down but no-one complained.

When I arrived at our destination, some of the women were busy preparing food, others were cutting wood with which to construct some makeshift beds, and others had gone to find some water. One young mother sat serenely feeding her tiny baby as though nothing unusual was happening. Everybody knew what to do and how to do it—except me. Even the little three- and four-year-olds were busy gathering sticks for the many fires burning beneath cooking pots. I never felt so aware of the cultural divide between us as on that day, for while this was going on, all I wanted to do was rest. I was absolutely exhausted. I didn't even offer to help.

We were all apprehensive, and so were glad when two men from the village arrived at 10pm to stay the night with us. They took it in turns to sleep and keep watch.

They had heard on the radio about the fall of Stanleyville, and the report had mentioned that thirty-seven foreigners had been killed. I desperately wanted to know if any of my fellow-missionaries were among the dead, but nobody knew. The announcer had given their names, but foreign names are not easy to remember, and they did not know who my colleagues were anyway. They had also heard that our folk at Aketi had been rescued.

None of us slept that night, in fact the adults didn't even lie down. We read and prayed, talked and wondered. Mercifully it was not the rainy season, though it was very cold at night. At last morning came, Wednesday November 25th.

The women returned to their chores. Some went for water, some for firewood, and others cooked, while the children helped cut back the dense jungle growth to let the sunlight in. I sat and watched, amazed by their industry and feeling very helpless and rather a liability to them all.

During the afternoon I sat with Mary's dog Simba at my feet. I tried to pray but I could not shake off a sense of great uneasiness. Around 4pm, the dog suddenly sat up with his ears pricked forward, and started to whine. We thought there must be a wild animal in the vicinity, and some of the women called the dog to go with them to investigate, but he wouldn't budge, and

Above: Mary Baker with her dog, Simba

stayed at my feet, crying as though in pain for about half-an-hour, then lay down again across my feet with a big sigh. I tried to comfort him, but with my own emotions being in such turmoil, I do not think I was much help. This of course was that time our friends in Banalia were being hastened into the presence of God. Bearing in mind how the jungle can carry sound, is it possible that the dog, whose hearing is more acute than ours, could have heard what was happening there? We'll never know.

I spent the evening reading and praying, but found it hard to concentrate. The men arrived from the village at 10pm with the latest news from the radio. Nothing outstanding to report. We fully expected the National Army to reach Bopepe any day. Bo's wife said she thought we would be in the forest for a week. I wondered if I could cope with such strain for a whole week. It would not be easy.

We all slept restlessly that night, and next morning I had only just finished washing when Paul Ponea, our young school director, came and sat by me and very quietly told me to pack my things quickly; as I was to be moved. Something in his eyes told me to obey and not to quibble. I suddenly became aware just how quiet and still the camp had become. In a few minutes I was saying my goodbyes to the women, many of whom wept, while others turned their back to me in the traditional way of showing deep sorrow. Paul had previously said something to them in their tribal language, which I did not understand. He had asked them not to discuss the matter among themselves until he had had the opportunity to tell me. Once again I felt so apprehensive it made me nauseous, but I did not dare ask why I was being moved.

We plunged into the jungle, Simba the dog still with me. After about ten minutes, Paul turned round, looked at me and just said, 'Oh Mademoiselle!' He looked absolutely broken. I asked him to tell me what the matter was, but he could not speak for emotion. My *Daily Light* that morning had said, 'Fear not…thou art Mine', but it was so hard not to fear in these circumstances.

I followed on in silence behind Paul. After about a mile two of the teachers came running breathlessly towards us. They spoke rapidly to Paul in their tribal language, yet all the time with their eyes fixed on me. Then they departed in the direction of the camp, and Paul called me to him. This was the moment. 'Mademoiselle Margarita,' he began. 'I do not know how to tell you, but all the white people in Banalia were killed yesterday afternoon. When we first heard, we sent a runner to find out if it was true. They are now all with the Lord. Now they are coming to kill you too, so Bo sent me ahead to fetch you. We will meet him further along, and he will hide you away on your own until the National Army comes.'

I was stunned. I simply asked, 'All?' Paul gently and sorrowfully replied, 'Yes, all of them, Mary included.' I felt totally numb inside. I do not know how I managed to follow him along.

Mary was dead! Mary, with whom I had lived and worked for the last two years. So too were Ian and Audrey, who were friends from my home church whom I had known for more than eleven years, and had watched their children grow up. Then Dennis and Nora, whom I had worked with at Maganga. Dennis had been my Swahili teacher and I had seen their children grow up too. I didn't know Ruby so well but…how could they all be gone? These thoughts went round and round in my brain.

At that stage I was incapable of praying. I just stumbled along behind Paul like a robot. We met Bo. He hugged me. 'Thank God you are still alive. Oh Margarita, my heart is broken! But come, there is no time for sorrow. You must be hidden because they are looking for you.' Up to this time Mary's dear faithful Simba had been with me, but now it was decided that it would be better to keep him with the women. It was sad to see him go back with Paul, his tail between his legs.

We walked on in silence through the jungle. Someone at home must have been praying specifically for me, for I do not know how I made it to the tiny clearing that was our destination. Bo had brought along a garden chair for me, and there I sat, overwhelmed by my sad thoughts, and unable to cry. Bo returned briefly to the village, coming back with a pineapple he had picked from his garden. It was midday by now and I was thirsty. We ate the pineapple between us, then Bo left me again, this time for several hours, as he had things to attend to in the village. He promised to be back by nightfall.

I was grateful for the solitude and eventually began to think coherently. Why? Why? Why? I asked. It just seemed so tragic, but after a while I started to think of them in glory with the Father, and was glad for them. I prayed for the courage to face a violent death as a true believer. At that stage I had no idea how they had died, but knowing the Simbas I could make a reasonable guess. Finally I was even able to praise God for taking them all to be with him. As Geoffrey Bull puts it so beautifully in his book *God holds the key*—'Departure is really only a transfer from one sphere of service to another, but the Master knows what he is doing and never errs.'

As he had promised, Bo came back at sundown and we talked for a long time together. He kept looking at me in a strange way, and with hindsight I now realise why. In their culture, a death is always marked by very loud hysterical screaming which may last several hours, but at this stage I still hadn't shed a single tear.

We shared *Daily Light* together. We read, 'The Lord hath anointed me to preach good tidings to the meek; he hath sent me to bind up the broken-hearted, to comfort all that mourn...to give them the oil of joy for mourning, the garment of praise for the spirit of heaviness' (Isaiah 61:1–3)

Bo lit a fire, and having brought himself a garden chair, we settled down for the night. Our shelter was a tiny roof about eight feet by five made of leaves and supported by four poles, although without any kind of wall. 'In everything give thanks' says God's word, so I thanked him for the dry season and a roof over our heads.

Occasionally, I would see Bo wipe away his tears, and wished that I too could find relief in crying, but the tears would not come as I was probably still in a state of severe emotional shock.

Bo wanted to go to Banalia to recover the bodies from the river, so they could be brought back to Bopepe for burial by the church. Dear Bo was not thinking straight; he had taken fifteen blankets from the dispensary for the bodies and was preparing to take them with him on his bicycle! Happily the village elders forbade him to go, as it was too dangerous with the Simbas still there, especially while they were hunting for me. He could well have lost his life on such a mission, for the Simbas were so full of hatred for the whites they would not waste sympathy on a pastor looking for the bodies of his white friends. I also heard that the entire population of Banalia had fled to the jungle, when they realised the enormity of the crime committed by the Simbas.

We stayed in the hideout for several days, and one by one the women came to visit me. They would weep loudly, holding on to me, and though this was the custom in their culture, I believe they were really genuine in their grief and concern for me. One woman, a deaconess, came and wept long and loudly at my feet; and when I tried to comfort her by reminding her that our friends were now with the Lord and they would not want us to grieve, she replied, 'But I'm not weeping for them, I'm weeping for us who are left behind.' As she said these words, it suddenly dawned on me that of all the group at Banalia, I alone was left.

One evening four or five days after the massacre, Bo said he was going to transfer me to the village as he felt sure the National Army would be along any time. The village was almost deserted, as all the women and children were hidden away in the jungle hideout. It was nonetheless good to greet the men, as they were associated with us in our work. As they brought me some food, many of them broke down and wept. It was at this point that I was finally able to express my sorrow with tears. That evening a runner came through bringing news from Banalia with the names of all the dead and how they had been killed.

That night Bo set up a folding bed for me in one of his outhouses, and he slept on guard, as he was not totally sure about the safety of the village. The next day I had to go back into the jungle to a place that he and his brother had made months before, which was like the previous one only larger. Bo brought one or two things from the house and it was relatively comfortable.

I stayed there for three weeks, during which time the Simbas came to the village several times, demanding that I be handed over to them. They eventually decided that Bo must be handed over too, so he too had to stay with me in hiding. He was so kind and thoughtful, going out of his way to find things to make me comfortable. I felt that I was becoming an increasing liability to these dear friends of mine.

During all this time, I would spend the better part of every day just reading my Bible and praying. The Psalms were a great source of comfort, as were the books of Isaiah and Jeremiah.

In thinking through my amazing deliverance from Banalia, I felt sure that in God's economy it had not happened by accident. My colleagues had completed their work and had heard the 'Well done thou good and faithful servant, enter then into the presence of the Lord,' but my work was not finished. The more I thought about this, the more convinced I was that the Lord would have me continue to serve him in the Congo, and one day, when I was alone in the solitude of the jungle, with only the insects and trees as witnesses, I rededicated my life afresh to the Lord, to go or stay, to live or die in his service.

On November 30th, the Africans heard planes in the distance, followed by the sound of bombs exploding. Their target was Banalia, as the National Army knew there was a pocket of Simbas there. The planes came every day for a week. They did not do much damage, but they did frighten the Simbas and anyone hiding in the jungle nearby.

On Tuesday December 8th, a plane twice flew very low over the village. One or two men said they saw that one of the men on board had a pair of binoculars. This may well have been true, but at the time I was hidden in the jungle and thus unable to signal to it. I made a note in my Bible diary, 'Still looking to the Lord to effect his deliverance.'

The Simbas in the locality were furious about the plane, saying I had called it to find me and bomb them. How they thought I could contact planes they never explained. After this they redoubled their efforts to find and kill us.

The following week, everyone was in a state of great excitement: the National Army had said on the radio that they would come to Banalia that very day. The Africans had heard gunfire and explosions, and expected them along our road any minute. Bo ran into the village with a white bandage round his head. All the men did the same. (The bandage had been designated by the National Army as a non-Simba symbol.) Unfortunately a bomb had destroyed the ferry, so there was no way for anyone to cross the river. I heard later that mercenaries working with the National Army had come to Banalia, but only stayed one night as they couldn't cross the river. They then went on to rescue the missionaries at Bafwasende. There were many wounded Simbas coming to Bopepe for treatment, but the men were too afraid to let me go to them, so I was not told about this until after they had left.

The next night one of the men heard a report on the radio from the National Army that all the white people at Banalia had been killed. This meant no-one would realise I was still alive. My hopes of being rescued

'The following week, everyone was in a state of great excitement: the National Army had said on the radio that they would come to Banalia'

were suddenly dashed to the ground. Now I was alone, caught up in a situation in which I was truly out of my depth.

My reading that day was from Micah, and as I read chapter 7, I felt very rebuked for my lack of faith. Verses 7–9 read, 'Therefore will I look to the Lord, I will wait for the God of my salvation, my God will hear me. Rejoice not against me, O mine enemy; when I fall, I shall arise, when I sit in darkness, the Lord shall be a light unto me… He will bring me forth to the light, and I shall behold his righteousness.'

The following day it rained, and in the tropics this means a deluge. Even during the so-called dry season these downpours do occur from time to time. It seemed like my last ray of hope had been being washed away. I had been glad for the dry weather, for the road from Stanleyville to Banalia was pretty awful at the best of times, but at least the army could have got their vehicles through. Now it didn't matter any more how much it rained. It was too late. Bo lit a fire as soon as it became dark, so we could dry out, as we were both absolutely soaked. He dare not light a fire during the daytime as the smoke would have given us away. However as no-one normally walks through dense jungle at night, we would be safe.

It was now the middle of December—only a few days until Christmas. My thoughts turned to what would be happening in England at this time: carol singing, putting up the Christmas tree lights, last-minute shopping for presents and so on. How I wished I could be there. It was unbearable to be thinking about it when I was so isolated. In Congo, as in many African countries, there is little build-up to Christmas. Life carries on more or less as normal and only a few places have any sort of celebration.

It dawned on me too that once I was reported dead, that would be the end of all my prayer support. I was appalled at this prospect, and asked the Lord that somehow he might get it across to someone that I was not dead and to burden them to pray for me. I prayed this prayer at least once a day until the middle of March, by which time I knew folk at home were aware I was still alive. I was not to know how wonderfully the Lord answered that prayer until I eventually came home six months later. It was indeed a humbling experience to hear from various prayer groups how they had continued to pray for me throughout all the troubles.

By December 19th, the Simbas began to be more insistent that I surrender to them and threatened war on Bopepe if I stayed in hiding. On Sunday 20th December, a whole crowd of them arrived in the village. Bo took me from our hiding place and hid me in thick, dark, damp jungle, with instructions not to move. I could hear the Simbas searching the undergrowth not very far away. Local people know their own patch of jungle but as the Simbas were not local, they were too scared to venture very far in. At some point during the day Bo crept back and without saying a word gave me some bananas to eat. We were so near that we could actually hear the Simbas arguing with one another in the village.

I thought of all the promises which the Lord had given me when I was first called to serve him in Congo, especially the well-known verse from Joshua 1 'Be not afraid, neither be thou dismayed, for the Lord thy God is with thee whithersoever thou goest.' I remember whispering, 'Yes Lord, I believe you are with me, but right now I'm both afraid and dismayed.' It did not make any sense to me. Why had I escaped the Banalia massacre if I was to die in the jungle like a hunted animal? Then my thoughts went back to the last leaders' conference we had held a couple of months earlier at Bopepe and how Bob McAllister had preached on 'Not my will but thine.' As I thought about this, I remembered that the Lord had said this after asking that the cup might pass from him. Had I reached that place where I too could say, 'Nevertheless, not my will but thine'? As I thought this over, I eventually realised that if this was God's will for my life, then the responsibility was his, and he would keep his promise to be with me whatever was to happen. There is a saying, 'in acceptance lieth peace'. I don't know who said it but as I surrendered to his will I was overwhelmed with a great peace in my heart. I need not worry about the future, for it was all in the Lord's hands.

It was not much longer after this that Bo came back. He was accompanied by his eldest son, Stetefano, aged eleven, who was to guard me for the rest of the day and then lead me back to our hideout when it got dark. He also stayed with us through the night. We had a time of prayer together in the hideout, and Bo read the evening portion of *Daily Light* for the day; 'With God all things are possible'…'Have I no power to deliver?'…'Lord it is nothing with thee to help, whether with many or with them that have no power.' As we read these words, we realised that we had no power apart from God. This turned out to be the last time we read that little book together.

We got up as soon as dawn broke, and after a short word of prayer, struck camp, and headed off to another place. Our route took us through the thick jungle again, always a struggle for me. For a while, we waded down a river to conceal our progress, before going back into the jungle again. We eventually stopped, and after Bo had made a tiny clearing, he and Stetefano went back to collect the rest of our belongings, while I cooked some rice on the little Primus stove we had brought with us. Bo later cut down a few small bamboo branches and some saplings so we would have a roof over our heads when night came.

Suddenly at 3.30pm we heard shooting and men yelling the unforgettable 'Simba! Simba!' We heard them running down the pathway and into the jungle towards the camp where the village women were hiding—the same place where I had spent two nights a while ago. Obviously there must have been a traitor as the Simbas were being lead straight to the camp. Then the war-drums sounded. Bo grabbed his briefcase, I picked up my small travelling bag, and we plunged into the thick undergrowth, back through the river, and on and on through thick jungle. We heard shooting and women screaming. The Simbas were calling my name and telling me to give myself up. Bo told me to be quiet and not to move. We lay low under the bushes until nightfall, not daring to move a muscle and hardly daring even to breathe.

Eventually, Bo led us out into a small field of maize, where we met some men from another village who had come to defend Bopepe. They took us to what had been the women's camp, except that by now the women had fled. Instead we found a few men engaged in an argument. When they saw Bo, they cheered and clapped.

They hid me behind a little leaf wall. There was a wounded Simba lying the other side of it, and they were arguing about whether they should kill him. Nobody had been killed from the village at this point in time, but Bo's eldest brother's wife Ruta and my faithful assistant midwife had been taken prisoner by the Simbas.

Bo, by virtue of his seniority in the tribe, was then automatically made judge and jury. He heard both sides of the argument. The Simba, a young man of twenty, an adjutant, had been ordered to wreck Bopepe, but not to kill anyone, only to frighten the villagers. He had been afraid to do this, but had been threatened by his senior officers with beating and demotion if he failed. He had been wounded, caught by the men of the village and was now on trial. Today we would call it a 'kangaroo-court'. Most of the men wanted to kill him then and there, while others argued against it.

Bo explained that as Christians, we had an example to give to non-Christians. We were here to build up the Church, and glorify the Lord, not to kill our enemies. If we were really Christian we would forgive them.

He finally had his own way, and was keen to let the man rejoin the other Simbas, but the other men disagreed with him, and all walked off except for Bo's brother. The Simba's rifle was taken from him and hidden. Bo washed his wounds, and after untying him we formed a small procession back to the village, the Simba in front on a lead—for want of a better word—which was tied round his neck with Bo's brother holding the other end. Bo was next while I followed on in the rear. Somewhere in all the excitement we had lost Stetefano, but I was assured that he was quite capable of finding his own way back. It was a beautiful night, with a full moon, and it seemed hard to believe that there could be so much natural beauty in such close proximity to the ugliness all around us.

We reached the river again. The Simba was allowed to bathe, then his rope was untied and he was free. After giving him five minutes' lead, Bo's brother left us, at which point Bo dived into an exceptionally thick and dark patch of jungle, and beckoned that I should follow him. We fell over logs, our arms and legs were scratched by bushes and we lost our way more times than I care to remember. Finally at 3am we arrived at the back of one of the houses in Bopepe, having taken three and a half hours to traverse half a mile of jungle

The Simbas were still in the village. We could hear them laughing and talking. We found out much later that they had been systematically looting every house before burning them down.

Bo's plan was to enter the jungle on the other side of the main road; but this meant crossing the road in bright moonlight, without being seen by the numerous sentries. In our flight through the thick undergrowth, Bo had lost his briefcase and I had lost my travelling bag, so at least we were unhampered by baggage, but on the other hand we literally had nothing apart from the clothes we were wearing—not even a Bible.

At 4am, the road seemed quiet enough for us to cross, and Bo instructed me to jump down into the road, run along in the shadow on the right for about fifty yards, then run across to a small pathway on the left. That was what we did. It was a sad sight to see Bo a fugitive from his own people in his own village. I felt more of a liability than ever, as all this was happening because of me.

Having crossed the road successfully, we quickly made our way deep into the jungle on the other side. How Bo knew his way through the jungle I do not know. By now, I was becoming aware of how thirsty I was, and I am sure Bo was too, as we had not had anything to drink since 8am the previous morning. Bo found somebody's sugar cane garden, and cut some cane, which we both ate gratefully. He then found two sticks, and made them into a cross, which he stuck into the ground where we had stolen the sugar cane so that the owner would know that it was a Christian who had taken it because he needed it.

We then lay down on the ground to wait for daylight at 6am. I cannot remember what my thoughts were, as I was too exhausted both physically and emotionally.

By daylight we were up again and on our way. Bo led on, and I followed blindly. We had no proper path to follow, and at times were wading through ankle-deep thick black mud. In Congo, the dew is very heavy, and it was not long before we were both soaking wet as well. My dress was clinging to my legs, and in addition, my sandal-strap was broken. It would be an understatement to say we must have looked a sorry sight! The broken sandal strap slowed me down even more, much to my embarrassment. Unlike the Congolese, I was not used to going barefoot, and had developed a blister. My legs were all scratched and the mud was making them sting. I did not voice my problems but Bo realised and was very patient with me. We stopped frequently for a breather, and several times he actually carried me over the muddy patches.

We found a pineapple garden and helped ourselves. Never has pineapple tasted so good! Bo must have had a penknife in his pocket to have to cut firstly the sugar cane and then the pineapple. Finally at 9am we met up with a Christian couple; my dispensary gardener and his wife. They gave us rice and peanuts, and some hot water to wash in. They even set up a little lean-to for us to rest in before continuing our journey. We were very grateful to lay down to rest, but it was cold and the ground was hard, and the emotional strain made any real relaxation impossible.

We were so tired that we ended up staying the night, aware all the time of what might happen to this couple if we had been caught on their compound. It was while we were here that we heard a message relayed on the drums saying that two men had been killed at Bopepe and every house had been burnt to the ground. They were beginning to burn down two adjacent villages, and Paul Ponea, our school director, was being led about with a rope round his neck in order to find me.

It was at this point that I decided I must give myself up, and we prayed that the Lord's will be done.

The gardener gave me two pieces of paper and a pen, and I wrote two farewell letters—one to my parents and the other to the director-general of the UK branch of the Mission. I asked the gardener to give them to the National Army if they ever came. They never did come, so my letters were never delivered.

We resumed our journey on Wednesday December 22nd. By now my feet and legs were infected and beginning to swell, so I could only walk very slowly. We also had to endure several spells of heavy tropical rain, which drenched us every time as there was nowhere to shelter.

After more than twenty-four hours of painful progress through the jungle, I was very weary, and asked the Lord that he might provide us at least with a roof over our heads for what I thought was to be my last night on earth. Miraculously we found a small leaf-shelter, and Bo found some matches in his pocket wrapped in a banana leaf with which he made a fire, so we were able to dry out. What was left of the night (it was 2am) I spent praying for my loved ones at home.

Bo tried hard to talk me out of giving myself up, but I felt it was wrong for me to hide while my friends were being killed and their homes burnt down. At least I was sure of going to meet the Lord.

Morning came, and we found we were fairly near the Simba camp. We found a young man to lead me in, and I sadly took my leave of Bo. Strangely, all fear of death had left me, in fact I was looking forward to meeting the Lord and the others who had been killed a month before. I even had the audacity to ask the Lord to tell them I was coming!

It was Christmas Eve 1964. I quoted Psalm 23 to myself as I walked behind my guide. Suddenly I was aware of such a presence of the Lord that I turned round almost expecting to see him there at my side. Of course I didn't really see him, but I knew with certainty that he was with me in this. I remember asking him to let it be a quick death with a bullet, and to help me die as a true believer.

At 9.30am we reached the village of Bopando, the Chief's village (although he wasn't there at the time), three miles from Bopepe, and the local Simba headquarters.

Someone went to call the major, whilst I sat down on a chair which a villager kindly offered me.

Thursday

24

December

1964

'I quoted Psalm 23 to myself as I walked behind my guide. Suddenly I was aware of such a presence of the Lord that I turned round almost expecting to see him there at my side'

Nurse-prisoner of the rebel army

The villagers crowded round as I waited for the rebels to come. They were not particularly hostile but neither were they friendly. I noticed that one man was wearing a pair of my shoes; and it suddenly occurred to me that the last time I had seen them was in my bedroom a month before. He saw me looking at them and said, 'They were in your house and fit me nicely. We have taken all your things away.' I asked what my crime was. He answered by pointing first to his own skin and then to mine. 'You are white and a friend of the American capitalists,' he said.

After a short while of this intense scrutiny, a car arrived and two rebel officers got out. They had come to collect me, and pushed me rudely into the car. The journey was very short, and did not really necessitate the use of a car, but the rebels did not want to get wet in the rain as this would result in the loss of the power of magic on their bodies. I was already soaking wet so it didn't matter to me.

I recognised the car as having belonged to the doctor who had been at Banalia. It still had a few family belongings inside it, including his daughter's chemistry notebook from school. For some reason, the sight of this book comforted me. I wondered if the doctor had been rescued during the liberation of Stanleyville.

When we arrived at the house they had commandeered as their base, I was pushed into a large room while somebody was despatched to call the senior major. I could see out to the veranda, which was full of dancing women, chanting all the time. Many of them were former patients of mine at Bopepe, but although they must have recognised me, they did not acknowledge my presence in any way.

There are many better ways of celebrating Christmas Eve than being in a room full of Simbas armed with rifles, spears and knives. Those with spears and knives were dancing round me, brandishing their spears and thrusting them almost into my face. Their dancing was very insinuating and

'There are many better ways of celebrating Christmas Eve than being in a room full of Simbas armed with rifles, spears and knives. Those with spears and knives were dancing round me, brandishing their spears and thrusting them almost into my face'

revolting, though I dared not show my feelings. One Simba, who was particularly repulsive in his actions came to me and said he was going to have the greatest pleasure in thrusting his spear through my face. I almost believed him. Another approached me with a long, thin hunting knife and said he had been delegated to cut my throat that afternoon.

How do you pray in that kind of situation? I just called, 'Help!' Almost immediately my fear left me, and I raised my head to see just how ridiculous the whole situation was—these big brave men dancing round me as though I was a prize elephant they had just killed.

'You are a Protestant missionary, aren't you? Well then, you will not mind dying, as you believe you will go to heaven.' I answered in the affirmative, and added that I hoped he had the same assurance. He then asked if I was afraid to die, and when I said I was not, he looked at me for a long time then slowly said he really believed me.

This ludicrous situation probably only lasted some fifteen minutes, but it seemed like an hour. Eventually we heard someone shouting orders, the door behind me was opened and the short stocky figure of the major entered, followed by his retinue. I must have looked a sorry sight, my hair wet, uncombed for four days and hanging round my ears, my dress dirty, wet and torn, my legs swollen from infection, and sandals only half on my feet.

His immediate reaction was to order a chair for me, and when I was seated, he turned to interrogate me. He was just over five feet tall, in other words the same height as me, middle-aged, clean-shaven and with a kindly face. He wore a leopardskin sleeveless jacket and khaki shorts. Round his neck, together with numerous medicine charms, was a human thumb.

'Are you the white woman from Bopepe? Where have you been? How did you get here?' I answered that I was indeed the white woman, and that I had given myself up in order to prevent further bloodshed. I added, 'If you want to kill me, go ahead, but please leave my friends alone.' To my surprise he said, 'You are not going to die; we want you to work.' He then turned on his heels and walked out leaving me quite deflated and wondering just what lay ahead. I could only pray silently, asking for grace to meet this next phase of my life.

One of his officers, a lieutenant, stayed behind and ordered the Simbas to leave me alone. He also arranged for some food for me. Lieutenant Dieu-Donné was very friendly, even sympathetic. He drew a chair up to a table, and motioned for me to sit across from him. He began to interrogate me about my life both before and after coming to Congo. He told me that he was a Catholic, but had spent four years in the UFM primary school at our station at Ekoko, and subsequently had been a bank clerk in Stanleyville. Everything I said was taken down to be used in their statement for or against me.

Half way through all this, the door reopened and a woman was brought in. The lieutenant asked me if I knew her. I certainly did. This was Mama Ruta, as we all called her, my faithful helper in the maternity unit and the wife of Bo's brother who had helped to release the wounded Simba.

When they were satisfied that we really did know each other, she was taken out again with her guard. I was disturbed at seeing Mama Ruta under such conditions, and asked why she was there. I was told they were holding her on two counts, primarily as a hostage until I gave myself up, and secondarily, because the villagers had taken a rifle from the wounded Simba. Until this was returned, she would remain a prisoner.

A little later a plate of pineapple was brought in for me, and proceedings stopped while I ate it. I must have been ravenous as the officer remarked on how hungry I was. Perhaps my table manners momentarily deserted me! The interrogation continued for a while, but stopped again when a plate of rice and mushrooms appeared, complete with a spoon to eat with. They also brought a mug of water.

When the interrogation was finally over, I was sent to the part of the village which had been turned into a prison. Mama Ruta had been told to prepare hot water for me to wash in, and they even gave me some soap. I was grateful for this, though I wished I had a towel. I put my dirty clothes on again, then combed my hair with a comb someone lent me. I now felt better able to face my captors. My legs and feet were the cause of much concern and a 'nurse' was sent to treat them.

I sat with Mama Ruta. Her 'prison' was a filthy hovel where she had to sleep on boards. We did not speak to each other at first, as many people were standing round us, but when we were finally left alone we started to talk. She was almost sick with worry, for they kept telling her that her husband was dead. She also asked me where Bo had hidden the rifle. She was very surprised when I told her that it was actually her husband who had hidden it, but if he was dead, how would anyone find it?

We discussed the fact that this was Christmas Eve, and were able to laugh at the incongruity of our situation. I dare not let my thoughts dwell too much on what was happening at home, such as carols, presents, parties and all the other Christmas celebrations. Were my parents mourning me? I expected they were, and in such circumstances would probably have cancelled any festivities that year.

I had hoped to be back home for Christmas, but for some reason God saw fit to allow me to share in the meanness and poverty of that first Christmas long ago, when Christ, the Babe of Bethlehem was born in a stable. I looked around me. Chickens were scratching everywhere, half-starved dogs moped about in the dirt, and the raucous voices of men who had been drinking grated on our ears. Was it possible that Joseph had led Mary to the stable in similar conditions when Bethlehem was overcrowded, and there was no room in the inn? Christmas cards depict the stable as being clean and wholesome, but I doubt if it really was.

'In everything give thanks'—I felt rebuked as I reflected on that verse, yet I was able to thank the Lord for sending his son into the world in order that the world might be saved, and for allowing me the privilege of sharing in some of his sufferings.

More food was brought which Mama Ruta had prepared—rice and peanut butter. She did not eat any herself, in fact I was told she had not touched any food for days. I was very hungry and ate heartily.

The rain cleared, and the women I had seen when I first arrived began to dance in the open. They were fairly near to us, and Mama Ruta thought it would be a good idea for me to try and speak to them. So I hobbled over, and as I approached, I recognised the young wife of one of our evangelists. She saw me looking at her, and turned her head away. Absolutely no-one would acknowledge me, so I sadly made my way back to Mama Ruta, who could sense how upset I was, and just sat holding my hand.

It was 5pm before the Simbas let the women go back to their villages, and then it was that one woman, who was 'president of the political group' in her village, came and asked me to go and see them. As I approached this time, the group suddenly broke up and they all came running towards me and hugged me. Many wept openly at my plight, and they were all concerned at how thin I was. I really valued their friendship in a world which had suddenly become so hostile. This show of affection made a lovely Christmas present especially after being ignored a few minutes earlier. I do not think they had ever been really against me. It was simply that they were very afraid of the Simbas, and had felt too vulnerable even to acknowledge me.

Shortly after this, the major came back. I could hear him calling first to one and then another of the officers to go to him. I was given some more food before being ordered to present myself to him. Mama Ruta took my hand and whispered that she would pray for me.

I was treated more kindly this time, being ushered—as opposed to being pushed—into a small bedroom in a mud-walled house. It was dark, with only two makeshift palm-oil lamps for light. The major was sitting on the edge of the bed in his underpants! By his side was his wife of the moment, a young arrogant girl. On the floor in front of them was their supper of rice and fish. They ate with their fingers and spat the bones on the floor in time-honoured fashion.

A chair was brought for me and I was ordered to sit down facing them. So I sat and watched them eat. The major then interviewed several other people and listened to their complaints before bellowing for Lieutenant Dieu Donné to come in with his report about me. I was asked leading questions and every time I tried to answer the major would yell 'Liar!' until finally I said it was not much point me telling him anything as he did not believe me, so I would not say any more. At this he looked quite astounded and quietened down considerably. Was Mama Ruta praying? I'm sure she was. He asked if I knew where Bo had gone, and told me they had killed eight men at Bopepe. I felt sick with grief and guilt when I heard this, all the more so as he didn't seem to know who they were. Later a friendly Simba said only two had been killed, but even that was two too many.

His wife then locked the door from the inside. I began to feel very apprehensive. The major pointed to the bed, which was a wide king-size, and said very gently, 'Do not be afraid, I will not touch you. Go right over to the other side of the bed, and my wife will sleep in the middle. Do not be afraid, I will protect you.' His wife then gave me a pillow which had come from Mary's bed, and one of her sheets too. I clambered over as best I could, as my legs were very painful and swollen, and after wrapping myself in Mary's sheet, lay down.

I prayed for protection for the night and grace to go through whatever was ahead of me. I also took time to thank the Lord for a roof over my head and a bed to sleep in. I fell asleep as soon as I had finished praying and slept soundly all night. When I awoke at 7.30am, I was alone in the room and judging by the noise outside, the day's activities had been under way for some time. Congolese are habitually early risers. How was I able to tell the time, as my watch had been confiscated at Banalia? Simply by observing the position of the sun, which on the equator is very predictable.

I opened a tiny window, and noticed in the daylight a number of details that I had not seen the previous evening. At the foot of the bed I saw the basket I had used for premature babies which used to be kept in my bedroom at Bopepe, and what was more it was filled with my clothes! There were some more hanging on a nail on the wall. The large mirror from our bathroom was resting on a chair by the bed, our cushions were being used for pillows, and the blanket used by the major had belonged to Mary.

As I tried to take all this in, the Major's wife came in to tell me I was wanted outside. There was no need to dress, as I hadn't undressed. I could barely walk, as the infection had caused my feet to swell up so much that I could not wear my sandals. The Major was genuinely sorry for me, and ordered the 'nurse' to treat me immediately.

Mama Ruta greeted me. She said that the rifle had been found and given back to the Simbas, so she was now technically free, but had been ordered to stay and look after the Mademoiselle. I was horrified at this and begged them to let her go. At about 4pm they finally consented, and she left me, very relieved to be going as by then most of the men were very drunk.

This was Christmas Day 1964, and while everyone in England was singing 'Peace on earth and goodwill toward men', I was sitting in the middle of a group of bloodthirsty Simbas. The Lord gave me peace in this situation, and even provided some good will in the shape of Lieutenant Dieu Donné, who brought out an accordion and asked me to name some carols. He then played 'Silent night', 'The first Noel' and 'Hark the herald

'I prayed for protection for the night and grace to go through whatever was ahead of me. I also took time to thank the Lord for a roof over my head and a bed to sleep in'

angels sing' over and over again for an hour and a half. Our primary school at Ekoko had clearly done him some good, for although he had been to Yugoslavia and Moscow for military training, and subsequently told me that religion was the opiate of the people, he played carols on Christmas Day to comfort the heart of a lonely Protestant missionary and a prisoner at that.

My Christmas dinner was not turkey and roast potatoes but elephant meat and boiled rice. They gave me enormous helpings and were upset when I found it too much to manage, but it was not only the huge portions that caused me to struggle—elephant meat is very tough and requires a lot of chewing.

Lieutenant Dieu Donné asked if I had hidden a case or anything with some clothes somewhere in the jungle, for by this time my dress was torn, grubby and very much the worse for wear. Bo had told me where he had hidden my suitcase, but I wondered if I could remember the way. Nor was I at all keen to take any rebels anywhere near Bopepe again. However, Dieu Donné promised that he would take me to find it, and would be my personal bodyguard for the trip, but not on Christmas Day. If my legs and feet were better we would go the following Monday.

Several women from various villages turned up, along with some of the village elders who had been my patients at Bopepe. It was good to see them and exchange greetings, but they were very guarded in their conversations with me. One man started to say something about Paul Ponea, but another man near him immediately put a hand over his mouth. He knew the Simbas wanted me to believe that Paul was dead.

Many of the women were wearing my clothes—often after making some alterations to them. My uniforms had been cut in half to make blouses and underskirts, and one woman appeared wearing the top part of one of my nylon nightdresses. I didn't make any comments. Whether I was meant to notice I am not sure, but I thought silence would be the wisest policy. It was not so easy to remain silent when three days later the major appeared wearing a pair of shorts made out of some material I had used to make things for the nursery. It came in two colour schemes: little pale blue puppies with yellow bows on a pink background or pink puppies, again with yellow bows, on a blue background. On this occasion he wore pink with blue puppies. He must have found a tailor to make them, and was so proud of this splendid new garment he even took roll call in it. The other officers were jealous, so he had to give them some of the material, and they too visited the tailor. So this was the new uniform for the rebel army! Some wore pink, some blue, while others were dressed in patchwork made from odds and ends. I dared not laugh out loud, but inside I was almost hysterical.

Another officer carried his spare bullets in one of our bright green cushion-covers. He took it everywhere with him. It was good that there was no fighting at that time, as he would have had a hard time reloading his rifle in a hurry.

One young Simba, who could not have been more than seventeen, turned up one day wearing three of my pink and blue hair-curlers on his wrist, and the polythene tubing and glass connection of a blood-transfusion set round his neck. As if this was not enough, he had fixed two of our bright orange nylon pot-scourers to his cowboy-style hat and was wearing a pair of surgical gloves on his hands and a very worn out pair of wellington boots on his feet. He actually went on parade dressed like this, but nobody took any notice of him, except me, of course.

Another day the major turned up in Ruby Gray's full-length pale blue candlewick housecoat. The other men were very envious! Later that same day, he came out in Mary Baker's pink bathrobe, wearing it back to front until someone pointed out to him, the buttons should be down the front.

Although these incidents were very amusing, the Simbas were very serious. It also underlines the huge cultural differences between us in the west and these men who were largely uneducated and had never travelled out of their own country.

On yet another occasion, the major's wife came to me wearing one of my own dresses and asked me if I would alter it to fit her. As I am small and slim and she was tall and buxom, it would have been impossible. However, it was not the logistics that made me refuse, it just seemed like the last straw when I was still wearing my filthy ragged dress. It would have been a better witness if I had at least made an attempt at altering it. This was brought home to me shortly afterwards when God brought Hebrews 10:34 into my mind. In this verse, the writer commended his readers for taking 'joyfully the spoiling of your goods, knowing in yourselves that ye have in heaven a better and enduring substance.' I felt very convicted as I reflected on this verse, and asked God to forgive me for letting him down. Unfortunately, by this time, the woman had gone elsewhere with the dress so the opportunity to make amends was gone.

This incident, minor as it was, really brought home to me how much we like to hold on to our personal possessions. The Lord was going to teach me even more about taking the spoiling of my goods joyfully. It was painful, but I found that he gives grace even in the hardest of situations.

I had lost contact with the outside world, I had lost all my local friends, and now I was shortly to see our house and the little hospital I had founded in ruins. All ties were being severed one by one. I was beginning to learn what it was to be completely dependant on the Lord.

When Monday came, the swelling of my legs and feet had gone down to the point where I could put my sandals on again, so it was agreed that I should go with Lieutenant Dieu Donné and four other armed Simbas to find my suitcase.

On the way we ran into a group of Simbas who were very obnoxious to me, and it took all Dieu Donné's time to keep them under control. We passed another group, and I noticed that several of them were wearing our house aprons, one had my bath towel round his neck, and another carried a blanket of Mary's in a bucket. Dieu Donné said that if anything belonged to me I could take it if I wanted. I took the blanket and the towel. The Simbas were furious and called down curses on me, but I was elated at such a find.

As we neared Bopepe, we had to pass several other villages, and the one immediately before Bopepe had been totally gutted by fire; not a single house was left standing. Dieu Donné said it had been done because I had not given myself up. We finally arrived at Bopepe. It was deserted, which was no surprise considering every house had been burnt to the ground except the three with permanent roofs, Bo's, Asani's, and ours. The church, which was built of brick, was also comparatively intact.

We entered our house. A lot of the things in it had been given to us by friends, so they had a sentimental attachment besides any considerations of monetary value or usefulness. I am sure that a missionary's home almost always seems to be a place of peace and happiness because even the furniture and furnishings emanate the love of the givers, but there was no peace or happiness now. Everything that was portable had been taken, and large things that were too heavy to carry like the refrigerator, stove, dining-room table, and the treadle sewing-machine had been vandalised by machetes. I was horrified at the wanton destruction. Food which had been in tins or containers had been poured out on the floor. As the Simbas could not read any of the books in English, they had torn most of them up and strewn the pages over the floor. I found a Bible more or less intact, along with a few other books, including several medical textbooks, and these were put on one side to go back with us. How they escaped the vandalism I do not know, but I was especially pleased to find the Bible.

Next, we entered the forest and retrieved the suitcase. I am sure there were eyes watching us all the way in. The camp bed, water filter and Primus stove were in the same spot as my case and the Simbas wanted to take them too, but I asked Dieu Donné to leave them for the villagers, as they had lost so much because of me. He agreed, and ordered the Simbas only to take my suitcase, although I expect they came back later and helped themselves to the other things. I was hoping that maybe Bo would be able to get there first, as he could certainly find a use for them.

We returned to the village, and I had time to look round. I felt as though my heart was weeping, as I had such a pain in my chest. The village always used to be full of life, but now it was deserted, every house a ruin. I wondered where the owners had gone. I thought of George my nurse and his five small children, of Mikaele who had four little ones, the last having been one of my premature babies, of Alumba, Bwanachui and their respective families. Where were the village elders, those saintly, hard working and brave men? I wanted to cry as it hurt so much. Dieu Donné stood behind me and said very quietly, 'It was all your fault for hiding in the forest.' If he wanted to make me feel guilty, he succeeded. I asked, more in anger than anything else, but also with some curiosity, 'And what has this profited you, or the People's Army? Do you really think that such unnecessary destruction of innocent people's homes is going to endear the population to your cause?' He had no answer.

I opened the case when we got back to find that the ubiquitous white ants had found their way in, but only just, so we were able to clear them all away. The major's wife was with me as I tipped everything out for inspection, and if I had not been quick enough I am sure she would have taken all those clothes too. She did help herself to a cardigan when I was away one day, but that was all.

That evening I washed and dried myself like a civilised person and was finally able to put on clean clothes. When I first emerged neat and tidy for the first time since giving myself up, they all applauded. I was rather touched by this, maybe even the Simbas weren't all bad, or was it simply that they were ashamed of my dirt and rags?

Now that I was clean and properly dressed, I was told it was time to begin work. I was to go to the hospital at Banalia, twelve miles away, and was to take or appropriate anything I thought would be necessary for dispensary work.

After my walk to Bopepe, my feet were very swollen again and the sores on my legs had not yet healed. The major didn't ask if I knew how to ride a bicycle, but ordered his men to find me one, so I could ride to Banalia. How did they find a bicycle? They simply stopped the first cyclist who had a lady's bicycle and appropriated it. It was almost brand new, and I felt quite sorry for the owner, who would have needed to save for months to buy it, unless, of course, it had been stolen.

We set out for Banalia at 6am next morning. The major had told me I would need a sponge bag and a blanket, as we would be staying overnight. As I was still sleeping in my clothes, I didn't need a nightdress. Two things were missing from my sponge bag; a comb and toothpaste. The major had taken them, so I simply took them back. When I told him afterwards, he just laughed.

About thirty Simbas were going to Banalia, including the major. On this occasion he was wearing a long button-through beige dress, with large red buttons, which reached to his feet. He walked all the way to Banalia in it.

It was wonderful to be able to cycle ahead of the crowd, I was pleased that the major trusted me to go alone. It gave me the chance to pray without being disturbed. It was hardly true freedom, but I made the most of it.

An incident occurred on the way which shows just how brutal even the youngest Simbas could be. A coloured boy of twelve years and another boy of eleven had been included in the group going to Banalia. They were my official bodyguards. The coloured boy had been brought up with his white father and Congolese mother, but when the troubles began, his father went back to his own country, leaving the boy with his mother, so he promptly joined the rebel army. A handsome boy, better educated and somewhat more cultured than most of the others, he was usually polite to me, though occasionally very cynical.

At one point of the journey, which he was also making by bicycle, he was quite a way in front of me and pulled up at a village to wait. The few villagers who were left promptly fled into the jungle, apart from an elderly blind man and his wife. The boy saw them going, and called them to come back, but they took no notice and continued to run.

The boy, who was called 'Panya' (the Rat) by the other Simbas, remounted his bicycle and returned to the rest of the group to tell them about this.

By this time I had reached the village and was talking to the blind man. He was very bewildered and when I told him I was white, he became very frightened and wanted to hide with the others. At this point, the Rat came back with several officers and the other young boy. They were very angry and grabbed the old man ordering him to show them the way to the forest. Only when I pointed out the obvious fact that he was blind did they eventually leave him alone.

The Rat then decided to look for himself and came back with a young woman who was in an advanced stage of pregnancy. To my utter horror and disgust, he kicked her in the abdomen, then hit her over the head with his rifle-butt as she bent over, while screaming at her to tell him where her husband was hiding. One of the officers—a grown man—then took over and hit her several times in the back with his rifle-butt until she was on the point of collapsing. When she had recovered sufficiently, she took them into the jungle and about five minutes later they flushed out an elderly man who emerged holding a machete. They then jumped on him, knocking him down and hitting him with their rifle-butts. The old blind man was absolutely terrified by all this, so I led him into the house where I assumed he lived. The rest of the group of Simbas arrived at this point and promptly started vandalising the village, breaking every window and door they could find.

I watched helplessly, feeling physically sick. The only crime the elderly man had committed was to be afraid of the Simbas and take to his heels when he saw them coming. As a punishment, he was forced to go to Banalia—at the run, and accompanied by my two 'bodyguards'. As he ran, the Rat would cycle behind him, deliberately causing his front wheel to run into the man's legs, which made him stumble, at which point the other boy would threaten him with a long knife. We were approximately five miles from Banalia, and he was made to run all the way under those conditions at the hottest time of the day. The pregnant woman was also taken prisoner on the same charge of being afraid, but she was allowed to walk.

There was an appalling lack of logic about the rebels. They terrorised everyone by their brutality, but seemed surprised that this made people afraid of them. What also saddened me was how young the Rat and his child accomplice were, yet they had already been trained to hate.

By the time we reached Banalia, I was beautifully sunburned. A pineapple was shared among us, and to my amazement I was given the largest piece, which was very welcome after the long, hot ride. We waited for the rest of the group who were on foot to catch up with us.

I wondered how we were going to cross the river as the ferry had been sunk by the bombs of the National Army. I was not left long in doubt. The major had it all in hand. He went down to the water's edge at a spot that was well shielded by the trees. They did not dare use the proper landing-stage as it was less sheltered and air-attacks were still a possibility. He whistled three times and was answered by three whistles from the other side. Ten minutes later, two large canoes arrived and we were conveyed safely over. The major told me not to leave him if I wanted to be kept safe.

I was dismayed when I saw how many Simbas there were. At a rough count, I estimated about two thousand. They were 'inspected' by the major, still wearing his beige dress. I also noted that their 'uniform' had changed. The fur pieces had given way to red strips of material worn either as armbands, belts, hatbands for those who had hats, or in some cases round their head, as little girls wear ribbons.

They were openly hostile to me at first, and I was grateful for the major's warning, but following the inspection they were very kind, some going out of their way to be helpful. I was a nurse and therefore valuable. They had realised too late the consequences of killing a doctor and all the medical staff.

That same afternoon, I witnessed a 'trial' by the people, or rather a kangaroo court as we would call it. Five men were accused of stealing, and the stolen goods, five trunks full of clothes, were also on display.

The first man was called forward and asked to state his case. He maintained that the contents of his particular trunk were his personal belongings. The trunk bore the name of one of the Catholic sisters who had been murdered, with her Banalia address painted on it in bold white letters. It contained her habits and some church furnishings, which must have come from the sacristy of Banalia Catholic Church. The man naturally lost his case, and the people decided he must go to prison and be beaten twice a day. The other four men had the same kind of 'trial', and were all found guilty and given the same sentence. Then, to my amazement, the contents of the trunks were distributed among all those present, with the major taking the largest amount. Before they were allowed to have them, the rebel witchdoctor was called forward to 'baptise' each item. The major claimed a pair of long white cotton stockings, which had belonged to one of the sisters. He then put them on, and thereafter frequently wore them regardless of how silly he looked, as he had nothing with which to keep them up!

At first the major always referred to me as his 'white-wife', and I was very indignant about it as it gave a misleading impression. Later, I realised he said it in order to protect me. The other men thought I really was his wife and did not dare molest me. In many ways the major was kind to me in a crude sort of way, and slowly I learnt to disregard the superficialities as I began to see the motives behind them. I knew that this man was being used by the Lord to protect me and I was grateful for that. The major always behaved like a Congolese gentleman with me. Whenever any amorous Simba officer tried to make advances to me, it was a simple matter to take the man to the major, who always upheld my cause, and I would then be left unmolested.

I was a source of confusion to the pagan Congolese. They understood that the Catholic sisters were unmarried, and thought that the white habit was a uniform which symbolised this, which I suppose in a way that was true, but I was not a Catholic and did not wear a habit. How, then, could I be single? After all, many female Protestant missionaries were married, and in that polygamous society, though the men often had several wives, only those who bore them children actually lived with them. So I could easily have been passed off as one of the major's wives, but to try to clarify the situation, I told them I was a Protestant 'sister' like the Catholic sisters.

The day after arriving at Banalia I was ordered to rob the hospital! I started off at the pharmacy, and soon had my uneasy conscience allayed. There were several people already engaged in the same task, albeit illegally, and quite honestly there was very little to rob. Books, cartons, and various instruction leaflets were all strewn on the floor. There were hardly any ampoules left, as the Congolese loved injections. I found a few dressings, but not a single bandage. I did manage to retrieve a large amount of very dangerous drugs such as insulin, along with some anaesthetics and a large stock of morphia and pethidine.

Next came the operating theatre, a scene of utter chaos and devastation. Thousands of pounds worth of equipment had been utterly ruined. There was not much worth taking here either, but I took a few things that I thought could be useful. I wondered if there might be some linen or towels, but all I could find were from five long operating sheets. The stainless steel sterilising drums, so essential for effective surgery in the tropics where sterile packs were unknown, had also vanished. They had a handle and the Simbas had taken them to use as cases.

Finally the obstetric department, and the same story. It was heartbreaking to see such wanton destruction simply because these men did not understand the function of the various pieces of equipment.

On the way back, I called into the wards. All the mattresses and pillows had been stolen. What I did see was a leg splint, a backrest, and a bottle with the tubing still attached to it, all poignant reminders of how the patients had fled in haste and terror.

We returned that night from Banalia to Bopando. Three trunks and one large box preceded me, carried by forced labour from the village, but some things I had packed never arrived at their destination.

I kept two of the operating sheets for my personal use. These sheets have a large hole in the middle to expose the intended operative area, but I was able to sew up the holes, and now I had two curtains, or one curtain and a sheet to cover me if I preferred.

One of the biggest problems was finding time to read my Bible. From daylight to bedtime I was in constant demand. Some times my services would be called for before I had time to get up in the morning. It did not matter to them what time it was, or whether it was convenient, they wanted treatment, and they wanted it immediately. This made Bible reading very difficult, so I demanded a room of my own. Apart from the major's wife, I was the only other woman, and although he was very amused by my request, the major conceded, turning out several officers from their room, and arranging for it to be cleared out and cleaned up for me. Without a twinge of conscience, I moved in.

Several of the Simbas wanted to stop me from reading my Bible, and made a big fuss about it, but the major took my part and told them to leave me alone. He was nominally a Catholic, but in reality had no time for anyone who believed in God. He often told me that our Congolese Protestant pastors and evangelists were reactionaries who preached against the People's Army.

We opened several bush-type dispensaries, but it seemed that just as soon as we were in full swing, the order would be given to advance, so everything had to be dismantled, repacked and moved on.

I was working solely in a medical capacity, and when at first I was told I could only treat Simbas, I refused to work at all. I told them that as the People's Army was fed by the people, and housed by the people, the people had as much right to my services as the Simbas. Also as a British trained nurse, I was committed to care for all types of patients, regardless of colour, class or creed, whether friends or enemies. They were angry at the thought of my helping their enemies, but I reminded them that I was a missionary and my Lord had taught me to love my enemies. Finally, they then agreed to my treating all and sundry, but only on the condition that Simbas had priority and were the first patients every morning. This worked well with everyone. The local population was scared of the Simbas, and so were quite happy for them to go first, and it suited me, for after making this arrangement I was able to get on with my work without any interference.

Numbers at my 'clinic' increased from one hundred to two hundred and fifty every morning, so they gave me a 'staff', a trained male nurse from Banalia who was also a Christian but had been forced to join the army. He had been present when the missionaries and the Catholic friends had been killed. Several other men started to wear a red cross and to designate themselves thus, but they knew nothing and certainly didn't want to learn. They were lazy and absolutely no help at all. It was obvious to me what their motives were, as several drugs and syringes would disappear overnight.

It was during this time I was ordered by the major to wear a red armband to indicate that I was a member of the People's Army. I refused, saying I did not wish to join the organisation, and that as a missionary my only allegiance was to God. He was distinctly unimpressed, but did not force the issue. I was given the rank of major, but when I refused to answer to it, I was demoted to a mere 'comrade'.

The Simbas really believed that the power of their magic medicine made them immune to death, and also to pain. Should they experience pain of any sort, they believed that all they had to do was to utter the magic formula and then the pain would go. It really was a form of self-hypnosis, but to my knowledge it never worked. For example, a tall, strong looking fellow in his early twenties came to me one day with toothache. The formula wasn't working, so would I take out the offending tooth? Dental work was not a favourite occupation of mine, and so when I peered into his mouth, my heart sank; for it was a lower molar, very badly decayed, but well and truly embedded. At Bopepe they had destroyed all my dental instruments and local anaesthetics and had stolen the special dental syringe. I had not trained as a dentist but had attended a course on emergency dentistry, and though I didn't mind doing extractions, the thought of doing it without a local anaesthetic made me feel more scared than the poor Simba. The situation was explained to him, though I didn't tell him how scared I was, but he was in such pain he agreed that I should go ahead. I said rather facetiously that he would have to try his native magic medicine and see if it would work. To my astonishment they *all* agreed.

It did not help that I only had one pair of forceps which were designed for extractions on the left of the mouth, as this offending tooth was on the right side. It took four hefty men to hold him down before I even started, and his

He would then be taken out to be executed, but always at the last moment someone would call them back and he would be put back into prison. They did not beat him. Seven of the judges were against his execution, and finally one day they said, 'We are through, we wash our hands of the whole affair. You know we do not approve of this man's death.' Then all seven walked out. The three remaining judges said jubilantly, 'Now we can do as we please. Tomorrow you will die'.

That night Bo did not know how to pray, so he just said, 'Lord you must choose for me whether I live or die, I cannot make a choice.' He then made a pillow of his shirt, lay down on the cold damp floor and slept peacefully until morning.

Early next morning there was a knock on the door, which was most unusual. A Simba came in and took him by the arm, which was also unusual. (Their normal approach was to push him round with their guns.) Bo was sure this was the end.

They led him not to the river, but into the office where the major was seated. Near him was an empty chair, which they told him to sit on. Bo could not believe his ears. The major asked him twice, 'Are you a pastor?' Bo assured him he was. Then the major said, 'Last night I was judged. I did not see who judged me, but a large picture of you came before me and a voice said, 'Why do you want to kill this man? If you kill him you will die." He carried on: 'I woke up and could not get back to sleep again.' He then went down on his knees before Bo, and begged him to forgive him for the way he had been treated. He then asked him to pray for him that he would not die.

He went to his typewriter and typed a letter saying that Bo was free, and not to be molested any more. He signed it, handed it to Bo, and told him to return to his village. When he arrived, the people just gasped, they could not believe their eyes.

Chapter 6

With the general

On one occasion during this second stay at Banalia, I had gone out to talk to the driver of a large lorry about the possibility of taking a patient to Buta, where there was a small hospital which was still functioning. He told me to wait by a tree until he had obtained the necessary authorisation. As I approached the tree, I noticed a blue book wedged in the branches. I went to retrieve it, and saw to my amazement that it was nothing less than my personal copy of *Edges of his ways* by Amy Carmichael. It has daily readings, so I turned to the reading for that particular day, which read, 'Maybe there is someone who is going through a special kind of trial and you do not think you can take much more but…he stayeth the rough wind on the day of his East wind'. I was so thankful to God, for I was very lonely at that time and wondering how much longer I could cope with this peculiar prison life, yet on a day when I especially needed encouragement, he led me to that book in the tree.

The very next day I was called out to the front of the house, and lo and behold, there were two white men! The major pointed to them gleefully and said, 'Your relatives!' They looked visibly shaken when they saw me. They had come from Buta where there were over fifty expatriate people, including many nuns and a Belgian lady with her two children. I was flabbergasted, for I had believed that I was entirely alone in the area. Truly 'he stayeth the rough wind in the day of his East wind.'

They were very interested in my story, as they had heard that everyone in Banalia had been killed. They too were being held prisoner, and had been sent to Banalia to repair the ferry. One was Belgian and the other Swiss. They were very kind, and shared their food with me. It was bread and cheese, which seemed the height of luxury in my present circumstances. They told me they nearly always ate European food at Buta, and said that on their return they would ask the 'colonel' if I could be sent there. Somehow I could sense the hand of God was in this.

I met Colonel (later General) Joseph a few days later. He was a young man of only twenty-six years of age and had been brought up in an orphanage run by Catholic sisters. At the age of ten he had been sent to

Above: A nationalist Army convoy on the road to Banalia

Belgium—presumably because he was obviously very intelligent. He went through High School and then on to college for two years, though I never did find out what he studied. He spoke beautiful French as well as Swahili and Lingala. He always addressed me in French. When he had been told about me, he decided I should be moved nearer to Stanleyville as the need was very great, with many sick and wounded civilians in that area.

As usual, I was only given half an hour to pack my few belongings *and* the dispensary. The general also gave me money to pay any debts I had incurred, much to my astonishment. I was very happy to pay the Christian couple for all the food they had provided, though no amount of money could repay their love and companionship.

It turned out that our journey was only as far as the other end of Banalia at least for the time being. My new home was to be the house that had previously been used by the administrator. I had a room, but anyone who needed to get to the bathroom or the kitchen had to pass through it. It was also where the supply of drinking water was kept, and I would often wake up at night to find someone in the room having a drink. As if that was not enough, whenever the general wanted to hold one of his frequent councils of war, he used my room, regardless of whether I was there or not. On another occasion several officers had supper with him there while I was in bed, though not undressed. They spat their fish-bones all over the floor in traditional fashion, which were duly scrunched underfoot by subsequent visitors to the bathroom.

Because the general lived in the house too, it was noisy, for all the officers needed to see him at some time or another. In many ways, it was rather like an officer's club. In consequence, the food was good—at least when we had any.

Under my bed was a trunk with thirty million francs in it. I presume it must have been stolen, for where else could they have found it? I asked the General if I could buy some fresh fruit, and he gave me some of the money. I needed to supplement my diet, as the African food had been making me ill. I eventually found that the problem was that I had developed an intolerance to rice. Unfortunately for me, rice was the staple diet in this area, as opposed to bread or potatoes, so if there was no alternative such as cassava or yams, as was often the case, I simply had to go hungry.

We began yet another dispensary near the river, abandoning our original site at the hospital, as it would be too far away in case of any air attacks. I met several of the civilian nurses from the hospital and they really did work well, though I felt sorry for them always having to have Simba 'nurses' with them.

One day, a man was found dead on a little-used track and I had to go and certify his death. He had been dead a long time judging by the smell and state of decomposition. No questions were asked as to how or why he died. Nobody cared. He was buried unmourned without any post-mortem. On the other hand when one Simba shot a colleague dead in a fight, the dead man was given a funeral with full military honours, and provided with a gravestone complete with a gigantic cross above it! I was told I must attend the funeral, take flowers, and wail in time-honoured Congolese fashion. I refused to go as the officer who had been detailed to escort me was drunk and I did not feel safe walking alone with him in that state.

Another day, I went for a wander. I tried to visit the house where we had been imprisoned in November, and from where our friends had been led out to be killed, but I was not allowed in for some unknown reason. I did get to enter the Catholic sisters' convent, which was in a state of chaos. Every room had been desecrated and vandalised, even their beautiful chapel. I saw a dead cat that must have belonged to the sisters, with all four of its legs dislocated. It looked like it had died of starvation, in great agony.

In one room I found a passport on the floor, and when I opened it, the face of one of the murdered sisters looked out at me. Furtively I tore out the photograph, and returned the passport to the floor, as I would have been beaten if they had seen me with it. I subsequently forwarded the photograph to their mother convent in Belgium.

From the convent I went to the Catholic Church. Here again, mindless destruction. Absolutely nothing remained intact. A beautiful leather-bound book stands out in my memory. It had been deliberately ruined by having paint poured over it.

I moved on to the priest's house where again everything had been destroyed. I did see a paw-paw tree with large ripe fruit just waiting to be picked, so I picked one, found a stick to cut it open, and ate it. It really tasted good. In Congo paw-paw can grow as big as melons!

The Simbas saw me wandering about and promptly declared these places out of bounds. They said the National Army was responsible for the vandalism. I did not argue as it would have been pointless, even though it was obvious they were lying. However, I had to live with them and wanted to keep a degree of peace between us.

The general decided I must go to the hospital and collect as much equipment as possible. He wanted an operating table, delivery table, trolleys, baby cribs and various other items. I wondered who was meant to use them, as we did not have a doctor, just myself. I did not expect to find anything still in working order but I found a few items worth taking. It turned out to be a pointless exercise anyway, as everything I had managed to retrieve was stolen by the Simbas before I could use them.

One day a lorry arrived with many Simbas on board. They had come from Buta, and had three men with them who had allegedly stolen twenty million francs. Simbas were allowed to steal of course, but no-one else. The men were badly treated; two of them were tortured for four hours before being freed, but the third man was tied up in such a way that his elbows and ankles met behind his back. He was left on the ground right outside my room, and beaten and kicked unmercifully every half an hour for three days and nights before he eventually died. It was agony to watch him there when I was powerless to do anything to help him. His screams went through me and made me feel ill. My concern for this man only provoked ridicule from the Simbas. The money he had supposedly stolen was apparently their pay, and as they had not been paid since August when the rebellion began, I could understand their anger, for it was now January.

I found out later that this man was one of the two officers who had ordered the killings of the missionaries. The other officer had been killed when the ferry was bombed in December.

During the heat of the day I would wander down to the landing-stage. Here I could find solitude and spend time with God. It is a beautiful river, and I could admire the loveliness of his creation as I stood there. Often I could not find words with which to pray, as my feelings were running too high, but in spite of my heartache and loneliness, I always went back strangely comforted and conscious of God's presence after visiting this spot, which became such a sacred place to me.

The time came for us to move on from Banalia. We had to travel by night in order to avoid being ambushed by the National Army. At 10pm we loaded up our belongings into a two-cabin Volkswagen Camionette, which looked exactly like the one we had been going to collect in Stanleyville before the revolution. It is quite possible it could have been the very same vehicle.

The general, his aide-de-camp, a cheerful major and the general's 'little Simba' called Victor all climbed into the Camionette. I sat between the aide-de-camp and the major in the second cabin. I recognised Victor from our prison days. He became my bodyguard. At only ten years old, his gun was almost as big as he was. We also had an outrider, Captain Jean Pierre, but his motorcycle broke down halfway.

At 2am we arrived at a place called Belgika, about thirty-eight miles from Stanleyville, and two miles past our UFM Station at Banjwade. Here I was to enjoy a greater degree of comfort than I had experienced for quite some time. My new home was a house that once belonged to a European professor, and the general allocated me an enormous bedroom complete with a real bed, though without any bedclothes. I went thankfully to bed without undressing. It was just as well I had not undressed for when I woke up, there were numerous faces peeping in through the four curtain-less windows at me. It felt rather like being the wrong side of a shop window.

My food arrived on a china plate, complete with spoon and fork, and even a glass of water. The General always ate apart from the other men. He preferred to eat like a Westerner, although I never heard him complain if he had to eat with his fingers or drink water from a communal bowl or even from a bucket, which was frequently the case.

That same morning, he took me by car to see the Banjwade station, as he knew I belonged to the same mission. I was appalled to see the same wanton destruction here as at the Catholic mission in Banalia. There were papers and rubbish scattered everywhere in practically every house, but amidst the chaos I spotted a copy of Geoffrey Bull's book *God holds the key*. I asked permission to take it and my request was granted. Apart from this book there was nothing else worth taking. All the buildings remained intact, although some rooms boasted big holes in the ceilings, but there was no furniture to be seen anywhere.

As I was about to get back into the car, a man emerged from a group of bystanders and grabbed my hand. He was one of our seminary students who had been stranded since the long vacation last August. It was like a breath of fresh air to see him and his wife. He was able to tell me what had happened at Banjwade. Most of the population had fled to the forest after the massacre at Banalia, but were gradually coming back to the village. As far as I could gather, nobody had lost their life from the station. It was encouraging to hear that they were meeting daily for prayer, and that they were able to hold a little service in one of the houses twice a week. My morale was so uplifted by our conversation that during the journey back, I started singing, albeit quietly, but much to the general's amusement. He was almost certainly a Roman Catholic, at least in name, but although he tolerated my religious views, he forbade me to talk to others about them, as it was 'reactionary'.

Later that same day we went to a beautifully-furnished home in a rubber-plantation. How it had escaped vandalism by the Simbas I do not know. It was located approximately twenty miles from Stanleyville, just before a fork in the road, where the new main road into the city diverged from one route, which was seldom used now, although the Simbas kept most of their arms and supplies there.

The general went off on his own, leaving me in this house to be looked after by a major and his wife. They were the epitome of kindness. He loaned me his radio, and when I finally found the BBC, the first thing I heard was that Winston Churchill was very ill and not expected to recover. He died the following day. On the day of his funeral I was allowed, in fact ordered, to take time off from work to follow the BBC commentary. The general said he was saddened by the death of such a great leader, although none of the other Simbas had ever heard of him. At the time I wondered if there had been any memorial service for me, and tried to visualise their faces if they ever found out I was still alive. I found out later that I had been included in several corporate memorial services and my home church in London had also held a service especially for me.

In this house we set up yet another makeshift dispensary in the basement, which was well patronised. It was so sad to see little children starving and ill when I had no food and precious little medicine to give them. All I could do was to whisper to their mothers about the Great Physician.

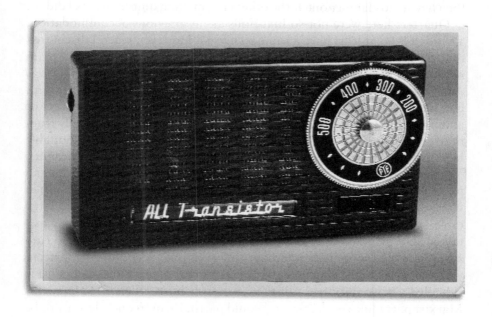

'He loaned me his radio, and when I finally found the BBC, the first thing I heard was that Winston Churchill was very ill and not expected to recover'

Chapter 6

It was soon time to move on again, this time to Bengamisa, thirty-two miles from Stanleyville. Transport on this occasion came in the shape of a tractor and trailer. I felt very undignified clambering up into the trailer, and then having to clamber out at the other end, making quite a fuss as I did so.

Quarters here were not so luxurious as my previous accommodation, although I did at least have a room to myself. However, when I discovered that the so-called bathroom was outside and right by the side of a main road in full view of everybody, I made it clear that unless something was done about this, I was not prepared to stay there. They were furious with me, but within two hours the bathroom was all enclosed with sheets of aluminium. Where they obtained these from I do not know, probably from the roof of a house. I did not really care. There was not much food available here, and often my only meal of the day would be a handful of raw peanuts.

I was allocated a large staff to help me, including several thirteen and fourteen year-olds. I had good opportunities to talk to them, and often when the dispensary was closed in the evening, we would sit around a large table and discuss things together. Most of them listened attentively as I talked about Christ. They knew that they could be killed any day, and I am sure this helped to focus their minds. There was one exception—a fourteen-year-old who would only talk about how he wanted to kill somebody. He ridiculed Christianity with all the scorn of a born atheist. He knew his Marxist party lines perfectly and would parrot them frequently, only to be told to shut up by the others who thought he was an extremist—which he was. It is a sad reflection on all of us who are Christian teachers that few youngsters are so devoted to Christ as this fourteen-year old was to Marxism.

One day, while I was busy at the dispensary, I heard the sound of men screaming in pain while others were laughing in the background. Nobody would tell me what was going on, so I went to investigate. I saw five men lying in a row in the middle of the road. They had each received the special 'command' treatment of the Simbas—first their arms were crossed and tightly tied behind them at the elbows and wrists, then their legs were crossed and their ankles tightly bound, before finally a cord was passed from the ankles to the elbows and pulled tight, so that their bodies were pulled into an oval shape, with their backs bent backwards. They were then kicked and beaten about the head and shoulders. The road was dusty and their faces were pushed into it.

What crime had these five men committed? They were civilians, one of whom had kept a little shop at Bengamisa, where he had sold various items including soap and cigarettes. When the rebellion began he wisely packed most of his stock in cartons and hid them in the jungle together with his wife, family and the other villagers. He was able to keep the villagers supplied, until somebody became jealous and reported him saying he was dealing in stolen goods. He and four village men were then arrested and given the 'command' treatment, while the Simbas confiscated all his stock. They had to suffer for five hours through the hottest part of the day. It made me feel sick when I saw them, but the Simbas laughed at me for my so-called tender heart.

At the house one night I was lying on the bed trying to sleep when a Simba started playing an accordion that had belonged to Viola Walker, one of our missionaries. He played the same four bars over and over again, until I was almost at screaming point. If I had asked him to stop, he would have carried on longer and louder out of sheer spite, so I prayed that the Lord would either stop him or give him another tune. Within three minutes he stopped playing and left. How slow we are to ask the Lord for everyday things!

Another day for some reason I had a longing for eggs, even though I knew there was no possibility of buying any, as the Simbas stole any chickens they saw and promptly killed and ate them. Nonetheless, I brought the matter before the Lord, and that same afternoon, a Simba appeared with four hard-boiled eggs that someone he had met on patrol in the jungle had asked him to give me.

Soap was getting very low, and when I only had a tiny piece left, I asked the Lord for some more—after all he had promised to supply my every need. Once again, that very day the major gave me three bars of Sunlight soap, and two of toilet soap. Truly 'over and above all we ask or think!'

The Lord was answering so many of my little prayers, yet it seemed as though he was delaying the answer for the one big prayer for deliverance. I had asked that I might be free by Christmas Day, then New Year's Day. I then set a date of April 5th—my birthday, and remonstrated with him,

Chapter 6

'After all Lord, you've had plenty of time to get the National Army organised if you want to do it that way.' However his ways are not our ways; and after all, who was I to reason with the Sovereign Lord? Strangely, when I prayed like this I could never find the assurance I was seeking, in stark contrast to when I prayed for the other things.

I did not forget to ask him to burden somebody at home for me, and would actually name certain individuals whom I knew would really pray if they thought I was alive. As for my prayer about deliverance, I suppose the Lord needed to teach me a few more things before I could be free. I always find it amazing just what the Lord will allow us to go through in order to teach us something. With the benefit of hindsight, I know the lesson I had to learn was patience. As James says, 'Knowing this, that the trying of your faith worketh patience. But let patience have her perfect work, that ye may be perfect and entire, wanting nothing.' (James 1:3–4)

One afternoon, the general came to take me to Banjwade for a social evening. I wondered what was in store for me! As we turned into the driveway, it was obvious that the station had been tidied up. The long grass had been cut, and every house appeared to be occupied, not with rebels but with the civilian administrative staff. These were men appointed by the general to run the territory, though where he found them I do not know. I noticed that newspapers had been gummed to the windows as a substitute for curtains. Even the electricity was running, although I wondered how long that would last. The main complaint was that the water system had broken down, but even this was not a big issue as the big River Aruwimi was at the end of the driveway and ran parallel to several of the houses at the back.

Our host for the evening was none other than the district commissioner, alias 'Monsieur, the Devil' from our prison days at Banalia. He was charm personified. He had lost his beard, having been shaved by the National Army in Stanleyville, and was not wearing his sunglasses. He said he remembered me, and could not do enough to make me welcome in his home, although it really belonged to our Mission, and had been occupied by the Muchmore family before they had gone home on furlough just before the rebellion.

The highest ranking officers met for a council of war at 8.30pm. Chairs were brought out on to the spacious lawn at the back of the house, and home-made wine was served. This is usually very potent, and has a distinctive smell, which I have always found nauseating. Cigarettes were distributed while their favourite cha-cha music was playing in the background. I had to sit there with them. I hated it, but had no option, as medical work was on the agenda, which obviously involved me. I was the only woman present. I thought about how unfavourably these men compared with the previous occupants of the house.

When it was all over, we went back into the house, where I met two civilian nurses, who hated this regime and were trying to work their way back to Stanleyville. As I was talking to them, I heard someone calling me, and when I turned round, I saw that everyone was seated round a large table except me, and 'Monsieur the Devil' was waiting patiently for me with a chair! Really, it was all so ludicrous.

He personally waited upon me at table. Our menu consisted of roast goat meat with rice, manioc, plantains and gravy—all cooked to perfection. Our chef had worked for an expatriate family before the rebellion.

It was 11.30pm before I finally left with the general. He drove me 'home' and actually came right into the house with me. I went into my room and was about to light the makeshift palm-oil lamp when suddenly somebody jumped up from my bed and yelled, 'Don't light the light yet, Mademoiselle, I must put my trousers on first!' I could hear the general doubled up with laughter outside the door. As it was so late they all had decided I would not be coming back until morning, and a Simba decided to commandeer my bed for the night, as it was much more comfortable than the floor on which he usually slept. I can't say I blame him.

Two days later, the general came to move me to a place just two miles from Banjwade. It had been a technical school specialising in agriculture and went by the initials ETSAFF, so we always called it 'Etsaff'. When the general came it was midnight and I was in bed, partly undressed. I did not have many belongings with me, so I was soon packed and ready to go. We reached Etsaff at 1am, but the general was called away almost as soon as we arrived, leaving orders that I was to occupy his own room in his absence.

This was another expatriate professor's home, and the general had somehow managed to preserve it intact. We had running water and electricity, a working stove and a refrigerator. Food varied—sometimes plenty, sometimes nothing at all. The general's European education and upbringing paid off as far as I was concerned for he clearly enjoyed the comforts of a Western lifestyle. This particular home we occupied had everything we needed to live a civilised life. Maybe this sounds rather arrogant, but I was grateful for the relative luxury at the time.

I had to make sure the house was properly run, rather like a housekeeper. Often we would have rebel officers for lunch or supper. They were not used to sitting up to the table to eat, and would spit their chicken or fish bones onto the floor. I found it quite a chore to keep picking these bones up after every meal. I tried to 'educate' them by placing an empty plate on the table for the bones, but this failed. When they saw the empty plate they promptly gave it back to the 'boy' with instructions to fill it with food!

I always insisted on eating with them, rather than on my own in the kitchen, and on one occasion an officer sitting opposite me decided I did not have enough on my plate. He grabbed a handful of meat and another handful of spinach, reached over and placed it in front of me on my plate. It was a delicate situation. To refuse food when it is offered to you is a great insult in their culture, but I was not very hungry and neither was I sure if this man had washed his hands. The general was amused and speaking to me in French, which the officer did not understand, said that it was an interesting situation, and that he would be intrigued to see how I would extricate myself without insulting the man. The wretched man watched every mouthful I ate, making comments about the small amounts I placed in my mouth and how slowly I ate. Why did I eat with a spoon *and* a fork? It seems very funny in retrospect, but I was terribly embarrassed at the time.

Once more I founded a dispensary, although there had been one here earlier before everything had been stolen. My 'staff' were transferred too. One case I remember from this period was that of a wounded Simba who had spent four days on the road, who came to me with a compound fracture of his lower leg. A compound fracture is a broken bone complicated by an open wound which has direct contact with the bone. It was by this time seriously infected and we were without any antibiotic or any other drug which could combat the infection. We did have plaster of Paris, which I had stolen from the hospital, and a very few dressings of doubtful sterility by this time. We went ahead and gave him a spinal anaesthetic (which I had also stolen from the hospital) and cleaned up the wound, the bullet had gone right through his leg and out the other side. We then applied a plaster cast.

Four days later his leg was worse, which was no surprise to me, but it was very obvious the infection was spreading upward, so I knew I would have to open the leg further up, as I thought he had a large abscess there. When it was opened, I found another bullet. It had lodged about three inches above where the other one had struck him, but had missed the bone. We dispatched him to the Catholic hospital at Buta as soon as we could find a lorry that was going in that direction. He made a good recovery and when I was re-arrested in May I saw him one day, walking with sticks.

A large number of Simbas had advanced to our UFM headquarters only five miles outside Stanleyville and they said I was to join them in due course. My feelings were mixed at this news, for although it would be nearer the National Army, I knew they would do everything they could to prevent me meeting them. It must have been obvious to them how I felt. They pretended to reassure me, 'Don't worry, we won't let the enemy find you. If we have to retreat, you retreat with us.'

Another of my many jobs was to reopen the Banjwade maternity facility. The two male civilian nurses there were coping well, but in that culture men could not do obstetric work. So twice a week I would walk to Banjwade, accompanied by the inevitable guard, to deal with the maternity and child welfare work. I enjoyed these days, for at the end of the clinic I was able to slip away and see my Christian friends in the village, which was a real blessing. I would tell my guard to wait for me at the station entrance and would then visit them on my own.

On my first visit, I saw an elderly man who had been a houseboy for many years. It gave me a real thrill to see that he and his dear wife were still alive. They were understandably tearful, and had suffered much, but they were more concerned about me, especially after the Banalia massacre. I was terribly hungry, having eaten nothing for twenty-four hours. I hated asking for food, for I knew they wouldn't have much to offer, but I was glad I did so for two reasons: firstly, they had something to give me, and secondly, it gave them so much pleasure to be able to give it. When I left that first day, I was loaded with sweet potatoes, paw-paw and bananas.

Before I left, the other Banjwade folk came round, mostly students from the seminary who had been unable to return to their homes. We had a wonderful time of rejoicing and fellowship together. It was lovely to be able to pray freely with each other. After this first visit, whenever I went there, one of the families always cooked something for me. They knew I could not repay them, but they gave so freely and lovingly.

Finally the day came in late February, when the general said I was to go with him to Buta, approximately one hundred and seventy miles away, supposedly to obtain supplies for the dispensaries. We were due to leave at nine o'clock on Monday morning, but nothing ever went to plan with the rebels—we finally left at 10pm on Wednesday night. I travelled in the leading vehicle of a small convoy, with Captain Jean Pierre again on a motor cycle as an outrider. After two miles, our car broke down and we transferred to a small van. As if this was not enough, after twenty miles, the outrider's motorcycle broke down. We reached Banalia at 2.30am and called for the administrator, whom I remembered from my prison days. He greeted me like a long-lost friend, and ushered me into his house. I knew my way around, as I had been there before.

The rebels never had set times for anything, so it was not that bizarre when they immediately demanded a meal even at that unsociable hour. At 3.30am we were presented with a scrumptious meal of elephant meat, rice and pounded plantains (cooking bananas). There was only one knife and fork, which I was given. I reflected on how times had changed since the administrator confiscated all our knives and other sharp implements when we were in prison.

We left Banalia at daybreak crossing the river on a makeshift ferry. After ten miles the back wheel of our van came off, so once again we had to transfer to another vehicle, this time a large eight-wheeled lorry. The day was hot and sticky and I was in the front of the lorry with the driver, the general and his aide-de-camp. Somebody had presented the general with a baby owl, which I had the privilege of caring for during the journey. Unfortunately for the bird, my hands perspire heavily when I am hot, and after an hour or two of being handled by me, it looked a rather sorry sight. I was also given the responsibility of looking after a large bottle of Scotch whisky. The general told me that I was the only person who could be trusted not to drink it en route.

We passed Bopepe, but it looked deserted. I recognised several people as we passed through the neighbouring villages, and I felt sure the drums were telling people I was on my way. About nine miles past Bopepe is a large coffee plantation called Zambeke. We were scheduled to stop here for the general to inspect the troops. I dismounted from the lorry with the owl, leaving the whisky under the seat, and was recognised at once by several women who were standing around. They seemed overjoyed to see me, just as I was to see them, and one of them told me that many of the villagers from Bopepe were close by. She then went off to find them for me.

I had been terribly apprehensive about how the folk from Bopepe would react to me. It is one of the customs in that tribe to give 'an eye for an eye and a tooth for a tooth', and thanks to me, two men had been killed, several others injured, and almost the entire village had been burned down. I was afraid they might hate me now.

I was sitting down with the general—and the owl—when somebody came in and asked if I could go outside as some women had come to see me. I hurried out of the house and my fears evaporated at once. First came Alphonsina, who put her child on the ground, ran over, flung her arms round my neck and wept loudly on my shoulder. Next, Cecilia took my hand in hers and wept noisily. Others followed, some weeping others laughing. The Simbas were angry with those who were crying and made them stop, but this did not detract from a wonderful reunion. Not only had I seen my precious friends again, but I feel that I had witnessed a miracle, for when I asked Alphonsina, 'Do you not have any hate in your heart against me for all the sorrow and loss you have suffered?', she simply answered, 'Mademoiselle, what we have lost can be replaced, for the Lord is able to supply all our needs, but if we had lost you after what happened at Banalia, I don't know what we would have done. Please don't worry, it's us who worry and pray much for you.' I was greatly comforted. She then went on to ask many pertinent questions about my life with the Simbas. They had heard many ugly rumours about me, and I was glad to be able to relieve their anxieties. They also gave me up-to-date news of Bo Martin and many of the others.

The Simba who had been delegated to guard me did not like the way the women would hold on to me every now and then, but I explained that these were all special friends from 'my' village of Bopepe. The women backed me up to the hilt. One held up her child and said, 'This is one of Mademoiselle's babies,' another said 'Look at me, didn't she make me better in her hospital?' and so on. The Simba then went in, probably to tell the general what was going on, for he came out, complete with his poor owl, and looked on, amused. He finally commented that I had more friends than he did!

The villagers fed us, and then the general did his routine inspection of his troops. They all had a piece of wood fashioned roughly to resemble a rifle, but there was not one real rifle between them. Their commanding officer was wearing Viola Walker's sun hat. It was back to front, and had been decorated with Christmas tinsel and fine white wiring, probably from a transistor radio aerial. He was also drunk, though the general didn't notice.

After the inspection, we made our slow way back to the lorry, surrounded by dancing women. The troops followed behind, all chanting about the general and his bravery in battle. He may have been a general but he had never been in a battle!

We resumed our journey. I held the owl in my hot sticky hands. The poor bird would not eat a thing, not that anyone had the slightest idea what owls should be fed with. I had forgotten all about the whisky, which remained still hidden under the seat. The general was telling me about how he planned to resign from the army and go into politics to sort the economy out. I was surprised at his self-confidence, but wisely held my peace.

At 4pm we stopped for water and bananas at a village approximately forty miles from Buta. I had perspired so much on a leather seat in an airless cabin that my clothes were so wet they could have been wrung out. While we were in this village, a car arrived from Buta, a beautiful Cadillac. The colonel at Buta had become impatient and had sent on an officer to collect us. I had no objection to riding in a Cadillac, especially after the discomfort of the lorry, and our belongings were transferred, including the owl and the whisky, which had again been put into my hands for safe keeping.

The driver of the Cadillac was a commander, and he drove like a maniac.

'After the inspection, we made our slow way back to the lorry, surrounded by dancing women. The troops followed behind, all chanting about the general and his bravery in battle. He may have been a general but he had never been in a battle!'

He pointed out the skid-marks he had made on the way there. I prayed very fervently, but to my horror, the general then offered some whisky to the driver, who drank almost a glass-full without stopping or slowing down. After this, I prayed even more fervently. The owl must have sensed my unease, for he hopped from the general's shoulder and squatted on mine for the rest of the journey. Perhaps he knew I had a Sovereign Lord and felt safer with me in consequence. The driver had a strange tale to tell. He had been a mere captain, and had fallen foul of his colonel. He was condemned to death and taken with several others to the riverside. The Colonel carried out all the executions himself, but he must have been a pretty poor shot or else drunk, for although he killed everyone else at point-blank range with a revolver, the driver only received a bullet in the back. The pain and fear made him faint, and being presumed dead, he was thrown into the river with the others. The cold water revived him, and he made his way on to dry land and stayed in hiding for a day. He was in great pain but was able to make his way to the hospital when night fell.

He firmly believed, as did all his Simba friends, that he really had died, but the power of the magic medicine had resuscitated him. He showed me his wound to substantiate his story, but it was actually only a superficial skin wound; the bullet had bypassed all his vital organs. He was consequently made the colonel's private secretary and promoted to commander. I made few comments as he told me all this, having heard many similar stories, but the general was clearly impressed.

We finally arrived at Buta at 7pm and drove into the Convent of 'Le Saint Coeur de Marie' (The Holy Heart of Mary). A Congolese nun was despatched to call the Belgian Sister Superior. The general took my things out of the car, and handed me the whisky, asking me to keep it until he came to collect it. He told me he would come to-morrow at midday and take me back to Etsaff.

The driver got out to shake my hand and as he did so I noticed, to my horror, that his right leg was in a plaster cast; it had obviously been broken at some time. It was as well I had not seen it before!

The general and driver went straight back into the car, and with a wave they were gone. As they left the convent grounds, the car overturned, but no one-was hurt. My prayers for safety had not gone unheard. Meanwhile I stood waiting for the Sister Superior, a Protestant missionary with a large bottle of whisky in my hand. How incongruous it must have looked.

Chapter 7

In the convent

The Sister Superior was not long in coming. I introduced myself simply as Margaret Hayes of Banalia. As she heard the word Banalia, she drew her breath in quickly. 'But we heard you were all dead,' she faltered. So I was right; everyone thought I had died with the others. Hastily, I told her I was the sole survivor and had been a prisoner of the Simbas since Christmas Eve. Gently she took my hand in hers and took me to their part of the convent.

She called another sister who had been hovering in the background, Sister Assisia, an elderly woman of nearly seventy years, who found me some water and a towel, murmuring to herself all the time 'toute seule, ma pauvre petite' (all alone, my poor child). After enjoying the luxury of being able to wash my hands and face, I spoke to the superior again. As I would be staying in a Catholic convent, I thought it best to tell her from the outset that I was a Protestant missionary. Her kind and spontaneous answer endeared her to me immediately, 'You are a child of God and are in need; we too are children of God and in that sense we are sisters in the Lord.' Such a gracious and heart-warming answer was most reassuring, as I really did not know how she would react to my Protestantism. I was then taken to the refectory.

It is almost impossible to describe my feelings as I entered and saw eighteen pairs of eyes turn to me in sympathy and love. It was suppertime, and a place had already been laid for me at their overcrowded table. After I had sat down, a delicious plate of soup was put in front of me. I hardly knew how to return thanks; words were so inadequate to express all I wanted to say. A sister was delegated to make a pot of tea for me, for after all, wasn't I an Englishwoman?

The nuns naturally wanted to know about their colleagues and the priest who had died at Banalia. We spoke in French, as nobody knew English; although most of the sisters were Flemish. There was also a Belgian lady staying in the convent called Madame le Gros, who was accompanied by her two little girls, Ann, aged four, and Chantal, six. They all spoke French.

I was amazed at how noisy it was at the table, and I commented about

'It is almost impossible to describe my feelings as I entered and saw eighteen pairs of eyes turn to me in sympathy and love. It was suppertime, and a place had already been laid for me at their overcrowded table'

this, saying I thought they always ate in silence. They laughed heartily, then added on a more serious note that due to the tension under which they were living, the rule had been waived. I was very grateful for that concession.

After supper, I took a shower and put on clean clothes. It all seemed too good to be true. I was then taken to a bedroom which had a hand basin and two mirrors. I had not looked in a mirror for two months, and what I saw was not a pretty sight—my hair was a disgrace and I had obviously lost weight. The room also had a real bed complete with mosquito net.

After tidying myself up, I was asked whether I was too tired to come out and tell the sisters about my captivity in Banalia and subsequent life with the Simbas. Not at all! I would gladly have sat up all night just to enjoy their company. After telling them my story, I then had to answer their innumerable questions. After a while, a bell rang across the quadrangle, which I later discovered was the nine o'clock retiring bell, but no-one moved on this occasion; we stayed up talking for another hour.

The superior—Sister Alberta—took me to my room and said she would call me at 7.10am for breakfast. After she had gone, I sat in the armchair, surveyed my surroundings and then prayed. I was close to tears, and my heart was almost too full for words. For the first time in four months, I was able to undress before going to bed. It felt such a luxury. I soon fell asleep, and it seemed like no time at all before I was woken up at 5.15am by the noise of the rising bell. The bell tower was immediately above my bed, so it really was loud. My immediate reaction was to jump out of bed, but when I remembered where I was, I returned to bed to wait for dawn half an hour later, when I got up and dressed, feeling really refreshed from the deep sleep I had enjoyed.

True to her word, at 7.10am the superior knocked on the door. I automatically called out in Bangala asking who was there, and she answered in the same language, 'Mama na yo' (your mother), much to her amusement. She said this because her full title was Mother Superior.

Three of the sisters were nurses and they arranged for me to go with them to the hospital to try and find supplies to take back, as that was the apparent reason for my being sent to Buta in the first place. The hospital had been built by the Government and was large by African standards. It had managed to retain its supplies and equipment, in spite of the rebellion, probably because various items stolen from other hospitals had found their way there. In the large pharmacy was a big trunk with Dr Sharpe's name and address painted on it, presumably stolen from Bongondza after the massacre. It was filled with things taken from the hospital there.

Having more or less collected my supplies—apart from a few items on my list which the sisters held back as they were too precious to be spared—they called for me and we went back to the convent in time for dinner at 12.30pm. After dinner they always took a siesta—at least during the time I spent with them. I did likewise, and on this occasion I slept heavily until 3.30pm, feeling greatly refreshed when I awoke. As I emerged from my room into the main corridor, the sisters were coming out of the chapel.

The superior showed me round the chapel, which was a beautiful place. It was uncluttered and modern, yet in its very simplicity there was a beauty which had to be felt rather than seen. The altar was simple. The only decorations were flowers, tastefully arranged, which appealed to the aesthetic taste of all present.

The superior genuflected and crossed herself with holy water; but if she expected me to do the same, she gave no outward indication. I was given an open invitation to all the services and times of prayer, and was told I could also use the chapel for private prayer at any time. This was a great honour for me as I knew it was an invasion of their privacy, so I gratefully accepted their offer.

They had mass in the mornings at 5.30am, followed by private devotions until 7.10am. Next came prayers at midday for fifteen minutes, with further times of prayer at 3–3.30pm and 6.30pm–7pm before retiring for the night. Often the sisters would be in the chapel at other times too. There was much for which we all needed to pray whether corporately or privately, and I went to all their prayer times except the early morning and late night sessions. As they prayed in Latin or Flemish, it did not disturb me, and I could pray in my own way undisturbed. The two children tended to be fidgety when they went to the chapel, so the superior arranged for me to have my special place behind everyone else, so that I could pray without being distracted. I really valued my little corner; it became a truly precious place for me.

During my first five days with them, I heard that two of their number had been given permits to go over the border and on to Europe for a two-month vacation. The colonel was under the impression that the sisters were all quite happy living in the middle of a civil war, but as he knew it was a European practice to have a holiday, he offered to arrange transport for two sisters and two priests from the men's convent to go home, promising that when they returned he would double the number for the next trip. He only made arrangements to take them as far as the Congolese border. From then on, their transport arrangements would have to be their own affair.

On the fifth day the superior came to my room during siesta and said a jeep had come to take me back to Bengamisa (the other side of Banjwade). My heart sank at the news, but there was nothing I could do about it; so I hastily gathered my things together, heaving a sigh as I bade farewell to my comfortable bed, and then went out to the jeep, praying for courage to face this next phase of my bizarre life. As I left, I scribbled my name and mission address on a piece of paper and gave it to the superior so that in the event of any of the sisters being allowed out of the country, they could let my friends know that I was still alive.

I had not met this officer before. He was quite small for a soldier, and wore a brightly coloured Moslem gown over his grey-green uniform, which looked quite ludicrous with his cap and rifle, all the more so as he was not a Moslem. He told me the colonel had instructed him to take me right through to the most advanced post held by the rebels. Our journey, predictably, was a nightmare. The vehicles broke down, I saw men being beaten for no reason, and had to spend the night in a village where every man became drunk. I barricaded the door of the room allocated to me and sent up numerous SOS prayers for safety. It was a great relief when morning arrived and we could continue our journey.

We arrived at Banalia in the middle of a riot. Everything was in confusion. Apparently the day after we left Etsaff the previous week, the National Army had begun to bomb the area, and the house where I had stayed received a direct hit. When I heard this I could only murmur a 'thank you' to the Lord, whose timings are always so perfect. The General's aide-de-camp turned up during our stop at Banalia with a suitcase full of my belongings. I really appreciated his concern and honesty.

As the air raids apparently lasted continuously from 6am to 6pm, the officer did not know what to do with me, but finally decided to continue our journey. We travelled on into the night, and finally arrived at Bengamisa at midnight. The night watch were called to find me accommodation, as the house I should have stayed in had been bombed. I realised these men were also to be my 'medical team'.

There was nowhere where I could have a room of my own. I was sent to a mud hut they called the 'ladies' house' where eight women were sleeping on an assortment of mattresses all placed together to create a communal bed. One poor soul was told to vacate her place and it was offered to me. I was tired, hungry and absolutely filthy from the thick red dust of the road, but was grateful simply that my journey was over. I lowered myself onto the mattresses with the other women who all went to sleep almost immediately.

As I was lying there, I began to wonder why the Lord had allowed me to spend five days with the sisters, enjoying all the comparative luxuries of a civilised way of life, only to transfer me to even worse conditions than before. I accepted that the Lord had much to teach me, but what lesson was I meant to be learning? I realise now how gracious he was in teaching me in stages, for at the time I did not know what lay ahead. So as I thought how God's hand was on me even if few of the recent twists and turns in my life seemed to make any sense, I grinned to myself in the dark and thought of Philippians 4:11: 'I have learned in whatsoever state I am, therewith to be content', and asked the Lord to make me content inwardly as well as outwardly.

Next morning the rebels found me an empty house. The reason it was empty was because it was not quite finished. The room I was allocated had no window, which meant I had to sit outside to read my Bible. There were guards around most of the time, and when I read, their conversation would drop to a whisper as though they were in church, and they would prevent anyone entering the house and disturbing me.

Two of the guards really went out of their way to make things comfortable for me. They had both been houseboy-cooks before the rebellion and their cooking was superb. I thanked God for this extra provision, though it was hard not to think of the sisters in Buta and wish I was back there with them.

During my third evening there, we were sitting together discussing the Christian life and beliefs when a runner arrived to say the major was coming and I must get ready to go to Banalia with him. He turned up at 10pm, having waited until dark to make the journey because of the air raids. There were no air raids when I was at Bengamisa but they resumed the day after I left. I heard later that the Simbas thought I had some sort of magic power, but I know this power was not magic but the providential power of God, and to him I gave all the praise.

We travelled through the night. I do not know when these rebels slept for they seemed to keep awake day and night. We were in a large lorry, which was fairly new and had obviously been stolen from the post office. The cabin was comfortable, although there were four of us all packed tightly in, for besides the driver and myself, the major had brought his first wife with him. Was I content? Well, it was comfortable, and I prayed for and duly received the gift of contentment as we went along. We finally reached Banalia at daybreak, and there we had to stay, as there had been air raids all the previous day, and it was therefore considered too dangerous to try to take our bright red lorry across on the newly-repaired ferry.

It seemed that tribalism had crept in even among the Simbas, for I witnessed a terrible fight between the Buta and Banalia contingents over the distribution of rifles. I was ushered into the very house where we had all been imprisoned in November, and saw a man lying on the floor and being tied up in the special 'Simba Command' manner. His screams were awful, but his tormentors took no notice; they seemed to enjoy being sadistic. I asked permission to leave the house, but did not know where to go because of the fighting. I was taken to the house which Ian and Audrey Sharpe had occupied, although by now it was completely devoid of any furniture. Who should I meet there but 'Mr Jingle' of our prison days, although now he was neither so cocksure nor so incoherent. He assured me he would deal personally with any Simbas who tried to bother me. In so many ways I could appreciate how over the months a good number of Simbas had really tried to be nice to me, but nonetheless I still remained very distrustful of any of them.

It was arranged that I should cross the crocodile-infested river in a dugout canoe and wait for the major on the other side. After arriving safely, I was led to a house near the ferry, where several ladies were staying, including the major's three wives and the lady of the house. The major turned up soon afterwards, but not long after his arrival, some Simbas came and told him that the Banalia Simbas had taken our lorry and hidden it. He was furious, and crossed back to the other side in a canoe. We heard shouting and shooting and then a young man was brought to me who had been shot through the hand, shattering most of his bones. I rendered first aid, but did not have any painkiller for him, so I sent him on to Buta for treatment at the sisters' hospital.

When things were a bit quieter, I made my way down a private path to that beautiful river, took off my sandals and stood in the water. It was lovely and cool, especially bearing in mind how hot and sticky my feet were. I sat on the grassy bank with the water lapping at my ankles. Everything seemed so quiet and peaceful. The sun was setting, the sky was cloudless, the shadows were long, and the opposite bank—the scene of November's massacre, was bathed in golden sunlight. As I looked at the landing-stage over there, I thought about my friends who had laid down their lives. Somehow, it all seemed so unreal.

In his book, *God holds the key*, Geoffrey Bull pens these lines, which he composed while in prison in China:

> O Lord to know, amidst this tangled skein
> Of men, events and things, 'tis not in vain,
> I seek that cord of gold, thy way decreed –
> Is comfort to my soul, O God indeed.
>
> To know amidst this maze of circumstance,
> Dead ends which cruelly stay desired advance
> Can turn my feet to tread with surer sense
> Thy way of truth—Brings peace when all is tense.
>
> To know that when these floods of grief subside,
> Throughout the soul's poor fields, the ebbing tide
> Must leave such silt as shall much fruit ensure –
> My soul sustains and says to faith, 'Endure'.
>
> So, Lord, I shall not fall, I shall not faint,
> Thy grace enough for every baffled saint,
> Still through the wind-thrashed sea, I glimpse thy form
> And know thou hast thy footsteps in the storm.

I had learned these lines by heart and had set them to music, and now by the water's edge, when everything seemed so futile, I sang them quietly. The author of those words had expressed so eloquently how he had felt in prison in China, and now they were comforting the heart of a lonely prisoner in Africa. As I sang the last line, I seemed to catch a glimpse of the eternal majesty of God, and duly started to sing that lovely hymn of praise 'How great thou art'. I felt overwhelmed by the very presence of God in that place; I was indeed standing on holy ground. Afterwards when words came, I made the most of my solitude and prayed yet again to be delivered in time for my birthday, and also that I could go back to Buta for the time being. I had assurance for the latter request, but not the former. Obviously I still had a lot to learn.

The major came back, this time with the lorry, and he said I could stay at Banalia in the house we were then occupying. I had investigated the house and had found there were no doors between any of the rooms, so as I knew that several men would be sleeping there too, I told him I was not prepared to spend the night there and insisted on going back to Buta. To my astonishment, he did not argue with me. 'Go ahead, jump in the lorry', he said. 'We are on our way!' I praised the Lord for answering my prayer so quickly and jumped in as requested.

We stopped for the night at the same village where I had met the Bopepe women before, but it was midnight and they were all in bed. The commander's wife let me use her spare bedroom, for which I was very grateful. I made sure I locked the door before going to bed, and was glad I had done so for about an hour later, I heard the major asking for me. He tried several times to open the door while I kept praying that it would not open. Eventually he was told to leave me alone as I was obviously asleep. Once again, I thanked the Lord for his deliverance.

We were meant to make an early start the following morning, but it was midday before we finally resumed our journey. We stopped at a place called Kolé, which is near our mission station of Bongondza. Somebody recognised me and came to tell me that Bo Martin had been through there the day before with his wife and family, and they were all in good health.

The major's wife was drunk when we entered the lorry again, and he was sleepy. At one stage his wife was asleep with her head on my left shoulder, while he was also asleep with his head on my right shoulder. On another occasion, he leaned against the door in his sleep and it flew open. I was just about able to grab him in time.

We came to a very muddy patch in the road. Other lorries had churned up the mud when they had passed through earlier on, and it was very slippery. Even our relatively new eight-wheeled lorry was finding it hard going, so the major pulled a special stick of Simba magic medicine out of his pocket. He held it up in his left hand at shoulder-height, and made strange passes at it with his right, while chanting the magic formula 'Mayi, mayi, Lumumba mayi, advancez, mayi Lumumba' at the same time. Its magic did not work. Perhaps it could not cope with new technology like the internal combustion engine or was it because I was on board? We found ourselves bogged down in the mud. His wife, who was awake by this time, made fun of his magic formula and suggested that his magic stick had gone flat, and needed recharging—rather like a battery. He said nothing, and I wisely held my peace though I was laughing inside. So we had to get out of the lorry, and as I clambered out, I sank almost up to my calves in thick, orange, sticky mud. I made my way to the nearest house, where the lone occupant kindly gave me some water to wash my feet, legs and sandals in. I thanked him, but had no money with which to pay him.

By this time I was hungry. We had not eaten since the evening before and it was now 4pm. The major found someone who had some dried fish and bought some from him. Raw fish is hardly my favourite meal, but we washed it down with some water from a bucket, and at least it allayed the hunger pangs. The major also bought a large bottle of native wine and put it on my lap; I passed it to his wife in exchange for three radios she was carrying.

We finally arrived at the convent at 9pm. I was so glad to see them again! The superior said they had frequently prayed that I would be sent back to them, and now the Lord had answered their prayers. It was so evident that someone had been praying for me as I thought about that bizarre journey, I felt very humbled. The sisters even had the faith to keep 'my' room ready for me on my return. After a meal of rolls and cheese and a large pot of tea, I thankfully retired for the night.

So began the next phase of my life. I was to spend the next three months in the convent. Of course neither I nor the sisters had any say in the matter, but again I can see with hindsight how it was indeed God's provision for me at that particular time.

As the newest arrival and a 'non-professional' in the Catholic sense of the word, they used to call me the Protestant postulant (in other words, a candidate seeking admission to a religious order). Madame le Gros was also teasingly called a postulant, much to her children's disgust. We shared the dining-room duties between us, such as washing up, setting the table and generally keeping the place clean.

Madame had experienced a sad time before coming to the convent. The Simbas had told her back in November that they had killed her husband and thrown his body in the river. The children were only told that he was in prison. Consequently, she was very nervous, and if a Simba showed his face in the convent, she would call the children to her and scurry inside the house to hide. The children were naturally spoilt by all and sundry, and at times it was almost more than Madame could do to keep them in order. Looking at things realistically, they were not really badly behaved considering the trying circumstances.

At the time of my arrival, there were sisters from two different orders in the convent. It belonged to the order of the Holy Heart of Mary, but some nuns from the order of the Holy Sepulchre had also been taken there as prisoners of the rebel army. Most were teachers, the majority being university graduates. The others were nurses with the exception of the eldest sister who was the cook. She had been in Congo for over forty years.

While I had been away, the two sisters who had been promised a vacation in Europe had actually gone back and had very kindly contacted my mission telling them I was alive and well. I was so relieved when I was told about this, as I knew that folks at home would begin to pray for me again.

I had returned to the convent on a Sunday, and on the following Tuesday a lorry came in bringing six Congolese sisters who had been in the forest for three and a half months without a change of clothes. They too had a wonderful story to tell of the Lord's protection.

A week later, another lorry arrived with three European sisters and a Belgian brother on board. They too had been through a terrible ordeal for the last three months, and were very glad to meet up with other expatriates, just as I had been. These sisters were from the Ursuline Order. In all there were twenty expatriates in the sisters' convent, and thirty-five in the men's, along with twenty-four Congolese sisters and eighteen Congolese priests and brothers. 'Our' convent made bread for them all.

Several priests spoke English and would come to me for practise. They also searched their library to find me some English books to read. The pervading atmosphere in the convent was one of peace, deepened by a sense of oneness we all had in the fellowship of suffering. I did feel a bond of real fellowship with them, for after all, we all loved and served the same Lord. I could not worship as they did, nor could I accept their beliefs, but they never tried to impose their doctrines on me. We had many discussions. I found out that I knew more about their faith than they did about mine, and they were always interested to hear what I had to say. One question I was asked very early on was whether or not I had been baptised, a big concern for them in view of the precarious life we were living. I told them that I had been christened as a baby but had been baptised as a believer when I was an adult. This led to a most interesting conversation.

One evening, the superior asked me how I became a missionary, so I explained first how I had become a believer, then how the Lord led me on to full-time service. She was most interested and asked if I would tell my story to the other sisters that evening at recreation, which I was only too glad to do. It was about this time that the superior mentioned the school they ran and how they had to employ protestant teachers—but said they were Protestant only in name. I was the first believing Protestant they had met. When I heard this, I prayed that my life among them would bring honour and glory to God, and that he would keep me close to himself.

The sisters were a grand crowd; they had a good sense of humour and loved fun. I commented on this one day, saying that many people had the impression that nuns were always very grave and seldom laughed. They laughed at this and told me they had had exactly the same opinion of Protestants. They added that they had so much to be happy about, that they should be rejoicing all day long, although they had to be serious when they were in church or walking along the street, which was when most people saw them.

They were disciplined. I was with them for four months altogether, and the last month was very stressful, but not once did I ever hear a cross word between them. I assume that if they had a difference of opinion they would agree to differ, or else one would give in with very good grace. I cannot be sure about this, but can only record what I saw and heard.

One sister who had been allowed to go to Europe used to make epaulettes for the senior Simba officers, and as I had taken her place at the dining table, and used the serviette holder with her name on, they said I could take over her work too. I was only too grateful to have something with which to occupy my hands. I would go to a sewing machine allocated for this work after we had washed up the breakfast things and tidied the dining-room, and would make those epaulettes that the Simba officers so loved. It was often their only piece of uniform. At first they varied in colour and shape but eventually we standardised them. Incidentally, it seemed as though every Simba we met was an officer.

As I had gone to Congo primarily as a missionary, I asked the superior if she had any tracts or pictures portraying Christ to go with the epaulettes. A sister was sent to look for some and she duly returned with several pictures of Christ along with some of Mary. Another sister saw me looking at them and made the remark 'Mademoiselle won't be wanting the ones of Mary!' I chose some copies of a picture of Christ surrounded by people of all nations, and packed one with each packet of epaulettes I made. It was a shame that there was no text to go with the picture. Still, we all prayed that the Simbas' thoughts would be directed to Christ, who alone could give them the real liberation they sought.

Often the Simbas from Bengamisa (Etsaff) would come in to see me. Two regular visitors were Captain Jean-Pierre, the general's motor-cyclist outrider, and young Victor, the little Simba who had been our guard when we were in prison in November, who was later transferred to the general's retinue. Another day a group of nine Simbas came, including Lieutenant Dieu-Donné who had played Christmas carols for me several months earlier. They were all officers, or should I say they all wore epaulettes. When these men came, I was given complete freedom to speak to them. They would frequently ask for a portion of the Word of God, but sadly I did not have any to give them. The sisters gave me a few booklets in Lingala on the life of Christ so at least I was able to distribute these among them instead.

The convent owned several animals, including cows, goats, pigs, a monkey, nine dogs, including three full-grown German Shepherds, and several cats, which I especially appreciated, being a great lover of cats myself. The animals had been left there by expatriates who knew the sisters were quite happy to open their doors to all strays—animal as well as human strays like me. After a few days everyone started referring to the cats as 'Mademoiselle's cats'—though I could not see why. I enjoyed teaching little Ann and Chantal how to care for them and they were willing pupils. There was also a grey and red African parrot called Koko, who could speak in five languages but English was not one of them.

One day I had a visit from the 'resurrected commander', the man who had driven the car the first time I came to the convent. He came to tell me that the general was in prison but wouldn't tell me what his crime was. I am sure it was a trumped-up charge; the Simbas' kangaroo courts were not too bothered about establishing the truth. He asked me if I had been the general's wife—in other words, had we had sexual relationships, for that was one of the accusations being made against him. I was only too happy to tell him that the general had always behaved like an officer and a gentleman as far as I was concerned. The commander appeared very disappointed at my answer, and left me abruptly.

The general was subsequently sentenced to death, but escaped from prison. He was finally recaptured and then shot when they thought the National Army was nearing Buta. I was sorry to hear this; for he had been kind to me and had personally saved several men from death.

We were informed one day that the self-styled prime minister/president, Christophe Gbenye, was going to visit us in Buta, as this was apparently the area he came from, and the Congolese bishop was told that they wanted a mass said in his honour. The sisters all put on their Sunday habits and went across the road to the cathedral (which was opposite to the convent) at the appointed hour of 9am. Madame le Gros, the two children, one sister and I all stayed behind and watched and waited from the windows. 10am came and went with no sign of Gbenye; then suddenly at 10.30am we heard orders being called out and saw him descending from his car (or rather the bishop's car). The Simba brass band which was waiting for him inside the Cathedral struck up the Congolese national anthem. It must have been deafening in there! Mass was said, and Gbenye was placated. He came out followed by the band who were playing the only other two pieces they knew. One was the Belgian national anthem which the priests had taught them, although only the Belgians would know what it was, and the other was 'It's a long way to Tipperary' which I knew all too well!

On another occasion Gbenye ordered a requiem mass to be said in honour of those of both sides who had died in the cause of the 'liberation of the people'. He also 'honoured' us with a visit to the convent itself, and gave a long speech on how well we were being looked after, and how lucky we were to be under the control of the People's Army. He went on to say that if we were called upon to die, there would be a martyr's crown for us. Were we suffering from not having enough to eat? (We hadn't said a word about this.) If so, why could we not be like our predecessors, whoever they may have been, who ate the grass of the fields? I wonder where he got this piece of information from. After his talk, one of the sisters picked a basket of grass, and put it on the table at supper time, saying that all who wished to eat like our ancestors could do so, but she would stick to normal convent food.

There was always an underlying current of tension. There was a very efficient 'grape-vine' and news would come in of increased National Army activity in the outlying areas, and we eventually realised that we were surrounded by them. We assumed that military operations had been stepped up because the sisters and two priests who had been able to go to Europe had told of our whereabouts.

To our amazement, another sister was able to get out on April 1st, and we spent a busy couple of hours writing letters. I wrote to my mission and my parents, and the sister was able to take them and post them. In May some sisters and two priests were sent over the border for supplies, and they too took letters. When they crossed the narrow frontier at Bangui in Cameroon, they were told they could not return, as the frontier was closed into Congo. They pleaded to be allowed to return as they felt that their continued absence would result in reprisals being taken out on those who were left. Eventually, they all came back except for one priest who had gone further inland to plead our cause to the officials there. By so doing, he saved his own life.

Birthdays and feast-days were always made a time of rejoicing, with

Above:
At the Convent, there was a grey and red
African parrot called Koko, who could speak
in five languages—but not English!

flowers and on some an extra treat for tea. When my birthday arrived, I found a lovely bouquet of flowers by my place at the table at breakfast-time together with a birthday card which I treasured. It was hand-painted, and showed an open hand from which grew a single flower—a marguerite. The words on the card were in Flemish and said: 'In Uw hand Heer, ben ik veilig' which means, 'In your hand Lord, I am secure'. Such a lovely thought when all was turmoil and tension around us!

I happened to mention my parents would soon be celebrating their golden wedding, and we had a celebration then as well. I heard that all the priests had prayed for them that morning in their chapel and later in the cathedral, and the sisters really went to town. We celebrated with golden flowers, golden decorations on the table, and also by all wearing a golden leaf. We sang songs in English, written by the English-speaking priests. Two sisters dressed up as Mum and Dad as they would have been fifty years ago when Dad proposed, then followed it up with a second 'scene' where they were celebrating their anniversary. We were all in hysterics, apart from little Ann, who kept asking, 'But where *are* Edward and Louisa?'

My days were divided between work on the one hand and prayer and Bible study in the chapel on the other. There was so much to pray for. The Lord had not answered my prayer for freedom by my birthday, nor Easter, nor my parents' anniversary, yet he was constantly answering other prayers. I now asked for deliverance by Whitsun.

By this time my hair had grown long and I needed a haircut, so I asked the superior if one of the sisters could cut it for me, and that was a hilarious time. Two sisters were delegated to do it, one to cut and the other to supervise or help. I could not see what they were doing but could hear the comments like, 'Oh dear, this side is not level with the other side' followed by, 'Now that side is higher than this side.' The sister doing the cutting was using an enormous pair of scissors normally used for cutting cloth. Finally they finished amid much laughter and I discovered I had been well and truly shorn; the lobes of my ears were now showing! Still, it would grow again, hopefully by Whitsun.

The superior had given me some material to make a dress with and a priest had given me two new dresses from his 'poor-box' so I was well adequately supplied with clothes. Indeed, we had all the necessities of life, but we were not free. It was certainly not through lack of prayer, so what was it the Lord wanted to teach us?

One Sunday when the sisters were going to mass, the superior asked if I would like to listen to the radio. It was in a tiny sand-bagged room, hidden well away from the rebels, and I was thrilled to be able to use it. I tuned it to Radio ELWA, a mission station in Liberia, and although they broadcast in many African languages, I had managed to pick a service in English. Stephen Olford from Calvary Baptist in USA was giving a Bible study on 1 Corinthians 3:12. His theme was service, and showed how gold represented sanctified service, silver sacrificial service, and stones steadfast service, while wood, stubble and hay were careless, useless and worthless service respectively. He then applied it, leaving the question open as to how we would evaluate our own service. When I switched off the radio and put it back in its hiding place, I had much food for thought.

On Sundays, we restricted the work we did to a bare minimum—only essential chores such as washing up. When the sisters and Madame went to the cathedral for High Mass, I would go to my room. I had made out a little form of service for myself, and would endeavour to have a time of praise and worship. I would start by trying to sing a few hymns from memory, although I would frequently get stuck in the first verse, then would come a Bible reading and a time of prayer. I would then read a chapter from *God holds the key*. I was so thankful to God that I had found that book at Banjwade. Geoffrey Bull became, in effect my preacher, and I can recall one Sunday in particular when I felt deeply challenged by the words of this young prisoner-of-war. Here is an extract from the passage in question:

My avowal surely was, 'Lord, I will lay down my life for thy sake.' Yet the words of the Master still come back; 'Wilt thou lay down thy life for my sake? Wilt thou… Wilt thou…Wilt thou?' The days slip by and I become a prisoner of the Communist army…I am taken out by a young official and he talks to me seriously about the question of execution…I am young and it is hard to think of dying alone out there in the hills; and I go back to the dark cell and fight on, kneeling in the dust and the darkness, trying to still my heart-beats and keep back the tears 'Wilt thou lay down they life for my sake? Wilt thou…Wilt thou?'

So then I was going to die and all I know is that I was not saying any more 'Lord I will lay down my life for thy sake.' Not that I would if I had to, he knows, but only if I had to. It was not my will really to die for him. The will to live was much stronger. Why was it? Simply that I was facing reality now, and not the make-believe of my daydreams. I had not yet understood the doctrine of departure. We talk about living for Christ. It is more profitable to speak of dying with him. There are probably too many of us today still living, who should have died long ago.

As I read these words I was deeply provoked, and wondered how I had really faced up to this challenge. When I left Bo Martin on Christmas Eve to give myself up to the rebels, had I really wanted to die? No, I do not think so. Of course, I recognised at the time that they could have killed me, just as they killed Mary and the others. I knew too that if they had been enabled to face death, so would I. Nevertheless, I do not think that I had thought of it as a deliberate laying down of my life for Christ's sake. I had been glad, indeed relieved, that I had been spared passing through the valley of the shadow of death while still young. As I reflected on this, these thoughts appalled me and filled me with shame. Led by the Spirit, I then read on in the same chapter:

This then is our heart's trouble, that in the conflict of the cross, we should fail to die. That we should still be in good health, and able to answer questions when we should have nails in our hands and feet; that we should have survived to face our shame rather than have died in the promise of his glory; that we should be accepted when we should be outcasts; that we should be accounted friends when we should be spurned as foes. 'Wilt thou lay down thy life for my sake?'

That day in my room, in the relative safety of a Catholic convent, I reached a spiritual crisis in my life. The Lord was teaching me to evaluate life in the light of the cross. Before, my consecration had not been complete; I had thought it was, but now, to my shame I saw the superficialities of it. I was appalled at my worldliness and my materialistic outlook, and getting on my knees I wept tears of remorse. I asked to be crucified with my Lord. I knew it would mean humiliation, degradation, self-denial, and death to self. God knows I prayed in all sincerity.

During May, tension began to rise; you could almost feel it. The

Congolese bishop warned us about making too much noise in the convent. If we must laugh, we were to do so quietly, as he did not want us to attract any undue attention.

During our last week in the convent we were visited by two Egyptian journalists. We could not work out why they chose to visit us, although their trip was obviously for propaganda purposes. They asked if it was true what the papers had said about all the missionaries having been killed. It was a pointless question, for we were living proof that not all had died. They took photographs, but we heard later that their cameras were empty. They explained that the reason for their visit was that they had been sent by the Egyptian government to see how they could best help the People's Army in Congo.

The bishop sent one of the Congolese priests to tell us that if we heard that the mercenaries or the National Army were fifty miles away we were not to sleep in our beds, nor to undress, but to stay all together in a small but safe place. He would not disclose what he had heard, but tension was at breaking point. The Congolese sisters were afraid for us, and for themselves too.

The superior and some others cleared a space in the attic, and put some food and various other items in there in case we had to endure a long siege. We each packed a case with the belongings we would need for a flight or a long overland journey. These were put together in the same store-room along with blankets, pillows and more food. We literally did not know what was going to happen next.

All day we would watch the lorries going past filled with trigger-happy Simbas, thrilled to be going to war and singing their songs of hate. Several came to wish us goodbye, and to solicit our prayers for the coming battle. We heard reports that mercenaries had been seen fairly near. It raised our hopes that rescue was imminent, although we all remembered what had happened in Stanleyville and Banalia, and realised that it could be the same fate for us here at Buta. Everyone spoke in whispers, and neither Madame le Gros nor her two children would leave the building.

One day I moved my remaining belongings from my isolated bedroom in the front of the house to a cubicle in the large dormitory occupied by the nuns themselves. However, I never did sleep in it. Father Alphonse, a Belgian and the nuns' father confessor, came over the same day to hear confession in the chapel. Usually he stayed and chatted until the sisters were called to supper, but this time he hurried back to the men's convent as soon as he came out of the chapel, which did nothing to ease the tension we all felt.

After supper the sisters filed into the chapel, but there were Simbas in the quadrangle so Madame did not want to go. Sensing her fear I stayed back with her and the children in the work-room. Two sisters stayed behind too, as they were feeling sick. The windows of the work-room had been closed but there were several little peep-holes, and I was looking through one of them when suddenly I saw a crowd of Simbas running down the road behind the cathedral, followed by a jeep full of Simbas who were all shouting and gesticulating with their rifles and knives. This road led to the men's convent.

Madame was very nervous, pacing up and down. She gathered the children to her. If I had told her what I had seen, it would have made her feel even worse, so I said nothing, although she must have heard the noise.

Five minutes later we heard shouting and screaming in the quadrangle. One of the sisters turned the key in the lock on our door. We heard Simbas banging on doors and windows, calling us to come out. They went into the chapel and forced the sisters out, and shortly afterwards we heard the superior outside the door of our room. She told the Simbas to be quiet, then called out to us, saying we had to unlock the door. No sooner had we turned the key when a crowd of Simbas swarmed in, and pushed us outside using their spears and rifle-butts for good measure. Madame went deathly white; I expect we all did, although the children were very good, and did not even whimper. 'March! March to the men's convent, all of you,' they screamed at us. We were all arrested on Saturday May 29th at 6.45pm.

Above:
Margaret with the Sister Superior, Madame Le Gros and her daughters,
Chantal and Ann

Imprisoned again

As we hastened to obey our captors' orders, I saw Victor, the little Simba, standing at the corner. We had to pass him, and he was waving his spear like a maniac. As I drew level with him, we looked at each other. It saddened me to think that this young boy was mixed up with so much hatred and savagery, so I said to him, 'What you too, Victor?' He put down his spear and hung his head. We were never to meet again.

The road leading to the men's convent was full of Simbas, all enjoying watching the sisters being hurried unceremoniously along. At the end of the road we saw the pitiful sight of the thirty-one men from the convent sitting in the mud on the ground, with their legs crossed. We saw first one then another, receive the butt-end of a rifle on the head or back of the neck. Such unbridled hatred was terrible to behold.

We were made to sit behind them in rows of four. Our pockets were searched, and the contents were seized. I only had a handkerchief, which they gave back. The sisters all had rosaries, as did the priests; and these were taken and broken in pieces before their eyes. Next they demanded all our watches. These were not broken but gleefully put on their own wrists. I had already surrendered mine in November.

After they had satisfied themselves that we had nothing else to give them, we were ordered to march. It was almost dark by now, and we were made to walk in pairs, though Madame was allowed to walk with her two children, who had kept quiet through all this, but clung to their mother. Anyone who was too slow to walk at the Simbas' pace was helped along with a push from the pointed end of a spear. The eldest sister, Sister Fredeganda, who was seventy, collapsed twice and was brutally kicked in the back before she was able to get up. We walked in silence, though I am sure they were all were praying hard, just as I was. My prayer was, 'Lord, we don't understand what is happening, but we believe we are in your hands, and that you alone hold the key to all of our lives. We only ask for grace to go through whatever is ahead of us now.'

The former police station building loomed up in the half-light before us. We had to line up two by two in front of it, with the priests at the head of the

'At the end of the road we saw the pitiful sight of the thirty-one men from the convent sitting in the mud on the ground, with their legs crossed'

queue. There were a number of Simbas standing by who taunted us. Several times they asked Madame le Gros. 'Where is your husband?' Interestingly enough on each occasion someone standing by would answer for her. Then they asked me where my husband was, and when I explained that I was not married, they asked from where had I come. As soon as I mentioned the word 'Banalia' they left me alone.

We were then ordered to take our spectacles off, at least those of us who wore them. The African viewed them as a status symbol, so taking them off meant we were losing status. As I was slow in obeying the order, mine were knocked off. The sisters then had to remove their distinctive headgear of wimple and bonnet. Several were hit because they hesitated. We could hear the men being searched, to the accompaniment of more blows. Slowly we moved up the queue.

Eventually it was our turn. One by one we had to stand between two Simbas who searched our clothes. The Simbas were trying on the spectacles they had taken. They complained that my short-sighted glasses had too much 'medicine' in them and knocked the lenses out. They even took the nuns' 'wedding' rings and pectoral crucifixes. My heart went out to these dear women, being deprived of the symbols which they held so dear. After thirty or forty years a professed nun, it was not always easy to remove the rings, and we all felt for one sister who almost had her skin removed as hers was pulled off.

Finally the search was over, and we were all herded together into one filthy room, which was empty apart from two small tables and two benches, which the priests gallantly let us use. We sat or stood wherever we could. The children were so good, and did not whimper at all. The only indication of how they were feeling was the tight hold they took of their mother's hands.

Without my spectacles I could not see very clearly, but I knew there were men standing outside the windows. They were singing, and their songs became increasingly focussed on us. After an hour or so a major came in with several hefty Simbas and ordered all the men to undress. As they stood in their underpants we were ordered to do likewise, and several of the sisters were brutally beaten as they were initially very reluctant to comply with these orders. The Simbas then gathered up all the clothes and deliberately mixed them up. For some reason they really enjoyed doing this.

Next, the priests were ordered to strip naked. We naturally looked away, apart from three sisters who were forced to watch by having their heads held. The Simbas were searching for transmitters and radios. Our turn came next. The father superior thought we were all going to be killed then and there, and so he turned to face the entire room and while still stark naked, loudly gave us all what I was later told was the absolution in Latin. The sisters and Madame le Gros were visibly comforted by this gesture, and I expect the priests were too. I had the assurance of salvation and forgiveness of sin through the merits of Christ my Saviour, and felt sustained in this hope even in the midst of all my fears during this terrible time.

When the inspection was over, they told us to put our clothes on and then departed in fits of laughter. The men turned and faced the wall behind them, and told us to get dressed first. As we scrabbled for our clothes, whenever we found any of the men's belongings we would throw them over to them. It must have looked like a scene from a jumble sale! Of course we still had our audience at the window. The Simbas had wanted to humiliate us and they had succeeded. Still, I recalled how our Lord had been humiliated too and knew he would give us grace to go through with it all.

When we were finally dressed, we were separated from the men and taken to a room which contained absolutely no furniture at all, so we had to sit on the floor. Two days before this episode, the superior had fallen and severely hurt the base of her spine, so this must have been torture for her, but she did not complain. She looked very pale, but was able to smile back at us when we cast an anxious or sympathetic glance in her direction. The elderly Sister Fredeganda also looked ill, but she too did not complain.

We had been in this room for maybe half an hour when the door burst open, and in came yet another major with his retinue of Simbas, accompanied by the Congolese Catholic bishop and two Congolese nuns. The rebels had decided that I had a transmitter and was contacting the planes, because the bombing raids at Banalia and Etsaff had stopped when I was there. Of course, I knew that the lull in the bombing was the protection of my sovereign God, but I was not given the chance to tell them. Instead I had to undress again so they could look for the non-existent transmitter, and then Madame le Gros was also put through this humiliating ritual after I had put my clothes on. The bishop was made to watch, and when one sister turned her head away, they punished her by hitting her.

Later, we were taken back to the first room to be with the men, whereupon the new major accused the bishop of having a transmitter. Of course the bishop denied the charge, which had obviously been invented for the occasion. He asked the men to confirm that he had spoken the truth, and bravely added; 'My dear brothers in Christ, if you have anything to say in accusation against me, please don't be afraid to say it. I am not afraid to die, and I will forgive you in advance.' Then the bishop removed his sash and cassock, turned to the officer and said, 'I am ready to die. If I am guilty, shoot me here.' The major laughed and told him to put his cassock and sash on again. He had done nothing wrong, and could go back to the men's convent. Then the bishop begged them to kill him instead of the fathers, but they would not listen, and hastened him and the two Congolese nuns out of the door.

The door was slammed shut, and we heard a voice through the key-hole telling us to get some sleep. Nothing was further from our minds, but we arranged ourselves as comfortably as we could in the circumstances. The men stretched out on the floor in their portion of the room, using their cassocks as pillows, and some of them even managed to get to sleep, judging by the snores.

I was sitting on a fairly wide windowsill with four of the sisters. The superior was next to me, and she looked so pale I thought she was going to faint. She must have been in considerable pain as well as going through great emotional trauma. There was a small pane of glass missing behind my back, and during the night a Simba came round and shouted at us from outside. He then poked me with his spear, and when I looked round, he bent down and whispered, 'Don't be afraid, you women will be all right. ' Then he quickly straightened up and began shouting again. I assume he was on sentry duty, for he came round several times, and once I was able to ask for some water, but he said he could not do anything until morning. The room was stifling, thirty-one men, seventeen women and two children all crammed in together with no window or door open. Little Ann, who was very tired by now, was fidgeting. Her sister Chantal had fallen asleep in the arms of one of the sisters. We changed position often, as our legs and backs ached so much, but nobody complained, and nobody spoke. We were all busy with our own thoughts and prayers.

I found it quite a strain without my glasses, and it did not help when the Simbas would come in and point at somebody and tell them to come outside. In the half-light I could not see if they were pointing at me or not, and I was not alone in my plight.

We were all glad when daylight came. The guards were changed, and those who were stationed outside the broken window were much kinder, fetching us several bottles of water, which were quickly passed round. One officer came in and offered cigarettes to anyone who would like one. Most of the men took one, which did nothing to improve the quality of air in that overcrowded room.

There were no toilet facilities, and we were taken outside, two men and two women at a time, and placed deliberately in full view not only of each other, but also of the Simbas and anyone else passing by on the main road which ran parallel to the building. It seemed they could not humiliate us enough.

After a while we were once again separated from the men, and returned to the empty room where they had put us the previous night. As we filed out, the men were being forced to remove their shoes and socks.

In this slightly larger room, we arranged ourselves around the walls. They were covered in yellow distemper, which rubbed off on to the sisters' white robes and veils. We were all terribly thirsty and asked for water, which they gave us, along with two cups, plus two mugs of hot milk for the children. In spite of their brutality towards everyone else, the Simbas were always kind to the two little girls.

Suddenly, we heard the main door to our section burst open and saw a Congolese man being dragged into a room opposite ours. He was unconscious, having had an eye gouged out and been severely beaten. What was his crime? He had sympathised with the fathers. Naturally, we were all very apprehensive, and could only find consolation in prayer. We prayed for the fathers, for their captors, for our Congolese friends, and for ourselves. My thoughts went back to that Sunday morning in the convent, when I asked the Lord to show me how to be crucified with him, realising even then it would mean humiliation, degradation, self-denial and dying to self. Had I really meant the Lord to carry it this far?—or more to the point, was I prepared to go this far with him? I do not think I had meant it quite in this way, but I knew beyond any doubt that he was with me in it all, and I had no regrets. With his grace, I could and would go through with it. As I considered these things, I must have smiled, for a Simba came over to ask what I had to smile about.

The man in the room opposite regained consciousness, and began to moan and cry. We longed to go over to help and comfort him, but we dared not move.

An officer came in to tell us the fathers had all been sentenced to death by the colonel, and when we heard machine-gun fire, we would know it was all over. The colonel also had said that they were not to kill us yet, 'So just relax and don't be afraid.' Some comfort!

Sister Fredeganda began to have malarial chills and started shaking. The nursing sister next to her said she was very hot. She had not felt well the previous evening, and had taken her own temperature before going to chapel. It had been 104°F. She had intended to report sick afterwards, but never had the chance to do so as we had all been arrested. It was no surprise that she had collapsed on the forced march to the prison-house, or that she had looked so deathly pale during the night. However, in spite of being elderly and slightly infirm, being kicked and imprisoned and being ill into the bargain, she did not utter a word of complaint all this time. We told the Simbas about her, and an officer appeared soon after with some quinine for her.

We could hear the noise of a roll-call in the distance, and we wondered what was going to happen next. Some of the Congolese sisters from the convent arrived about 3pm, bringing bread and butter, black coffee and sugar. We were allowed to eat, and to be honest, we ate heartily as we were very hungry, but the men had not been allowed a thing, not even water, for the Simbas said they no longer needed such things. The Congolese sisters whispered that they had seen the fathers as they passed the window. They had been told of the death sentence passed on them, and were apparently very calm and resigned to their fate. The sisters added that they were very worried for them. So were we. The sisters added, 'For you, we have no fear, but for them there is fear, for them there is no hope.'

When we had finished our meal, the Congolese sisters went back to the convent, and we returned to our prison-room. Suddenly at about 4pm, we heard shouting and people running, then somebody screamed hysterically, 'Give them the command', which was followed by a loud cheer. It made my blood run cold. The sisters did not know that the 'command' was the special Simba torture, and I did not want to tell them either. My heart was pounding; it seemed as though it was trying to get out of my chest, as it was beating so rapidly and loudly.

The injured man in the room opposite was dragged out, and the Simba guards kept us informed of events with a running commentary— obviously relishing the situation. The priests were dragged out into the street, and the 'command' was administered. How they endured it is beyond human comprehension. As the ropes around their legs and arms were tightened, making their bodies into a backward arch, one of them screamed in agony.

Some of the sisters were crying quietly, but most stood like marble statues. Only the movement of their lips as they prayed showed that they were alive. They had known some of these men for years in the course of their work and worship. Some men were old; two in particular were well over seventy and had long white beards. Others were in their late twenties and thirties and the youngest was only twenty-four.

A lorry pulled up outside, and we heard more beatings. Then the lorry moved away, and shortly afterwards an uneasy silence fell. Our guards told us that the priests had been released from their bonds, and after being stripped naked were now being marched down to the river Rubi. We were all praying for them, obviously, but how do you pray in this situation? I think it was beyond our mortal comprehension to understand such barbarism.

After a short while, we heard more shouts, this time from a distance; and then came the rattle of machine-gun fire. We knew the thirty-one men were now in eternity. The time was 5.30pm. The sisters surreptitiously crossed themselves. I asked the Lord to forgive the Simbas as they surely did not know what they were doing. Later we heard that the priests had been lined up on the river bank, called forward one by one, stabbed in the left of the chest, and then when they fell, machetes were put to their necks. Any still

'After a short while, we heard more shouts, this time from a distance; and then came the rattle of machine-gun fire. We knew the thirty-one men were now in eternity'

alive when thrown into the river, were given the coup-de-grace by Simbas in canoes, which explained the machine-gun fire we had heard. The general population of Buta, realising the enormity of the crime, fled to the jungle to hide. An unnatural silence fell upon the town.

It must have been about 6.30pm as it was twilight by now. The light was on in our prison-room, but nobody had moved or spoken since the men had been killed about an hour previously. We were all in a state of shock. Suddenly the door was kicked open, and before our horrified eyes, there stood a half-naked Simba, with perspiration running down his body in rivulets. In one hand he held the dripping leg of a white man which had been crudely severed at the knee. His long two-edged hunting knife was in his other hand, still covered in blood. I wanted to take my eyes off the leg, but could only stare at it transfixed. All the sisters did likewise. Nobody in the room had moved, but we were all very conscious of one another's reactions.

The Simba advanced into the room, still out of breath from running. He stood there holding the leg, as though it were a trophy, making sure we could all see it clearly. He asked what it was, and on failing to receive an answer, asked again, directing his question at me, as I was the nearest to the door. I gave the obvious answer, 'It is a white man's leg.' Satisifed that we had been identified it as white, he asked one of the sisters what she thought of it. She calmly replied that the man was dead, and this was only a part of his body, so it didn't matter. At this, he thrust the leg into her hands, and made us all take turns to hold it in two hands, even the children. Chantal asked her mother, 'What is it?', and Madame answered 'It is something they killed today', giving the impression it had come from an animal. The children were satisfied.

The man then put the leg on the floor, and gave us a long harangue on the fate of those who communicate with the National Army. He then went out, taking the leg with him, leaving a bloody stain on the floor. We were glad we did not know which priest had been the owner of the leg. It was a grisly reminder of what had happened to all thirty-one of them

Shortly after this, an officer came in, and stood in front of me asking for Mademoiselle Margarita. It was Captain Jean-Pierre, the general's outrider. I made myself known as he had not recognised me without my glasses, even though I was one of only two women who was not wearing a habit. He solemnly shook hands with me, and then went out telling the guards to take care of me as I was a Protestant. I apologised to the sisters, adding that under these circumstances we were all in this together, regardless of religious beliefs. Later, when we had Catholic guards, the sisters had to apologise to me!

Having sustained the pain, grief and shock when my friends had been killed at Banalia in November, I knew what was going through the sisters' minds. I had not known the men personally as they had, and though I had felt the pain and shock too, I longed to be able to help them through their grief.

We were left alone for several hours. The guards said we could sleep if we wanted. They gave us each a sheet of A4 paper to put our heads upon, a pretty poor pillow, not that it mattered, as it was very hard to sleep after the traumatic events since our arrest. We tossed and turned, and only the children were able to sleep at all, and they only fitfully. Some sisters wept quietly. I tried to pray, but it was hard.

Some time before midnight, an officer came in with two men of mixed race. They appeared to be horrified at the condition we were in and our squalid surroundings, although their horror could well have been play-acting. The officer told us he had received orders from the colonel to hide us in the forest until the National Army and the mercenaries had gone. 'Now don't worry,' he added, 'We won't let the barbarian National Army find you.' I'm sure we would have hugged a National Army man if he had shown up—barbarian or otherwise!

Then they left us to digest the full import of his words. They were going to hide us in the forest. My heart sank yet again, at least until the words of Job 23:10 suddenly ran through my mind: 'But he knoweth the way I take, when he hath tried me I shall come forth as gold'. I had read this verse only a day or two before in my devotions, and had had the temerity to ask the Lord to make me 'as gold'. Was this the only way my prayer could be answered? I silently accepted that this latest turn of events was yet another part of God's plan for my life, even if I was struggling to make sense of what was going on.

The children were wakened, and promptly said they were hungry. A sister had saved two crusts from the bread and butter we had been given that afternoon, and the children ate them even though they were rather dry by now. I must admit we were all so grateful for that sister's foresight.

A few minutes later we were ordered outside for our trek into the forest. The officer of the guard said it was 12.30am, and the date was May 31st 1965.

Back to the jungle

The Simbas lined us up outside our prison-house to be counted. Once they were satisfied that all seventeen adults and two children were present, they arranged us in pairs, apart from the children who were kept with their mother, then off we went to the jungle. It was a dark, moonless night, and I tripped up several times, as I could not see the holes and ridges in the road. The superior asked permission to rearrange the party, as she realised that five of us could not see properly without our glasses, and we were each paired with a sister with good eyesight. I was grateful, for I can only describe it as like being in a perpetual fog, straining one's eyes in a futile attempt to see just a little further. It did not help that it was dark.

The superior herself was suffering greatly with the pain in her back, and Sister Fredeganda was also feeling very unwell. She was allowed to head the procession and thus set the pace. Kindness was hardly a Simba strong-point, yet they were exceptionally kind to the elderly sister at this particular point of time, always letting her go first whenever we had to walk anywhere.

The road we took was called the Basali Trail, and ran alongside Buta at right angles to the main Stanleyville road. It was new territory for me, but the sisters knew it well, and as we walked on past the now silent river, our hearts grieved for the men who had suffered such a brutal death only a few hours earlier. We kept silent as we walked; every one of us deep in thought or prayer.

Our first stop was the now deserted hospital. A nursing sister was sent in to find blankets, but she only found three, along with four small baby cot sheets. These would have to be shared between seventeen women and two children. We then continued our journey. We noticed as we walked that even the insects and small forest animals seemed to have gone silent. Although our journey was probably no more than three miles in total, it seemed much further, for firstly it was dark, secondly we had two sick sisters and the children to care for, and thirdly we were all exhausted both physically and emotionally.

SIMBAS KILL 75 WHITES IN CONGO

DAVID BAXTER : Leopoldville

A DESPERATE search is on in the Northern Congo for possible survivors of white hostages by Simba rebels.

Among the missing is an English missionary nurse, 39–year–old Miss Margaret Hayes, from London—the only survivor of a massacre last December.

But the hope is dim. A rescued couple, both wounded, who were flown to Buta from Paulis today, said that about 75 whites had been murdered.

Daily Express Thursday June 3 1965

Eventually, we arrived at a village, and the first person we met was Patricia, the colonel's latest 'wife' whom he had abducted from the convent a month before and forced to renounce her vows. Apparently she knew we were coming, and had laid some mattresses—stolen from the convent—on the ground for us. We were so thankful to be able to lie down, and the children fell asleep immediately. Patricia told us quietly that the colonel had run away over the border. He was hoping to reach Sudan, where he planned to stay until the trouble died down. She told us that the time was 3.45am.

We huddled together as best we could under the blankets and sheets. I appreciated here for the first time how modern clothes were less effective in these conditions than the nuns' mediaeval attire. My legs and feet were cold, and so were my arms. Madame whispered in my ear that she too was feeling cold.

Dawn broke just over two hours later, and we arose and shook ourselves, wondering what the day would bring. Was it really only thirty-six hours since we were arrested? It seemed far longer, as so much had happened in such a short space of time. We were given a handful of rice and a few half-ripe plantains, but apart from the children, no-one was hungry. They did give us plenty of water, for which we were grateful, being very thirsty. The Bible says, 'In everything give thanks' so we thanked the Lord for the water and the warm sunshine, and asked for grace to face another day.

It was decided to walk us back to the hospital, which was on the outskirts of the town. Our hopes rose slightly. Maybe the mercenaries would find us after all. We arrived about midday, when the sun was directly overhead, leaving no shadow. Somebody came with several hot cobs of sweetcorn which he had been ordered to cook for us, and we had a quarter each. The children were given bananas. The nursing sisters were sent to find some mattresses, but only found three small ones, along with four pillows. These were quickly made into beds, one for the superior, who was in great pain by this time and looked very pale, and the other for Sister Fredeganda who was also given some anti-malarial drugs. We were glad that they also managed to find some codeine tablets for the superior.

Our guards were changed frequently, and some of them would harass us from time to time, depending on their religious or political beliefs. We were allocated a filthy room where we had no option but to sit on the floor. Late in the afternoon we heard a plane overhead. It was flying very low, probably looking for us. The guards rushed in and shut the one and only window we had opened. They were almost beside themselves with rage, genuinely believing we had communicated with it, for why else would it fly over the very place where we were sitting? We did not bother to answer them. We listened for bombs, but none fell. It then occurred to us that the National Army would not bomb the town in case we were still there. The plane had been sent to look for fifteen nuns all dressed in white, who would have been easily spotted if we were outside.

As the sound of the plane vanished into the distance, we heard other ominous sounds. Bloodthirsty Simbas were outside, demanding that we should die. Our guards somehow kept them at bay. As I looked round the room I saw that everyone was praying except me, so I quickly joined in. We were not afraid of dying; it was the manner of our death that was the issue. It is one thing to die in bed from an illness or old age, or even to be shot, but being speared to death or dismembered is another matter. Bearing in mind the Simbas' brutality, it was hardly surprising my thoughts were running riot, especially having only recently survived two massacres. Only after much prayer was I able to bring them under control again.

An officer came in, who harangued us in both Swahili and Lingala, saying he was going to kill us. As he wielded his long two-edged knife, I recognised him as the man who had come in with the severed leg the previous evening. He said that this time he would take the sister superior first, and whereas yesterday he had shown us a leg, today he would bring in her head, as they had done to John the Baptist, only without the plate. Somewhere in his past he must have been taught the Scriptures. He said he would be back in half an hour, but in the meantime, he wanted everybody's stockings or socks, whatever they wore. We took them off, and he took them out with him, saying he was going to set a guard on the bridge and gather some men to help him with our forthcoming executions

We sat in stunned silence after he left, then the superior spoke to us. She spoke in French, as opposed to the Flemish they usually spoke among themselves, so that Madame and I could understand. She said, 'Today, sisters, we have not eaten, but never mind; tonight we will have supper with the Lord.' If the sisters had anything in their hearts against another, it was to be confessed and forgiven openly. I thanked the superior for her kindness to me, and thanked all the sisters for their love and for accepting me into their community. Madame did the same. Ann, who was only four, remained oblivious to what was going on, and sat quietly eating a banana, but Chantal, being that much older, could understand Lingala and knew what the man had said. 'Mummy, I don't want to die yet,' she whimpered. Her mother promised her that she would see her beloved papa and the little one was comforted by the thought.

So, once again I was facing death. I prepared my soul to meet the Lord, and was at peace. My only regret was that I had given so little time to serving him. I could not understand why he had allowed me to live through two massacres only to die in another, but I knew without doubt that he was the Sovereign Lord who never makes a mistake. It is not necessary to know all the 'whys' and 'wherefores' with God. If we believe in his sovereignty everything will eventually appear in its proper perspective.

Half an hour passed, then an hour, but the man did not come back. It was getting dark now. Our guards eventually told us he had run away, in fact everyone had fled apart from these four men who were left with the responsibility of guarding us. I am sure that prayers must have been going up for us at this time.

It really rained hard that night, and next morning when we were lined up before starting our next journey, we noticed a large puddle where the roof had leaked. We saw this as God's provision, and knelt down one by one to wash our face and hands, drying them on our skirts and handkerchiefs. Being so filthy, we were not able to wash particularly thoroughly in just one small puddle, but although we were all left with 'tide marks', it refreshed us somewhat.

We set out once more with Sister Fredeganda at the head of the file. Our baggage now included three blankets and the three mattresses. I carried one mattress on my shoulder. It had been rolled up and tied with the belt from my dress, and was not that heavy, although a bit awkward. We walked approximately four miles to a small village, and were directed into a tiny hut. The guards positioned themselves outside the door. Planes flew overhead, obviously looking for us. We tried to relax but it was not easy. Even praying is difficult at times like this.

CONGO MASSACRE

CONGO REBELS
MURDER WHITES

British nurse
still missing

Just before midday somebody came with a large pot of boiled rice and some bananas. We were ravenously hungry, having not eaten for twenty-four hours. As we began to eat, we became aware of a hurried conversation outside our door between the guards and someone who had just arrived. All the Simbas had fled from Buta, and the mercenaries had entered the town. Even as we eavesdropped on this conversation, they were looking for us at the hospital, only four miles away. It was no surprise when shortly afterwards we were ordered to get our things together as we were to be moved deeper into the forest.

It was a hot, cloudless day, and as we began the next leg of our journey, we knew it was midday as the sun was directly overhead. I shouldered one mattress as before. Our guard had been doubled; there were eight of them now, all armed with machine guns. If a plane was heard approaching, we were ordered to hide under the trees, otherwise we had to keep on walking. The sisters all developed quite nasty blisters, for their stockings had all been confiscated, and they were not used to walking without them. Madame was wearing a fragile pair of sandals, and after three or four miles the strap of one of them broke. My own sandals remained intact, even if they were not in particularly good condition. At least I was used to walking in them and thus managed to avoid developing blisters. In spite of all these problems we were made to keep up a steady pace throughout the rest of that day, which must have been agony for the sisters, although not one of them complained. We were also extremely thirsty. It was no help to think that each step was taking us further away from the mercenaries.

At last we reached a village where we could rest. The shadows were lengthening and the sun was going down, so I knew it was now 6pm. We had taken six hours to cover just twelve miles. Some kind soul in the village found us some native-type beds and we all sank down wearily. The poor sisters took off their shoes to behold badly blistered feet. The children were in the same position. One sister was so weary she wept. The sister superior and Sister Fredeganda both smiled, but said nothing.

Some fruit was brought, and one of the nursing sisters divided it into nineteen portions. I had the privilege of taking it round the group, as I was one of the few without a blister.

One of the men had been ordered to prepare a small room for us, and while he was setting it in order, we were some given soap and water. It was only enough for a basin-full each—and a small basin at that—but it felt so good on our hot and dirty bodies it could equally have been a full bath.

While all this was going on, a group of Simbas arrived. They had fled from Buta, and were in a very angry mood. They wanted to kill us, but our eight guards were able to keep them under control, and after stealing a few chickens they left us.

We were very thankful when we were finally able to enter our room, which had been cleaned and swept. We spread out the three mattresses and the three blankets on the floor, and after barricading the door with our bodies, and a short word of prayer, we lay down. We did not sleep, for we were overtired and the mud floor was cold, hard and uneven.

Next morning at daybreak we were each given a handful of cold boiled rice and a mug of piping hot black tea with no sugar in it. It still tasted like nectar to me! After half an hour we were on the road again. Several of the sisters had torn the hems of their dresses to make bandages for their feet, but even with their feet bound up, progress was slow and painful.

By noon we had covered a further eight miles in six hours; and we were tired, hot and very thirsty. Suddenly as we passed a group of houses, I heard someone call out, 'Mama Margarita, Mama Margarita!' I turned to look, but without my glasses I could not recognise who it was. The owner of the voice came up to me and took my hand in his, saying yet again, 'Mama Margarita!' I was now able to see that it was Ndimu Gaspar, one of our UFM evangelists, and the first protestant I had knowingly met in over three months. I was so thrilled to meet someone in the area who knew me. It really boosted my morale. He asked me to stop and talk to him, but I hurriedly whispered that we were all prisoners, and therefore not allowed to stop. He said he would follow us and find out where we were going to stay.

We trudged on for another mile before being told to make our way into the next village. We were only too glad to comply, for the sun was directly overhead on a hot, cloudless day, and we were all very thirsty. Several of the sisters were by now in real pain because of their blisters.

We squeezed into a little mud hut which had been given over to us, grateful for a rest and a break from the hot sun. Several men came in who apparently knew me from Bengamisa and Banalia, so I assume they must have been Simbas, but they were too far away for me to recognise them clearly.

The evangelist was as good as his word. After we had been in the hut about an hour and a half, he came in without even asking permission and asked for Mademoiselle Hayes. It was very unusual for the Congolese to use my surname, in fact I wonder how he knew it, for he had not met me that often. He called 'Yaka' (come), then, as if to reassure the sisters who were a little perturbed by his authoritative voice, he added, 'It's all right, I am an evangelist and she is one of our own missionaries.' They were very impressed by his charming and courteous manner.

He had brought a large bowl of hot sweet potatoes, and a three pound tin of powdered milk. Powdered milk is very expensive in Congo so I can only assume that this was something he had been keeping for use in an emergency, which it certainly was as far as we were concerned. He gave it all freely, and as we ate and drank I was able to catch up on news of the other evangelists. He also reassured me that Bo Martin was definitely still alive, as was Pastor Masini Phillipe of Bongondza.

He said he was holding services in his little village church every day; but the congregation had shrunk somewhat as so many people had fled to the jungle, but he was still trying to persevere faithfully with his work.

He paid us a second visit, and on this occasion he asked why I was having trouble with my eyes. When I explained to him that the Simbas had taken our glasses, he immediately brought his own pair out from his pocket and offered them to me. I was very touched by this magnificent and unselfish gesture, for glasses were regarded as a great status symbol by the Congolese, and I knew he had only bought them fairly recently when we had an optician visiting our part of Congo. The sisters too were most impressed by his generosity, and I humbly gave thanks to the Lord for such a dedicated Christian as Ndimu Gaspar, but I returned the glasses, which were for reading, explaining that the 'medicine' in the lens was the wrong type for my eyes.

Ndimu whispered to me that one of the guards was supposedly a believer. Later I understood why he said 'supposedly', for he was the cruellest of them all. His name was Pascal, and he was believed to be a deacon in his local church. I was given an opportunity to ask him if he had ever believed, but after quoting several scriptures to me, he told me to shut up, saying he did not want to talk about religion.

Several villagers came to see us bringing gifts of fruit and vegetables, for which we were grateful. We did not know whether they had been forced to feed us, but recognised that this was nonetheless God's provision for us.

The Simbas gave us permission to collect some leaves to put on the floor, so that we could lie down in relative comfort at night, although it took a considerable quantity of leaves to make us any more comfortable. We were provided with water, and somebody from the village gave us some soap, so we could wash. Two of the sisters were allowed down to the river—with a guard, of course—to wash some of our clothes. There was nothing to do except to draw pictures in the sand to amuse the children. We took it in turns to walk up and down to pray.

We stayed in our little hut two days and three nights, during which time we heard that Buta had fallen to the National Army, and that the mercenaries were on their way to us. During the third night our guards came in and unearthed some things they had stolen and subsequently buried. One of the guards, Alexis, told us that the mercenaries were now only a few miles away, but the Simbas had chopped down some trees and blocked the road with them, which would slow their progress. He thought they would be along by 8am, in which case the Simbas would run off and leave us behind to be found.

Unfortunately Pascal, the Simba who was supposedly a Christian, was also the leader of our guards, and he refused to go along with this idea. He emphasised that the colonel had given orders that the sisters were to be surrendered to him alive and well in spite of the fact he had fled the country. We must not be handed over to the mercenaries under any circumstances, so we would have to move on again at dawn. The other Simbas had no option but to fall in with this.

During the early hours of that same morning, a crowd of Simbas turned up demanding that we should be killed. Alexis, the young guard, was able to prevent them breaking down the door, while half of the sisters formed a human barricade on the other side as the rest of us prayed urgently for help. The Lord rapidly answered prayer, for they disappeared as suddenly as they had come, and silence reigned yet again. As they were moving away we heard them threatening to destroy the bridge nearby, but whether they carried out their threat I do not know.

Finally Alexis called out to us to relax as the Simbas had gone. We lay down again, our thoughts once more in a whirl. Strangely, it was during this time that the thoughts of writing this book first materialised in my mind, and as we lay waiting for the dawn, hoping this would be the day of our deliverance, I made some notes in my head and even worked out the chapter headings.

When dawn finally came, we all tried to explain how simple it would be for them to run away while they still had the opportunity, leaving us in the hut. The Simbas were all in favour of this apart from Pascal. We cajoled, promised and pleaded but he would not budge, and eventually he became exasperated and ordered us to pack up our few belongings and march directly into the jungle, at right angles to the road. We were powerless to do anything but obey.

We all felt devastated as we marched in single file down the narrow track. Once more our hopes had been raised only to be dashed yet again. We walked in silence, carrying the mattresses and blankets, every one of us wrapped up in our own thoughts and prayers. After about ten minutes we came to a shallow river. We took off our shoes and waded through it, keeping our shoes off until we had waded through the mud on the other side.

In this unfamiliar patch of jungle it was hard to work out the route we were taking. Alexis led the procession, and eventually we arrived at a clearing where a little leaf shelter was in the process of construction. The clearing was very small, surrounded by tall trees, so the sun did not penetrate, making it cold and damp.

We were made to sit on the ground in a group, while the men started to smoke cannabis, which soon began to affect their personalities. They began to shout and rave at us, even Alexis, who had previously been so nice. We were not allowed to speak. They decided to take us one by one into the jungle, but we refused to go; and when they tried to drag one sister away, she struggled so much they decided to abandon this idea in case the mercenaries heard the noise. We heard later that only a few hours after we had left, the mercenaries had reached the hut where we had spent the last three nights. This news did little for our morale.

The Simbas worked hard to complete our shelter before nightfall. Some went back to the village after the mercenaries had gone and commandeered two African-type beds made of bamboo slats on a frame from some of the villagers. At least they were about a foot off the ground, and whoever lay on them would not need a mattress or blanket.

That night it rained heavily. The 'roof' leaked badly, and it was cold. There was only room for fourteen of us to lie down, so the other five had to sit crouched up in a small space. We took turns to lie down, although it was scarcely more comfortable than being crouched up. Once again the sisters' long robes proved far more practical than the dresses Madame and I were wearing. The sisters could wrap their feet up and cover their arms, whereas mine were exposed both to the cold and the ubiquitous mosquitoes. In spite of all this, I do not remember anyone complaining. We were glad when the new day dawned, for it had seemed as though the night was never going to end. We were given a piece of cold manioc (cassava) and a quarter of a ripe plantain for breakfast. Some of us sat huddled together for warmth, while others lay down and tried to get some rest. The day passed terribly slowly.

We could laugh at how filthy we were. The sisters' white robes were stained and torn, and we all looked very grubby. Madame and I were also aware of how unkempt our hair was, for we could neither comb it nor hide it under a veil like the sisters. During the day we experimented with washing our faces and hands using wet leaves. They obviously didn't remove the dirt, but at least made us feel fresher.

That night we took it in turns to lie down, as on the previous night. At least this time it did not rain, which was a blessing. Speaking for myself, I found that my prayers were tending to become very self-centred at this time. All I could think about was our own particular needs. It was also very difficult to concentrate for any length of time.

Sunday morning dawned bright and clear, and we reminded each other that it was the feast of Pentecost or Whitsun as we call it in Britain. We wished each other a happy day. I reflected how Pentecost was the day when the disciples were filled with the Holy Spirit and the Christian church began. They were enabled to speak and preach in a diversity of languages. Here we were in a clearing in the Congolese jungle, as opposed to an upper room, but still a remarkably multi-lingual group. Between us we could speak three European languages, (Flemish, French and English), we all knew Lingala, I knew Swahili and several of the sisters knew the tribal tongue of their particular area, yet for all this we were only allowed to talk to each other in a whisper, and were most definitely forbidden to speak to our guards, who represented four different tribes between them. As I pondered on these facts, I wondered why it had been necessary for us to go through this particular experience, and what God was saying to us, and to me in particular, through it all.

I also remembered that I had asked the Lord to be rescued by Pentecost. So far all the special days of the Christian Church had come and gone; firstly Christmas; then Easter, Ascension Day and now Pentecost. As each of these days had drawn closer, I had prayed that I might be liberated beforehand. I had also added dates like my birthday and my parents' golden wedding to the list, so why had the Lord not answered my prayer? I had prayed in faith as commanded in the Word of God, and I knew that nothing was impossible for him who was sovereign. Suddenly it dawned on me as I meditated there in the jungle, that I had been asking for my liberation in my time and in my way. I had everything nicely planned out, but in wanting God to do my will, I was forgetting that prayer I had prayed so often: 'Not my will but thine be done'. What right did I have to tell the Sovereign God what to do, or how to do it?

I felt so ashamed I wanted to crawl away and hide. Humbly I confessed my selfishness, and then told the Lord that I was willing to be a prisoner as long as he required it of me, provided he would grant me the necessary grace to go through each day. As I prayed, I was very conscious of the burden being lifted, and my peace was restored once again.

The guards were complaining of the cold and damp, and decided we could not stay in our current hideout any longer, but would move to a place with more adequate shelter and plenty of warm sunshine. Once more we picked up our few belongings, and followed the guards through yet more jungle until we finally arrived at a very large clearing, which was actually a cultivated garden, although it was the size of a field. At least the sun would be visible here.

We soon warmed up in the sunshine, and one of the guards collected some wood and lit a fire. We had kept some corn and plantains from a previous meal, and were able to cook them over the fire. We had managed to acquire various odds and ends during our travels, including two cooking-pots, one serving spoon, two aluminium plates, and two hub-caps, one from a car and one from a motor-cycle, which made excellent deep plates serving three people at a time. Those without plates used banana leaves, which, when folded properly, were perfectly adequate for most things apart from soup. We ate with our fingers, hygiene being in abeyance for the time being.

We washed the dishes in the water with which we had boiled the corn, and even worked out ways of scouring the pots. A handful of grass rubbed in the soil did a reasonable job, but the best pot-scourers were husks of corn, dried in the sun. There was no need to dry our 'dishes' as the sun did that for us. We must have all learned a thing or two from the native women! We also possessed a plastic bucket and one beaker. How we acquired all these things I have no idea. The sisters would never steal anything. It must have been the Simbas.

We found that whenever the bucket was empty we were all very thirsty, but when it was full nobody seemed to want a drink. The sisters who had good eyesight would take it in turns to go to the river for water, always accompanied by one of the guards.

We found it hard to keep the children fed. The food we had was very inadequate and not very filling, and now that the tension had lessened somewhat, both children had developed voracious appetites. We all felt terribly hungry for most of the time, but as there was nothing we could do about it, we said little and did not complain. However, it was most distressing to hear the children repeatedly and tearfully telling their mother how very hungry they were, for there was nothing nutritious we could give them. Even the Simbas were sympathetic, and they would sometimes scrounge or steal some bananas for the children. One day young Ann ate so many she had an upset tummy for days afterwards.

When we had arrived, some of the Simbas had disappeared to the other side of the field. They were obviously up to something, but we had no idea what it was, until during the evening they proudly led us across the field to a place they had spent most of the day building. It was a long, low hut, with bunk-like shelves made of tree-bark. The shelves were about three feet off the floor. The sides were open at first, but later they made walls of tree-bark which covered one end and half the length of the back. The two wooden beds were brought in, which we gave to Madame and the children. The hut was something of an improvement on our previous accommodation, for at least there was room for us all to lie down, but we were still very tightly packed together, and it felt rather like being in a hen house.

I was given a place between the sister superior on my right, who was feeling very much better by now, and the mother superior of another order who was on my left. Our feet dangled over the end of our bunks, which was not too bad for a small person like me but a different issue for some of the sisters who were much taller. Their feet and lower legs had no support at all. We always went to bed at 6.30pm when it got dark, and would each have to wiggle into our allotted perch. There was no room to curl up, and if one of us turned to the left, then like an advancing wave, we would all have to follow suit, one by one. At first this was quite amusing, but the novelty soon wore off.

The bunks were hard, and as we became progressively thinner they seemed to get even harder. During the day we would gather leaves and make mounds that we could lie on the following day, but by morning the leaves would always be scattered across the floor underneath. None of us slept very much, it was always too cold and hard.

The Simbas had built a small hut for themselves too. I doubt if it was any more comfortable than ours. They kept us constantly under observation during the day, but once we had settled down on our perches for the night, they usually left us undisturbed. The rigid discipline of the sisters' life was a great benefit at this time of the day, for being used to silence at bedtime, they automatically stopped talking as soon as the last person had settled down. I think we all looked forward to this opportunity of praying without being disturbed. I could see the sisters crossing themselves, and then folding their hands, and I knew they were seeking solace in prayer. It was a very blessed time for us all; we were able to unwind, and more importantly, we could enjoy communion with the Lord.

I would reflect on various aspects of the Lord's earthly life. If I could find a parallel between his situation and ours, not only would it draw me away from being so self-centred in my prayers, but it also would comfort me, for if my Lord had trodden this same path, experiencing hunger and discomfort because of the nomadic life he lived during his three-year ministry, then he could understand how we felt.

One day the owner of the field where we were staying paid us a visit. He turned out to be a UFM church member. Ndimu Gaspar had told him about me, and now he had plucked up courage to come and find me. He really needed courage, for the Simbas were so unpredictable. They gave him permission to talk to me, and during the course of our conversation, he asked if I had a Bible, to which I sadly replied, 'no'.

A few days later he came back to tell me that Ndimu and his family had fled into the jungle, but in the opposite direction to us. However, he had sent us a small copy of 'The way of salvation', a Scripture Gift Mission booklet written in Lingala. We were all very grateful for this, and we all took turns to read it, even some of the Simba guards. Such a gesture was very moving, and such a contrast to the attitude of the men we were with, who were unlovely and cruel in the extreme. We kept the little booklet tucked into a crevice in the leaf-roof, and someone would often take it down and read it.

We devised a regime for our day. We all rose at dawn, and one sister would light the fire, usually by taking a burning piece of wood from the Simbas' fire. Meanwhile others would go off to gather pondu leaves. Pondu was a Congolese vegetable much like spinach, and we would use the leaves to make soup. I stayed back with some of the others and we tidied the hut generally, and swept both the inside and the surrounding ground using a 'broom' made from a bunch of unripe rice. Without my glasses, I could not see well enough to recognise pondu leaves among all the other jungle vegetation, and my sandals were not in particularly good condition by now.

When the sisters returned with the leaves and whatever else they could find, such as the occasional wild tomato, we would all work together to prepare the food. The villagers were forced to supply us with manioc and plantains—without ever being paid, incidentally, and occasionally we were also given peanuts, corn-cobs or onions, which we boiled. It took several hours to prepare our food, as we had so few kitchen utensils. It was hard to peel or cut without a knife, and hard to pound without a pestle or mortar. We did have two spoons, so at least we could stir.

About 9am we would stop for breakfast—cold manioc left over from the previous evening and maybe a banana too. Water was our only drink, apart from one occasion when somebody brought us some coffee-grains, which we roasted, pounded and finally made into a brew that approximated to coffee. We had neither milk nor sugar, but we did have some honeycomb, so we used that instead.

We were quite filthy by now, so much so that the Simbas were as ashamed of our appearance as we were, and from somewhere they produced a large box of soap. They said we had to wash ourselves and our clothes, and took a group of five sisters to the river with some washing. Determining what exactly should be washed was a major logistical exercise, for none of us had a change of clothing. The sisters whose dresses were being washed stayed in the hut all day while their clothes were spread out on a large tree trunk to dry. I am sure the sisters had never washed clothes in the river before. I had learned how to do it during my time alone with the Simbas before coming to the convent, and had found it a most laborious job. The sisters, however, took to it at once, as though they had always done it that way!

The Simbas always insisted on going with us to the river, of course, so we did not feel free to wash ourselves as thoroughly as we would have liked—only our hands, feet and faces. Only a few of us were allowed to go on any given day, so we had to work out a rota. I seldom went because of the difficulty of seeing my way through the dark jungle. I did make three visits to the river on my own—apart from my inevitable Simba escort, but this was just to fill a bucket with water. Each time I tripped and stumbled so much, causing the water to splash out, that the Simba eventually took the bucket in one hand whilst leading me with the other. I was therefore restricted to washing myself in a small basin, about the size of a sugar-bowl, but was quite amazed at what a thorough job I was able to do with so little water. Because of our understandable reluctance to wash ourselves in front of an audience, one of the Simbas really thought we did not know how to bathe, and asked me one day, 'Do white people never wash all over?' If only we could have done so! The Congolese are meticulously clean, and will bathe in the river twice a day, but if I had tried to explain why we did not do likewise, it would have only made them more insistent than ever. However, as I had failed to answer his question satisfactorily, he brought over a bucket of water, called us all together and began to demonstrate how to wash all over. We tactfully withheld our grins until he had gone.

At midday we would eat whatever had been prepared that morning, and I would then help with the washing up. This was followed by a so-called siesta; for the hot sun was overhead, and our hut was too low, to cast any shadow. We would lie on our bunks until about 2.30pm when the shadows would be long enough to afford protection.

Afternoons followed the same pattern as the morning—preparing food, keeping the fire going, getting water, and keeping the place swept and tidy.

At approximately 5.30pm we would eat whatever food we had cooked, apart from some manioc or plantains that we put to one side for breakfast the next day. However, we found that no matter how much we ate, and it was never a great deal, we were always ravenously hungry again after an hour or two. As always, it was the children who suffered the most. They were not used to African food, and would hardly touch it at first, but later on they would eat and eat, yet after only a little while they would be complaining again how hungry they were.

At sundown, those who could see clearly would all gather to watch the monkeys in the treetops as they made their way home each evening. I could hear the crashing of the leaves, but could not see the monkeys, although I tried to visualise the scene in my mind. It was a good morale-booster for us all simply to see the look of utter delight on the children's faces. Considering they had no toys, books, paper or pencils, and were restricted to a limited area around the hut, they were really very little trouble.

Like the monkeys, we retired to rest as the daylight faded, and each evening Chantal would ask, 'Mummy, is this our last night here?' and Madame would answer, 'Perhaps, only the Lord knows.'

In our day's programme I have not mentioned prayer or Bible reading. We did not have a Bible and it was impossible to organise times for prayer, for the Simbas would be furious if they caught a sister crossing herself or trying to pray. So we had to work out a way of praying without it being obvious what we were doing. We came up with the idea of three or four of us walking about with our hands behind our back, which would indicate to the others that we were praying and that we were not to be disturbed. After some fifteen or twenty minutes, another group would do likewise.

Personally, I found it helped me to concentrate if I was able to walk as I prayed. We were all finding it increasingly difficult to concentrate for long periods, and it seemed as though physical exercise helped to focus the mind for prayer. When we were sitting down, whether on the ground, a low tree-trunk or on the bunks in the hut, we found it hard to think about anything else apart from how uncomfortable or hungry we were.

One day we heard the Simbas talking to one another about how the mercenaries had gone back to Buta and had given up the search. Whether they said this in our hearing deliberately, or whether or not it was true we did not know, but if they wanted to make us despondent, they certainly succeeded. Yet even in all this I knew that God would never abandon us. His word says, 'Lo, I am with you even unto the end of the world' (Matthew 28:20) and I shared this verse with the sisters as it came to my mind. I knew it was true, and nothing could shake my faith in God. Looking at our situation from a human point of view, it did seem as though there was no more hope; we felt that we had been abandoned by man. Yet we had the Lord's promises; we could comfort one another with them, indeed we should be counting ourselves privileged to have been allowed to tread this particular pathway. Our times were in his hands, and nobody could alter his plans for us. We knew that when it was his time, we would be liberated, not a moment too early or too late.

During these days and weeks, there were a total of nine Simbas guarding us. Several would go out on patrol in the daytime, but we were never left without an armed guard. We were not allowed to speak out loud, which suited us for it meant they could not hear what we were saying to one another, which was just as well. They objected strongly if three or more of us were talking together.

They liked to humiliate us from time to time. Sometimes they would force us to walk without shoes for several hours; at other times we were all made to sit on the ground while they insulted us. On another occasion they made us all stand in a line. One particular indignity they seemed to enjoy inflicting on us was pulling our noses. It may sound funny in retrospect, but it was very painful and humiliating at the time, for this was no playful tweak.

Twice a small twin-engine plane passed overhead, flying fairly low, more than likely looking for us. We pretended not to show any interest in it. When it had gone we were accused of having been in contact with it, and were threatened with death. They just could not think logically when it came to planes. After our release we learned that there had been two flights to Buta every day during the time we were held in the jungle, but in the Lord's providence, they always chose a flight path away from us.

We were told by the guards that the mercenaries would never find us, as they did not know the jungle and would thus not be able to penetrate very far. I knew from my own experience that progress in the jungle could be very slow for anyone unfamiliar with it. They also added that at the first intimation of any mercenaries coming near, we would all be killed, which we all knew was no idle threat.

It must have been terrible for Madame le Gros to hear the Simbas saying that when they came to kill us, they would spare the two children and take them back to live in their villages before eventually taking them as wives. In fact, to further torment Madame, two of them went so far as to say they had decided which child each of them would take.

The villagers who had been forced to supply us with food were frequently in trouble because they hadn't brought enough or what they had brought was too poor in quality. On one such occasion we were lying down during siesta time listening to a poor villager being harangued yet again about this when we suddenly heard the word 'command', followed by the cries and groans of the poor fellow as they tied him up in their barbarous way. At this point we were all ordered out of the hut to watch the spectacle, apart from Madame and the children, who were told to stay inside.

The poor fellow was lying on his side, and in front of his mouth was a small unpeeled manioc, which incidentally has a very thick skin, several uncooked palm-nuts, and a raw unpeeled plantain. The man was made to eat them all including the peel and some earth, the Simba using the point of his spear to push them into his mouth. When he had finished, he was untied and they made him drink a large bowl of water, maybe a couple of pints in all. By the time he had completed his 'meal', his stomach was sticking out from his abdomen, rather like a large displaced hernia. Following this, to our utter amazement the Simbas then shook hands with him, and invited him to sit with them in their hut for a while, so that he could recover before making the long journey back to his village. They chatted and laughed together as though they were bosom pals! This swing of temperament was always something we were up against. One minute they would boil over and become extremely vicious and then, just as quickly, they would cool down again. They were so unpredictable.

One Monday, which turned out to be our last Monday in the jungle, Alexis and two other Simbas went out on patrol, and at 4pm came back each with a new machine-gun and plenty of ammunition. Judging by their conversation, it seemed they had acquired their new weapons by robbing some fellow Simbas. They sat up that night handling their guns and regaling each other with accounts of the wonderful acts of bravery they were going to perform.

On Tuesday they went out on patrol once more, this time suitably armed, but when they came back they no longer had their guns! The commander had taken them back, and punished the two boys with the inevitable 'command' treatment.

On Wednesday, we received a 'letter' from the commander, written in pencil, the gist of which was, 'We know you are trying to contact your white relatives,' (meaning the mercenaries of course) 'but you will not succeed. We do not want to hear of any more trouble in your camp. You are our prisoners and you will obey your Simbas—or else. Remember that if one Simba is shot in an attack, you will all die.' We had no idea why the Simbas had reported trouble in our camp; we thought we were model prisoners.

As we read this letter, it felt like our death sentence. Not being military strategists, we could not imagine how it would be possible for us to be liberated without an attack on the villages beforehand. The sister superior said we must live from now on as though each hour was our last.

On Thursday it was chilly and drizzling with rain, so we stayed in the hut. The sisters sat along the length of the bunk, and as it was my turn to pray behind them, I suddenly felt a desire to pray for our liberation, which I had not done for the whole month since Pentecost. I lay down behind the row of sisters, prostrate before the Lord, while the sisters drew even closer together to protect me from prying eyes. As I prayed, I was overwhelmed with the presence of God, and no sooner had I asked him for a word for me when the text from Mark 5:36 came to my mind, 'Be not afraid, only believe'. I knew with renewed assurance that the Lord had everything, absolutely everything under his control. The verse was repeated in my mind three times in all as I waited before him. The sisters noticed the look of peace on my face and I shared the verse with them.

On Friday the Simbas were restless. Up to this time our food supplies had been reasonably adequate, usually with enough left over for the next meal, but now supplies were running low. The Simbas had heard that the villagers did not wish to supply us any more, which was no surprise. They had been feeding twenty-eight of us, including the Simbas, and had not been given a penny for their efforts. Not surprisingly, their stocks were severely depleted by now. The Simbas talked among themselves, but loud enough for us to hear that they were considering moving us somewhere else.

That night as we lay down to rest, I felt very burdened, in spite of the assurance of the day before. I argued with the Lord, and told him how precarious our lives were, as if he didn't already know. I reaffirmed my faith in him and his word, but I remember so clearly saying, 'Lord, we are at the end of our tether; we cannot go on much longer under these conditions. Please burden the folk at home to pray for we feel so tired and battered mentally, we cannot see our way clearly to pray for ourselves.' As I prayed, the words of the previous day came back into my mind: 'Do not fear, only believe.' How patient the Lord is with us!

It rained in torrents all that night, and the roof leaked like a sieve, which resulted in most of us getting very wet, including me. None of us slept that night for we were so uncomfortable. I just lay there fidgeting, feeling very cold and really sorry for myself. My feet, which were rarely warm at the best of times, were so cold they felt quite painful. The superior on one side of me arranged her skirt so that it covered my legs, while the superior on the other side arranged her veil to cover my arms and shoulders.

Such was our last night in captivity, though we did not realise it at the time.

Rescued!

Saturday morning, June 26th, was cloudy, cold and damp. As we began to stir ourselves, two of the sisters and Madame told us that they had heard the noise of vehicles on the road. As sound can carry very far in the jungle, this was by no means impossible, especially as the Simbas had heard something too. They thought it was the National Army coming to the villages to look for food for their men in Buta.

That morning as we stood around talking in whispers to each other, the two superiors told me that it was the feast of Corpus Christi. They used to keep a record of their various saints' days, and would pray to the appropriate saint on their particular feast day, so when they told me about Corpus Christi I assumed this was another saint, but never having heard of such a person, I asked them who it was. They said it was not a saint's day, but the day when Catholics everywhere worshipped Christ for who he was and for what he had done for us. So I said, 'Right, today I can join you in prayer, but you pray your way and I'll pray my way.' I had been very conscious that God says in Isaiah, 'My glory I will not give to another', and it had bothered me that if we had been rescued on a particular saint's day, they would have said, 'Saint So-and-so liberated us.' So on this particular day, I could honestly join in and worship Christ with them, for if we were liberated, the glory would go to the Lord himself.

The morning passed like all the others, except we were not at our best after our bad night, and we were more tense than usual after hearing about the lorries. Our Simbas went off into the jungle. They told us they were going on patrol, but as most of them were not local men, I was always puzzled as to how they knew their way round this particular area of jungle.

The sun came out during the morning, which lifted our spirits and warmed us up. We discussed whether the lorries we had heard belonged to the mercenaries or the National Army. As we speculated on these matters, one of the guards returned after having had a haircut. A haircut is always a fairly time-consuming process, and the Congolese can make it last anything up to an hour, but as this man was supposedly on patrol, and would have known who had been driving those lorries, as the 'grapevine' in

25 WHITES FIGHT THEIR WAY OUT

DAVID BAXTER : Leopoldville

TWENTY-FIVE whites who fought off Congo rebels are safe tonight, but four others are missing, three of them probably dead.

The whites, among them 10 women and two children, were surrounded yesterday at the timber plant of Nicki, 220 miles from Leopoldville.

Radio messages received in Leopoldville today said that 25 of them have arrived by boat at Kutu, 40 miles up the Fimi river.

Daily Express Wednesday June 23 1965

Congo was usually very reliable, we decided regretfully that there was no possibility of any immediate rescue. The guard would never have stayed around for a haircut if there had been any mercenaries in the vicinity.

We concentrated on the job in hand, which was the preparation of the midday meal. We peeled, pounded and cooked, then ate up—literally so, for we had absolutely nothing left for the next meal—not even a banana.

We cleaned up, washed the pots, and retired for our siesta as usual. Several villagers arrived, and we heard the Simbas demanding food from them, although whether they had brought any we did not know. Then the Simbas began to argue among themselves about what to do with us. As the supply of food had seemingly dried up, it seemed there was no option but to move to another area where hopefully food would be more abundant. As they argued their voices became louder and louder.

Because these men could become so violent, even towards each other, we decided it would be wise to keep a low profile for a while, so we stayed in the hut until 2.30pm, by which time things seemed to have quietened down. Madame started to make her way out of the hut at one end, and one sister was just putting her head out at the side. The superior lying next to me had sat up, so I had an uninterrupted view out of the hut. The time was 2.31pm exactly.

Suddenly the air was rent with bloodcurdling shrieks and shouts of 'Tirez! Tirez!' ('Shoot! Shoot!') We heard the rattle of machine guns and I heard several bullets land on the roof of the hut. Even without my glasses, I could make out a pair of white legs coming over a small hilltop and running down to us. Bullets whistled, and the noise was terrifying. One superior called out 'Don't shoot! Don't shoot!' The sister who had been about to leave the hut jumped back in saying 'C'est les blancs, c'est les blancs!' ('It's the whites!') We literally held our breath. Little Chantal, who had been just about to follow her mother out of the hut, threw herself under the African-type bed. Then came a lull in the gunfire, and a white, unshaven, bespectacled face peered down under the roof and said with such a cheerful grin, 'Bonjour mes soeurs, bonjour mesdames venez, vous êtes liberées!' ('Good-day sisters, good-day ladies, come, you are liberated!') We all immediately burst into tears with the sudden release of literally weeks of tension. The time was 2.35pm.

We jumped off our bunks and streamed outside to behold our liberators—a crowd of tired, bearded, dirty but very happy men! We all shook hands in the time-honoured European way, and each said a very tearful 'thank you'.

The man with spectacles who had just greeted us turned out to be the Catholic chaplain. There was a doctor with him, and both men were unarmed although they were wearing camouflage uniforms. They were able to tell Madame the wonderful news that her husband was out on the road waiting for her, which made us all even happier. We set off immediately through the forest, without as much as a final glance back at our hut.

God's timing was so perfect. Our assumption had been correct; the lorries we had heard that morning were taking the mercenaries along the main road deeper into the jungle. They were accompanied by some Congolese soldiers from the National Army, which turned out to be a blessing, for the mercenaries wanted to kill anyone they found in the villages en route, but the Congolese knew the mentality of their countrymen only too well, and warned the mercenaries that if our guards heard gunfire, they would kill us all immediately, in order to save their own lives. The mercenaries, to their credit, recognised the wisdom in this. So when they reached the village nearest to us, they took two men prisoner, discovering in due course that both men had been to our hiding-place the day before and knew the way there.

By this time the mercenaries had divided into two groups, half going to the left of the road and half to the right, and it was the group on the left who had come to the village and found the two men. It took them almost the whole morning to reach us from the village, for there were twenty-three of them in total, all having to make their way through the jungle as silently as possible. At one point, they began to doubt whether the two men were telling the truth, and considered turning back, but the chaplain and the doctor volunteered to go on ahead with two villagers while the others rested. They came to the little hill near us, peered over the top and saw us all tidying up after our meal. They then went back to tell the others, who promptly sprang into action.

It was God's gracious providence that the Simbas on patrol heard nothing. This alone was a miracle and we gave him all the glory. Of the four Simbas who had been arguing, three had been severely wounded, but the fourth escaped. As we walked on, surrounded by the mercenaries, we passed one of the guides who had been fatally wounded in the crossfire. He was not a pretty sight, lying on the ground jerking his legs in the last throes of death.

The mercenaries fired three mortar-bombs, which was the signal to the other group that we had been found and they should now make their way back to the lorries and wait for us. We were in a state of 'reverse-shock' as we tried to adjust to our new situation. The graciousness of the mercenaries made such a contrast to the Simbas. They were all negotiating a patch of unknown Congolese jungle, some of them walking backwards, simply to protect us.

One sister guided me over the tree roots and helped me to keep to the pathway, as I could not always see it clearly. We crossed the river, which had been swollen by the overnight rain, and eventually came out on to the road. We found an empty house and went in. The occupiers had probably run away when they heard gunfire. The mercenaries gave us some of their biscuits and some rather cold coffee.

Our conversation sounded like music to my ears. We all marvelled at the way God had effected our rescue. Someone was sent to find a bicycle for Sister Fredeganda, as it was a good three or four miles walk down the road to the mercenaries' vehicles, which were parked the other side of a bridge which had been destroyed. It was a good thing she knew how to ride one.

The other man who had guided the mercenaries to our hut was still with us, and we thanked him for being so courageous. He begged to be allowed to come to Buta with us, as he was understandably afraid of reprisals from the Simbas. His request was duly granted. Once the bicycle arrived, off we went again. We did not feel the slightest bit weary and all felt far more emotionally stable by now. The journey seemed to take no time at all, even though our progress was halted at times by large trees lying across the road. The Simbas has felled them deliberately to stop the mercenaries' vehicles, and the men had to help us climb over them.

As we neared their vehicles, we saw the other group of mercenaries. They had obviously heard our signal and had made their way back. One man detached himself from the rest and came running towards us with his arms outstretched—it was Monsieur le Gros, Madame's husband, and Madame soon disappeared in his embrace, and remained there for several minutes while the children bounced up and down saying, 'C'est Papa! C'est Papa!' ('It's Daddy!') The sight of this little family being so wonderfully reunited made us all burst into tears again.

The first vehicle we saw was a jeep which was named 'Maggie' (my Congolese name). The sisters laughed and said it was mine. We were bound to have been rescued if they had named a jeep after me!

There were also three or four covered lorries, and we clambered on board the first one, with Sister Fredeganda being put in the cabin in front. We talked, prayed and wept together, even pinching each other just to make sure all this was real. Monsieur le Gros had Chantal on his lap, with his free arm around his wife, while Ann snuggled up close to her mother. The children were quiet and hardly took their eyes off their father's face. Madame looked radiant.

Shortly before arriving at Buta we had to clear yet another tree from across the road. The lorries stopped and all the men jumped out, although Monsieur le Gros was made to get back inside with his family; they weren't going to risk losing him now!

The combined strength of the other men proved sufficient to remove the tree and in due course we resumed our journey. As the convoy approached the bridge at Buta, we fell silent, remembering the thirty-one men who had died there just four weeks earlier.

There was a hole in the canvas near me, and three of us peered out all along the way. Once we reached the outskirts of the town, the drivers all sounded their horns continuously, and we stuck our white arms out of the hole. As we made for the convent, it felt like we were the Pied Piper of Hamelin for behind us came a procession of people, all running, laughing, or waving headscarves.

We disembarked to a truly fantastic and emotional welcome—not only from the six Congolese sisters, two priests and two brothers, but also, so it seemed, the entire population of Buta. The Congolese flag was flying, the quadrangle was full of military vehicles, and there were mercenaries and National Army personnel everywhere. We were brought in to see the commander of the entire operation. He was so moved by the sight of seventeen women and two children who had all been rescued safely that he could hardly speak—mind you, nor could we; words are so inadequate at times like this. As we proffered our hands, he took them in both of his.

Almost automatically we went into the chapel, and each offered up our praise and thanks to God in our own way. Again the tears flowed. The chaplain and Monsieur le Gros joined us. We then were led to the refectory to be greeted by an amazing sight. The table had been laid for nineteen people! It had been set like this when we were arrested, as an act of faith that the mercenaries would eventually find us, and there it had remained until we turned up. I felt so rebuked for my own lack of faith.

While we were eating, the chaplain, who was also short-sighted, lent me his spectacles so I could see all the sisters clearly. Their clothes were incredibly filthy, but their faces had a radiant happy smile. I returned the spectacles suitably contented.

Having eaten our first decent meal for four weeks, the next thing to do was to get cleaned up. There was an ample supply of hot water, soap and towels. We went to see if our cases were still where we had left them, and found everybody else's except mine. We searched everywhere, but to no avail. However, whoever had taken it had left behind one dress, my good sandals and, to my great joy, my spare pair of spectacles!

We could not all take a bath at the same time, so while I waited my turn, I found an iron and an ironing board and had just started to iron my newly-found dress when the Congolese mother superior came to find me and gently took the iron out of my hand. She said she wanted to do it for me. It was a lovely gracious gesture, and I let her do it. The sisters also supplied me with underwear, as all mine had disappeared.

The mercenaries just stood around, looking awkward. It must have been a strange experience to find themselves in a ladies' convent, but they were grinning from ear to ear like a cat who has just stolen the cream! I expect that the satisfaction of rescuing us successfully had made up for all the disappointments and difficulties they had faced during the previous weeks.

When we had all washed, combed our hair and put on clean clothes, we were told there would be a service of thanksgiving in the chapel led by the chaplain. Surely this was the Lord's doing and was marvellous in our eyes.

We gave him and him alone all the praise and glory. He had brought us through the fiery trial unharmed.

One of my favourite chapters of the Bible is Deuteronomy 8: 'And thou shalt remember all the way the Lord thy God led thee…in the wilderness, to humble thee, and to prove thee, to know what was in thine heart, whether thou wouldest keep his commandments or no. And he humbled thee, and suffered thee to hunger, and fed thee with manna which thou knewest not…that he might make thee know that man doth not live by bread alone, but by every word that proceedeth out of the mouth of the Lord…' How very, very true that had been for us.

We had yet another meal and then were sent off to bed. The Congolese sisters had moved out in order that we could have their beds, as the mercenaries were sleeping in the other part of the convent. I never did find out where the Congolese sisters slept that night. I doubt that any of us slept except maybe the children. One sister vomited several times in the night, and some of the others wept; the rest of us were tossing and turning, even though the bed was comfortable and we had blankets and pillows.

During that evening the commander sent a radio message to Stanleyville asking for planes to be sent to Buta to evacuate us as the roads were still unsafe. It would have been a long, hot and dangerous journey by road, and there were not enough vehicles anyway.

It must have been one of the happiest messages he ever sent!

Coming home

S unday dawned fine and clear, in tune with the euphoria of the previous day. I assume we had breakfast, but I remember nothing about it. I suppose we should all have been on the proverbial 'cloud nine', but we felt very emotionally divided. None of us wanted to leave the Congo, our adopted land, and the place to which God had called each one of us to serve him. We all loved the Congolese, and many of them had become our dear friends, although I had not seen my closest friends for four months. It made it even harder to think we were leaving them to the mercy of the Simbas, yet we knew without doubt that at this particular time we were an embarrassment to them. I felt I had no option but to leave, and the sisters were in a similar position—the convent had been reduced to a state of total confusion. Our whole lives had been turned upside down due to a situation beyond our control.

As the sisters made their way to the chapel to pray. I joined them, making for my own 'private' pew. As I prayed, I was aware my burden was being lifted, and I felt a great sense of God's presence with me. I had given him the responsibility for running my life the day I committed myself to him all those years ago, and although the road had been hard at times, I could see that he had always remained in control. Even though I could not see the way ahead, I knew I had to step out in faith, believing that all things work together for good for those who are the called of God (Romans 8:28).

A mercenary gave me a small khaki knapsack about the size of a lady's handbag, which was sufficient for me to pack my possessions. The few personal effects that the rebels had left behind when they took my case were all I now possessed apart from a handbag.

It was about this time that I began to worry about how I was going to enter the UK again, for I had no money, and my passport and all my relevant papers had disappeared when my case was stolen, so how was I going to prove my identity or nationality? Knowing we were going to Leopoldville, I wondered if there would be time to contact the British embassy to ask for some form of confirmation of my nationality, but this would mean borrowing some money to ring the embassy, and how would I be able to do

'A reporter from the Daily Express was on the plane in the first-class compartment, and the air hostess told me I had been invited to join him there, and he very kindly looked after me during our flight'

this? Then again, suppose there was no time in Leopoldville, would I be able to convince the authorities in Belgium? When I look back over all my worries at this stage, I am amazed as to why it did not occur to me that the Lord who had arranged our rescue in such a miraculous way could surely be trusted to finish the job and get me safely back to England.

The authorities despatched a plane and a helicopter from Stanleyville for us, but the helicopter never arrived; it was shot down by the rebels. The plane, which belonged to the military, and was rather small, could only fit half of us in, so the rest of us, myself included, had to wait at the convent.

We were given an enormous lunch—our fourth meal in less than twenty-four hours—but we were too excited and emotionally overwrought to do it much justice.

At 2.30pm we heard a plane in the distance. We jumped into the back of an army lorry, and arrived at the little airstrip eight minutes later. We noticed the sandbags and the men spread out along the entire length of the runway manning their mounted machine guns—all reminders to us that we were still in a war zone.

After a final wave to the mercenaries, we strapped ourselves into little tip-up seats which were situated all round the inside walls of the plane, then the engines started and in next to no time we were airborne. The plane was not insulated, being a military aircraft, so we were unable to speak to each other above the noise from the engines, but we could easily see out through the windows. The plane circled Buta, and flew fairly low over the convent; a kind gesture from the pilot, but a very poignant moment for the sisters.

We flew on, looking out over the tropical rain-forest, which was broken here and there by a small red-ribbon road or a small river. We sighted the large River Aruwimi and I knew we were flying over the vicinity of Bopepe and Banalia. I crouched by the window and whispered farewell to all my loved ones who were still hiding in the jungle, and was not ashamed of the tears on my face as I did so.

When we arrived at Stanleyville's big international airport, it looked just the same as usual, except that the nearby market place was deserted. There was a welcoming party for us when we touched down. Firstly a group of priests rushed across the tarmac, followed by two US Army soldiers, whom I greeted in English. They knew who I was, and were there especially to meet me and to pass on messages from folk in Leopoldville. A young civil engineer from Lancashire who was working in Stanleyville had also received permission to come and greet me. We did not know each other, though he knew a lot more about me than I did about him. Even now I do not recollect his name, but I was very touched with his gesture—the only Englishman in Stanleyville taking time simply to greet a fellow-countrywoman who had just been rescued.

A number of cars appeared from nowhere, and we all squeezed into them to be taken across the city to the residence of Colonel Mulamba (he was a real colonel, with the National Army). Here again, we had a wonderful reception. We met up with the rest of our party who had left in the morning. Champagne was served all round, though I personally did not partake. Photographs were taken, we were all given vaccinations, and the conversation in the house was a mixture of English, French and Bangala. It was a delightful confusion. An hour later, we were taken back to the airport. We just went where we were told without asking questions. This may sound like being herded around like a flock of sheep, but we were all beyond asking questions at this stage.

We boarded the plane for Leopoldville along with some other civilians. This was the first time we had ever boarded a plane without tickets or baggage! We were all so excited that none of us could think coherently. Several priests came onto the plane with us, and showed us newspapers and magazines telling of the deaths of the thirty-one men at Buta in May. I was able to have a lengthy conversation with a priest who was of the same order as Rev. Hermann Bischoff who had died at Banalia, although I felt sad as I told him about the circumstances of his death, of which he had not been aware. There were two men from the Protestant University of Stanleyville, one Congolese, the other American. I had a long conversation with them too. Many years later I met Mr Habgood, the American, again, and he still remembered me, although I didn't remember him until he mentioned our conversation on the plane.

We finally arrived at Leopoldville's busy international airport. It seemed to be seething with people all intently looking at our plane. The air hostess told us to keep our seats until we were called. We probably only had to wait two or three minutes, but it seemed interminable. Finally came the call, 'All the sisters from Buta to leave first, please.' I assumed I came under the heading of 'sister', as did Madame le Gros and family, and as we appeared on the gangway, we heard the cheers and applause of those waiting to greet us. None of us expected such a welcome and found it almost overwhelming. It was hard to cope with yet more excitement with our emotions in the state that they were. We were surrounded by nuns, priests, embassy staff, Protestant missionaries, newspaper and TV reporters. Miss Jenkins of the Baptist Missionary Society greeted me with a hug. Mr Drake, the BMS field leader was there too, plus, of course the British consular staff.

Someone decided that I should stay at the home of Mr and Mrs Drake, so I bade farewell on the tarmac to my beloved Catholic sisters, who left even sooner than I did. They were going to spend the night in a convent in Leopoldville before flying back to Belgium the next morning.

At the airport were four priests who were going home to Europe on vacation. They very graciously gave up their seats to enable Monsieur and Madame le Gros and the two little girls to go home straight away, so they were able to leave Congo only forty-five minutes after touching down in Leopoldville! We were thrilled for the family and grateful to the priests for such an unselfish gesture.

Mr and Mrs Drake did not spare any aspect of hospitality. I could have been lodged at the United Missions House—rather like a motel but with limited facilities—but instead I enjoyed the luxury of a private home. I took a long, luxurious soak in a hot bath, and put on some clean clothes that someone I did not know had provided for me. I relaxed to soothing music, enjoyed some delicious food and appreciated the opportunity of wonderful fellowship. Staying with them was very like being in an oasis in the middle of a desert of confusion. I could escape from the crowds, the noise, the press and the tension. I remain to this day eternally grateful to them for their kindness and thoughtfulness.

While we were seated at table I heard for the first time that Lyndon Johnson had been elected president of the United States. We had been arrested in November on the day the election took place, so Mary Baker never knew the result. I was also told, to my great delight, that my parents were both alive and relatively well. I knew they must have suffered a great deal emotionally on my behalf.

'None of us expected such a welcome and found it almost overwhelming. We were surrounded by nuns, priests...newspaper and TV reporters...'

Then, as we sat quietly together after the meal, I was given various mission magazines and press reports to read, and I was both shocked and saddened when I read of how many had died from my own mission, all of whom I had known personally. In reading these reports I realised more than ever that my own deliverance was a miracle. I read two copies of my own obituary; an unusual experience to say the least!

Next day I found myself at a press conference at the British consulate, and everyone was most kind. I was also given an emergency passport and a ticket home. To think how much I had worried about all this when God had it all planned out right down to the last detail!

I spent one more night with the Drakes and then on Tuesday at midday I boarded a plane bound for Paris. Apparently the sisters had left at 8.30am that same day on a flight to Belgium.

I found the only vacant seat, which was next to a lady reading a newspaper. On the front page was a long account of our rescue and subsequent arrival at Leopoldville. As she was reading it, the lady turned to me and said, 'You boarded this plane in Congo' (she had boarded in South Africa) 'and this woman was in Leopoldville; have you, by any chance, met her?' 'This woman' was myself! I laughed and said that Leopoldville was a big place and then changed the subject.

A reporter from the Daily Express was on the plane in the first-class compartment, and the air hostess told me I had been invited to join him there, and he very kindly looked after me during our flight. Unfortunately, the hostess also told my neighbour who I was, and when I rejoined her just before touchdown, she offered me a job in South Africa in one of their pretentious hospitals. I did not have the slightest desire to work in South Africa anyway, but unfortunately found myself drawn into an argument with her about apartheid.

We touched down in Paris at 8.30pm. I said goodbye to my well-meaning South African neighbour, and wondered about the final stage of the journey home would bring. Having no luggage, I was not delayed in the baggage reclaim area, and the reporter who had been on the plane hurried me through to the transit lounge for UK passengers. He felt sure the press would be waiting, and his idea was to get me past them as quickly as possible. His suppositions were quite correct, for after walking down endless corridors we were suddenly confronted by a battery of cameras, but as we rushed past them, I heard a voice call out, 'Hi Maggie, aren't you going to say hello?' As I turned to see who was speaking to me, the press closed in! To my immense joy and relief I saw the Rev. H. Jenkinson, affectionately known as Kinso in Congo, where he had been UFM's senior missionary. He had flown out to Paris in order to meet me.

After another press conference with endless questions and photographs, the reporters eventually went off to catch their plane to London, leaving Kinso and myself in peace and quiet. We should also have been on that plane but the airline authorities thought I would be pestered by the press all the way home, and offered us seats on the midnight plane instead, which would be free of reporters. Kinso gratefully accepted the offer, and we were given seats in a quiet enclosed section of the airport, in order to talk privately, and were promised that we would be collected at the appropriate time.

I had only found out two days before that Kinso was still alive, as the rebels told me they had killed him. He was much older than me; indeed I regarded him and his wife as 'parents in Israel', honoured and trusted by missionary and national alike. It was sheer relief to be able to unburden myself to him, as he knew what I had been through, having himself been a prisoner of the Simbas before being rescued in November 1964. We were also able to exchange news of others whom we loved.

Our final plane journey took just an hour to deposit us at London Airport, or Heathrow as it is now called. Again the press were out in force, as well as men from Scotland Yard. At the bottom of the gangway was that wonderful invention England has perfected—the London 'Bobby'. 'Welcome home into the arms of the law of England,' he said. Opposite him was a woman I did not know who said, 'On behalf of all British nurses welcome home!' I remember saying to her, 'But how did you know I was coming?' to which she replied, 'My dear, the whole world knows you are coming!'

I was keen to leave the press and their blinding flashlights behind me as quickly as possible, for I had spotted a group of people which included several members of my family. Words are inadequate to describe that reunion and I will not even try.

I was taken to a VIP lounge for yet another press conference, and as I entered the room, I recognised yet more friends from my church and the mission. By this time it was well past 1.30am. I noticed that they were all wearing summer clothes, but I was cold and very glad of a heavy winter coat given me in Congo.

Once that press conference was over, which I think was for the BBC, it was time to go home. My family had been allowed to park their cars fairly near to the VIP enclosure, which was a lovely gesture on the part of the airport authorities, who were so wonderfully kind and understanding in all they did to make my homecoming such an unforgettable experience. We drove away with two police outriders for part of the journey, which was just as well, as it prevented my brother from speeding.

When we turned into the road where we lived, the windows of several houses opened and people called out their welcome. I was greeted by my mother at the door, who seemed very much older and thinner and looked very tired. My father seemed very well, though he was now lame due to an accident two years before. I had not been aware that he had to use a walking stick. There were more brothers, sisters and in-laws there too, and everybody was talking at once.

Mum and Dad had acquired a black and white television, which was still a novelty at the time. They told me they had been watching it a few days earlier and actually saw me getting off the plane in Leopoldville.

I did not finally get to bed until 4.30am, by which time it was daylight. I only had three hours' sleep before my youngest sister came in to call me. She dumped onto my bed a beautiful chubby eighteen-month-old niece whom I had not met before, but she seemed to be more interested in my cup of tea than me. I was not able to enjoy my first day back in England in peace and quiet, for the press congregated outside the house and it was quite a job trying to evade them.

Gifts had come from family and friends, mostly clothes, for which I was more than grateful. Letters came too, some of which were addressed 'c/o GPO London'. Our postman was impressed that the Post Office had worked out where to send them, and so was I!

Opposite: Tea with Mama Kinso

DAILY SKETCH

Monday, June 28, 1965 Price Fourpence * WEATHER: Sunny periods

Congo patrol reports: 19 saved

MASSACRE TOWN NURSE IS FOUND ALIVE

MARGARET HAYES

From Sketch Correspondent: Leopoldville, Sunday.

MISSING British missionary nurse Miss Margaret Hayes, held by Congo rebels for ten months, was reported tonight to be safe—and on her way to Leopoldville.

Miss Hayes, aged 39, from Islington, London, was said to be among a group of 19 Europeans rescued by a Government patrol in the northern Buta area.

Yours for the Congolese,
in His joyful service,
Margaret Hayes

From Margaret Hayes—"in His joyful service"

The others are believed to be 15 Belgian nuns and a Mrs. Legros and her two children.

'KILLED'

Unconfirmed reports from Stanleyville say Miss Hayes told the authorities that another missionary—Miss Mary Baker, from America—had been killed.

Little hope had been given for Miss Hayes's survival.

It was first feared that she died when rebels swept through Banalia, 100 miles from Stanleyville, killing her British and Belgian colleagues.

Then came news that she was alive and being forced to do medical work in a rebel camp.

When troops and mercenaries reached Buta the rebels fled taking Miss Hayes and the other 18 hostages with them.

LETTERS

Recently three letters from her, written on tissue paper, [illegible]

They were sent [illegible]

Cochran with Vickie Saxe, a witness in an assault case against him last December.

Actor's mystery sea death

By HENRY THODY
New York, Sunday.

[illegible]

Several days later I went to buy a Bible and Daily Light, and read the evening portion for June 26th, the day of my liberation. It said, 'It is a night to be much observed unto the Lord for bringing them out from the land of Egypt' (Exodus 12:42). How wonderfully appropriate.

It is impossible to describe my innumerable emotions the following day (Thursday) when I entered the church in East London which I loved so much. It was wonderful to meet Pastor Paul Tucker again, along with many other friends, and to hear how so many of them had kept praying during the past months, and had never given up hope, in spite of all the sad news coming out of Congo. They never really believed I was dead, and had held meetings especially to pray for me, I found it both thrilling and humbling as I saw how the Lord had answered prayer over and above all I had dared to ask or think.

Shortly after these early days back home, we heard that Pastors Bo Martin and Asani were alive and well and that the rebuilding of Bopepe had begun. Later, we heard that Pastor Masini Phillipe had been released from prison and was back home with his family.

I spent the next few months travelling the country in the time-honoured way of missionaries on furlough (home assignment) and was amazed to hear how many people had been praying regularly for me even though they had never met me! I even went to Belgium for a reunion with the nuns and it was so good to hear them say again and again, 'C'etait le Seigneur' ('it was the Lord').

Truly 'The Lord has done great things for us and we are filled with joy'. (Psalm 126:3 NIV.) Yes, that joy is tempered with sadness as I think back over these past events, but that psalm is so true.

The return to Congo

I was kept busy for much of the ensuing year with deputation meetings, and was away from home for much of the time, although in the providence of God, I was home when my father collapsed as a result of suffering a massive stroke combined with a coronary attack. He died four days later. We managed to get my mother into a 'granny-flat' in Hertfordshire, which was only a few minutes' walk from one of my brothers, and in the same town as one of my sisters.

I had wanted to return to Congo once the troubles had died down, and eventually a date was fixed for the journey. My tickets were bought, a visa obtained, and all inoculations completed. Five days before I was due to fly out, I was in the house of one of my brothers in London as part of my round of farewells to the family, when he returned home from work with a copy of the evening paper and said, 'Have you seen this?' There on the front page in heavy type was news of yet another uprising in Stanleyville. I couldn't believe it, yet there it was! Hastily we called UFM HQ, who had heard nothing, but promised to ring the Foreign Office and then call me back. An hour later they called saying, 'Sorry, Margaret, your flight and departure are cancelled.'

Having gone through the emotional upset of preparing to leave my family again to go back into a situation which we knew would be politically unstable, it was hard to come to terms with this news. Had I made a mistake? Had I mistaken my own desires for God's will? I was not alone in my confusion. I had been due to travel out with Olive McCarten, a teacher, who had also been held prisoner by the rebels, albeit in a different area to me, and not for so long. She too felt a leading to return. We obviously talked to each other about this, although we had come to our decisions independently. God, however, must have had other plans for us. Had he just wanted to prove our willingness to obey? He knew how much we could take on the emotional level, and maybe in his sovereign will he had allowed this uprising to take place because we were not as ready as we thought for the challenge of living amid the instability of Congo.

The mission said, 'No women to go to Congo for another year.' So we

waited. Olive managed to get a teaching post, but although I was offered many hospital jobs, I did not feel it was right to accept any of them. I was eventually led to apply to another mission—the Sudan Interior Mission (now called SIM International) on a short-term basis. I was given a year-long assignment at a mission hospital in a place called Galmi in the Republic of Niger. UFM seconded me for a year, but for a year only.

I found it hard, for the climate was very hot, the workload heavy, and Galmi was in the middle of nowhere. However, I learned a lot professionally during that year. The hospital was situated on the main west-to-east highway and a great deal of traffic passed by. At the time there was a big military movement going on, and whenever any lorries filled with soldiers went by, I would feel very disturbed. Obviously I still had some residual fear from my time with the Simbas, and God, who knew all about this, had engineered my circumstances so I could overcome it, for by the time the year was up the fear had gone and I had also incidentally made some lifelong friends.

I returned to England and was issued with a lifetime visa by the Congolese embassy in London. (Pity passports don't last that long!) It was arranged that I should fly out to Congo during January 1969 and after spending Christmas with my family, I eventually arrived in Stanleyville, or Kisangani as it was now called, on the 26th after having been delayed in Kinshasa (formerly Leopoldville) for four days.

Pastor Bo Martin came to meet me, along with several missionaries, including Olive McCarten. He still had his well-known smile, but looked very gaunt and thin. I actually thought he was his twin brother, Pastor Asani at first, although he forgave me for calling him by the wrong name. It felt so good to be back on Congolese soil, it was almost as though I was coming home again.

Kisangani still bore unmistakeable scars from the rebellion. We went to our new headquarters as the previous one had been destroyed. Later that week we toured the city and visited the communal missionary grave and memorial, pausing at the grave of Hector McMillan, who was killed on the day the city was liberated (see chapter 3).

On February 1st we finally left for a tour of some of our old mission stations, aiming to reach Bopepe, 125 miles to the north, that same day, even though the roads were terrible. Six of us set off in a Land Rover, Rev. and Mrs Jenkinson, Bob and Alma McAllister, Olive McCarten and myself. We knew my old friends in Bopepe had already heard of our forthcoming journey, and were expecting us any day. Pastor Asani was due to follow us in a lorry with all our baggage, plus an extra supply of petrol as there were no filling stations en route. Unfortunately, it broke down almost as soon as he set off.

We had to cross the river at Banalia, but before we boarded the ferry, we went to the memorial erected on the old landing stage, a sad and poignant moment for us all. Then we crossed the river and heard the drums heralding our approach to Bopepe.

We stopped at Chief Fidèle's village and saw him standing by the roadside, just as he had been when Mary and I went to prison. This time our reception was different. He hugged me and almost danced with me; and his servant Paul burst into tears as he too hugged me. For some unaccountable reason I found I was crying with him.

We got back into the Land Rover and continued on our way until about half a mile from Bopepe, when our progress was impeded by crowds of people surging on to the roadway. The door of the Land Rover was pulled open and I was lifted out bodily and carried to a flower-bedecked carrying-chair called a tipoi, which is rather like an open-sided armchair on carrying-poles, although not particularly comfortable. My squeals were drowned out by laughter, singing, clapping and even tears of joy as I was carried to the village in triumphal procession, the women waving their headscarves in the rhythm to the singing. I was carried round and round the village while the crowds got bigger and bigger by the minute. The other missionaries tried in vain to take photographs while all this was going on. Finally I was taken up the little hill where our old house was situated and was thankfully lowered to the ground.

Perhaps at this point I should mention something rather strange—at least to me. When an African would greet me, I would mirror their greeting, and so did Olive and Mrs Jenkinson. If they greeted me with laughter and dancing, we laughed and danced. If alternatively they burst into tears we cried with them. This peculiar phenomenon happened to me many times during that first year back.

We entered the house, which was now rather battered and looked very bare. Our emotions at this time were just as unpredictable as those of our African friends. We would be laughing one minute, then crying the next. At other times we just sat in contented silence.

By 8pm there was no sign of Asani or his lorry. Eventually at 8.30pm, another missionary, Betty O'Neill turned up in her little VW Beetle with Asani as passenger, who told us about his breakdown.

It seemed at first as though our trip would have to be abandoned as all our baggage was still in Kisangani, but as we talked and prayed about the situation, Betty graciously agreed to lend us her VW Beetle, which Olive would drive, taking Mrs Jenkinson, Alma McAllister and me as passengers, while Bob would take Kinso and all the baggage in the Land Rover.

Therefore, the following day, after the morning service, (which was basically a welcoming service for me and lasted for three hours) Olive and Bob set off for Kisangani to take Betty and Asani back and to collect our baggage from the lorry. It was not going to be easy for Olive, who had never driven a left-hand drive vehicle before. She would have to cope with dreadful roads, taking the car across a river on a pontoon bridge, and then the rest of our proposed journey of some 600 miles.

We stayed in Bopepe while we waited for Olive and Bob to return. Mrs Jenkinson—or Mama Kinso as the Congolese called her—went for a walk round the neighbourhood with Alma. I stayed in the house, but less than half an hour after they had gone, several women came round to tell me of a lady who was in labour and seemingly in great difficulty. They led me to a house nearby and I ended up dealing with my first Congolese patient since the rebellion. I had felt led to pack some obstetric forceps in my baggage and this proved to be a real blessing, for I was able to use them to deliver the baby within an hour. I then returned to our house and was cleaning the instruments when Alma and Mama Kinso came in. They could hardly believe me when I told them what had happened, so I took them to see the mother and baby. How wonderful are God's ways! Why did I feel I needed to bring the forceps with me? Surely it was because the Holy Spirit had prompted me.

The next day Olive and Bob arrived and we set out for Bodela, where the

Above: Villagers arriving for a service—Alma McAllister on the right

Above: Reception given at Banjwade for Margaret and the missionaries

Parry family had worked, and stayed there overnight. Bob preached at the early morning service the next day, and the little church was packed.

We felt very humbled by the amazing courage of the Congolese. Their indomitable spirit and resilient nature astounded me at the time and still does even now. Against seemingly impossible odds they had come though these troubles not only smiling but with their faith in God deepened. The proof of this could be seen in the churches which were full to overflowing. Extensions had to be added to pre-rebellion buildings, while new ones were going up as fast as they could build them. However, at the same time many schools were devoid of blackboards or textbooks, while dispensaries had to keep going with little in the way of supplies, although at least they were able to offer plenty of love and a real concern to help the community.

We visited many villages; Olive inspected the schools while I looked round the dispensaries. We based ourselves at Bopepe during the week and were able to attend a conference that was held there the following weekend, which culminated in the baptism of no less than 127 new converts in the local river, followed by a communion service. It was very moving to listen to the sound of hymn-singing coming nearer and nearer as each village arrived for the service en bloc, walking several miles and singing the songs of Zion as they came!

The people had been hit hard by the rebellion. Many of the clothes they were wearing were obviously second-hand, but still clean and worn with pride. They showed us their new homes, and my heart ached when I saw their poverty, although I knew they were spiritually rich, for they had come into vital contact with the living God. Everywhere we went we heard time and time again, 'Only God brought us through.'

We visited the memorial to our dead at Banalia again and took photographs this time. Already on that spot eleven ex-rebels had professed faith in Christ—surely a triumph of his marvellous grace.

Everywhere we went we were fêted, almost like royalty. Another large gathering of all the Christians from the area took place at Bopepe. They all marched past, then they formed a square round us and presented us with gifts: an antelope, nine live chickens, eight dozen eggs, sugar cane, a large bowl of uncooked rice and three pineapples. We felt embarrassed at the thought of accepting all these presents from people who were so obviously poor, but we knew that it was the only way they could say 'Thank you for coming back to work here.' To them it was incredible that we wanted to return at all after the way the rebels had treated us, and in a way it meant more to them than all the previous fifty years of preaching.

From Bopepe we moved on to Bongondza where Ian and Audrey Sharpe and Ruby Gray had worked. Our vehicles coped with the main highway relatively easily in spite of pot-holes and wash-board surfaces, but when we turned in the side-road leading to Bongondza the little VW Beetle came unstuck. As if the road was not bad enough, the bridges consisted of three or four tree trunks which the drivers had to negotiate hoping the wheels would not fall into any gaps between the logs. It was no surprise that about six miles from Bongondza the little VW refused to go any further and Bob had to tow it the rest of the way behind the Land Rover. It took him all the following day to find and repair the fault.

There were not that many people here, but Olive was able to visit and inspect both the secondary and primary schools. She felt disheartened by what she saw. Apparently all the desks and books had been destroyed by the rebels, so the children, mostly dressed in rags, were sitting on anything they could find, mainly tree-trunks. The teachers were struggling to teach from memory, and there was no blackboard or chalk, no pencils or notebooks, and certainly no money.

We also went around the hospital. I had worked here for two years during my first term, and I found it very depressing to see the building derelict, empty and almost hidden by the encroaching forest.

On our final evening before moving on, we had a bonfire and the boys from the secondary school sang songs in French, and some gave their testimonies. We retraced our journey to the main road at Kole where Olive was encouraged to find a thriving primary school of 500 children! There was also a growing church, which was thrilling to see, as Kole was originally only a very small outpost of Bongondza.

While we stayed at Kole we were able to travel down the main highway and visit several village churches. We received a warm welcome in all of them, and also had the joy of seeing ten people come to the Saviour during the course of the meetings.

From Kole we moved further north aiming for Buta, Aketi and hopefully

Ekoko. As we were travelling with all our equipment, we could just set up camp wherever we found ourselves. The people on the whole were thrilled to have us stay in their villages and we noticed that they seemed starved of both Christian fellowship and Bible teaching.

We travelled down the Basali trail, where I had been held with the sisters in the forest. The trail was aptly named, for it was only slightly wider than our little VW Beetle with long grass growing all over it. Olive said she was driving more by faith than by sight! We decided to stay the night in a village and after setting up our camp, we had an evening meal followed by a service. Then a man was brought in with a bad head-wound and though it was dark, we drove him ten miles to the nearest hospital. It had been a bad enough journey in daylight but now it was pitch black and poor Olive had not only to drive to the hospital in the dark but all the way back again as well.

The following day we set out for Aketi, a journey of about 100 miles, of which the last forty were on very bad roads full of ruts and mud patches. We also had to cross a railway line on no less than four occasions, twice at a proper open level crossing, but on the other two occasions we simply had to bump our way across the raised rails. We stayed at Aketi for a couple of days then went on to our former station of Ekoko. Somewhere along our way I was asked to go to a small town to test people's eyes to see if they needed glasses. Olive came along to help, and was also able to inspect a school in the area, and encourage the staff there.

We arrived at Ekoko and set up home in what was once Jean Sweet's house. Jean had been a special friend of Olive's and had been killed while on a visit to Olive at the beginning of the rebellion, together with some other UFM missionaries. This house therefore was full of painful memories for Olive. It had been riddled with bullet and mortar shell holes, and the windows were all nailed up with boards, so as Olive said, it wasn't exactly the Hilton.

It had rained heavily throughout our final night in Aketi, which had done nothing for the condition of the roads. We took a different route back, and if we thought the previous roads had been bad enough, this one was even worse. Twice the little VW stuck in the mud and sand, and we had to get out and push while Bob tried to tow it with his Land Rover, which was also stuck. The VW was looking much the worse for wear by now.

On our way back we had to pass through Buta, and I asked if we could stop somewhere near the convent so I could drop in to see the sisters, assuming they had returned too. Everyone was happy for me to do this, and the two cars stopped on the road while I went in. I made my way to the refectory where the sisters were having a coffee break. At first they did not recognise me, as I had put on weight and had a decent hairstyle, but when they realised who I was, they greeted me with hugs, kisses and lots of questions. They also invited the others to come in and have a coffee too. It was a refreshing time, a renewing of a friendship which has now lasted many years. I think the sisters were as excited by my unexpected visit as I was. We stayed overnight in Buta at the Norwegian Baptist Mission compound and enjoyed fellowship round a bonfire in the evening.

On our travels we stopped in villages and would hold a service wherever possible, and would talk to and fellowship with those who were believers. We stayed in one place where they had got together a most ingenious 'band'. They had some trumpets which had lost their insides, so the players 'trumped' the tune through them, and also a car radiator which they would hit with a piece of metal. It made different sounds depending on where it was hit. It was not very harmonious, but loud and joyful. They played one song over and over again, but we didn't really recognise it until they told us what it was, and now whenever we sing that particular song here in Britain, my mind is immediately transported back to that campfire in the jungle of Congo.

We also stayed at a village called Panga where we were saddened to see just how poor the people were. We attended a couple of services there, and frankly I felt ashamed that I had a complete and brand new Bible in my hand, when they did not have a single copy between them. I ended up giving mine to the evangelist, much to his delight and to the envy of the others. By the time we left, any Bibles that we had with us that these people could understand had all been given away.

We stopped off at Bopepe on our way back, and stayed there four days. It gave our two drivers Bob and Olive a chance to have a rest. We finally arrived in Kisangani after a journey of over 1,000 miles on very bad roads which had caused us to be jolted practically all the way. The VW looked rather the worse for wear, with a bent fender and a knock in the front wheel, and needed a good clean inside, outside and underneath. We were glad of a rest, a bath and the chance to put on clean clothes.

A count was made of the many gifts we had received, although some of these items had been passed on to our various hostesses on the way. The final total was 800 eggs and 120 live chickens, along with fruit, plantains, manioc, sweet potatoes, and peanuts. Plants grow remarkably quickly in the lush tropical climate of Congo, and in spite of the way the rebels had stripped so much bare, it had not taken long for the supply of fruit and vegetables to recover.

A couple of weeks later I set off again in the little green VW, this time with Olive, another single missionary called Sue Schmidt, and an African named Ambroise. This time we were going on to a different road towards Boyulu, which was the station where Olive had worked and from where she and some other missionaries who were subsequently killed were taken prisoner.

We called in to the station at Maganga where I had started my career in Congo. Rev and Mrs Jenkinson were staying there for a week prior to attending the Easter Conference. Sadly all the houses had been destroyed by the rebels. All that remained was a small fragment of the house where the Parrys used to live. They had built a cement fireplace-surround and had carved the word 'Immanuel' into the cement. Although the house had been flattened, the cement surround saying 'Immanuel' was left standing. Even today whenever I read the word in Scripture or hear it in song, it takes me back to Maganga and the image of that empty fireplace.

As we continued on our travels we saw similar sights all the way, ruined villages totally devoid of people. We arrived at Boyulu on the Saturday evening and were met by Pastor Ferdinand, Pastor Anziambo and Paul Mugundi. We set up camp in an empty house and Ambroise prepared a meal, helped by some women.

On Sunday morning we drove into Bafwasende, where six of our missionaries and one teenager had been killed. It was good for Olive to meet up with many of her Congolese friends again and they were thrilled to see her. At the morning service Olive was asked to preach and Sue and I gave our testimonies.

We were driving back to Boyulu for a meal when Olive noticed oil dripping from the engine of our car. As none of us were mechanically minded, we decided to return to Bafwasende. In the providence of God we found a Greek trader who knew a bit about cars. He looked at the engine and realised that one of the gaskets had been loosened—probably by excessive shaking on the bad roads. He made a new gasket out of cardboard, filled it with oil and off we went. We broke our journey at Maganga and had a meal with the Kinsos, and then set out again for the final 70 miles to Kisangani. After a while, we spotted a large muddy hole in the road and decided to stop to see how deep it was. As we got out, we noticed smoke was pouring from the back wheels. On investigation we found that both wheels were red hot. We took off one wheel and found the brake lining had seized up. We spent about half an hour trying to release it, but even with the help of the handbook we did not get very far. There was not a soul in sight, as all the villages had been flattened, the afternoon was getting on, it was hot and none of us had any mechanical knowledge. What could we do? We prayed, firstly together and then on our own, and suddenly we heard a lorry in the distance. As it came into view we read the name written on it: 'Depannage de Kisangani'—the equivalent of our breakdown services here in UK. We hailed it, and out jumped six mechanics. Only God could have brought the one and only recovery vehicle in Kisangani along that road, in that place, going in the same direction, with a full complement of mechanics and all the necessary equipment! They quickly adjusted all four wheels, gave the car a test run, and when they found out we were missionaries who had returned after the rebellion, they refused all payment in gratitude that we had come back to their country. They steered us round the mud-hole and then waved us off amid great rejoicing. Was it a coincidence? Of course not—rather an act of our Sovereign God. No doubt folk were praying for us both at home and in Congo, and God answered in that most wonderful way that he does from time to time.

Following all this excitement and rejoicing, life settled down for us all. I was given the task of reopening the Banjwade dispensary and maternity unit, and was allocated the house where David and Sonia Grant from Canada had formerly lived.

Before the revolution, I had only visited Banjwade for conferences or maybe for a few days rest, but now I had been assigned there to work, and it was to be my home for the next three and a half years. All the buildings were in a sad state of disrepair. The water system had broken down, the secondary school had not yet reopened, and the Bible school had closed down. The dispensary was open, but was operating under tremendous difficulties. The primary school was in a sorry state but at least it was functioning. The houses where the missionaries had lived were in a filthy state with damaged walls and broken windows. Then there was the church, with a roof that leaked like a sieve because of all the bullet holes in it.

This was where God wanted me to help pick up the pieces and turn into a place for his glory. It was wonderful to meet the Christians, and to hear all that God had done for them during the rebellion. They had a real spirit of eagerness about them as they faced the future, and it was a privilege to share in worship with them, to pray with them and to discuss our programmes together.

I was to share the house with Jean Raddon, an English teacher who was to head up the secondary school. Neither of us had ever done any interior decorating before, and our new home certainly presented a challenge. It had been used as a lookout by the mercenaries after they had driven out the rebels. There were holes in the doors and walls, and many panes of glass were missing from the windows, thirty-two to be exact. There were over a hundred bullet-holes in the wall between the living-room and what was to become my bedroom, which may have been good for ventilation but not for privacy.

We had bought a roll of brown paper in Kisangani—the type that was used in big stores as wrapping paper, and after making paste of flour and water, we set to work. Nothing like learning the hard way! The first sheet of paper I tried to hang was a disaster because I had not taken my short stature into account. It missed the top of the wall by eighteen inches. We had to place a chair on the table and then books on the chair in order for me to reach the top of the wall. We also wasted quite a bit of paper and paste simply in the process of getting the hang of it, but eventually the interior walls were all covered with brown paper and the holes in the exterior walls were filled in with cement which Barrie Morris had taught me how to mix and apply. Then we painted over it all, using a different colour for each room and white for the outside walls of the house. At the end of our labours, it looked like a new house. We bought locally-made furniture and moved in just a few days before Jean was due to open the first year of the secondary school.

The whole place came alive! Primary school children and secondary school students appeared from everywhere. The other teachers also arrived and suddenly we found ourselves living a very full and busy life.

Leon Abende was the head nurse in the dispensary and at first I would go there to help him, but as my own obstetric work developed, I could only help at the dispensary when I had some spare time, although we always worked as a team, and supported each other whenever any serious case cropped up. I came across a lady who used to help with babies before the rebellion and gave her a job, along with a lovely Congolese trained midwife who had worked with me during my first term of service. It was so gracious of God to send her along just when she was needed! What was more, Banjwade was her home village.

It was quite remarkable in the aftermath of the rebellion to see how some Christians had really stood up to the rebels and suffered for it. We met an evangelist who had no ears because the rebels had cut them off, leaving the open canals and a tiny vestige of cartilage round them. When we first saw him, he was leading a meeting in a little village church. Another evangelist was taken prisoner and made to walk on red-hot embers. During the night following this incident, he had managed to escape into the jungle and kept going until he reached a friendly encampment. He told me, 'All the time I was running I had no pain until I reached help and then the pain hit me.' I saw his feet, which would remain scarred for the rest of his life.

Some ladies told how they had escaped in a dugout canoe with several very small children on board, yet miraculously none of them cried or made any noise as they skimmed over the water in the middle of the night.

Shortly after my arrival at Banjwade, I needed to go to Banalia to get a work permit, and on arrival at the administrative headquarters, I made my way to the administrator's office. I knocked on the door and received permission to enter. When the administrator looked up he was speechless, for he was none other than Paul the Christian nurse who had worked with me when I was with the rebels. He burst into tears, rushed over and hugged me, by which time I too was in tears. 'We heard you had been sent to Buta to be killed,' he said. 'I knew there was a Margarita at Banjwade, but I didn't realise it was you!' We had a time of prayer and praise together and then I received my work permit.

Because there was no dispensary-cum-maternity between Banjwade and Bopepe, apart from Banalia, which most people avoided if possible, I found that I had a major problem on my hands. Because of the extreme poverty of the people around us, we kept our fees to the absolute minimum, indeed without my allowance from the mission our unit would not have been viable at all. Whenever I asked for money everyone pleaded poverty. I knew I could never be sure if they were all telling the truth, but my natural reaction was to give them the benefit of the doubt and therefore frequently waived the fees or at least reduced them. My staff, who knew everyone, at least so it seemed, were not so forbearing. They would make many of these people pay up and gave them a lecture about deceiving me.

I decided to exempt pastors, evangelists and their families from the charges altogether, but I had forgotten about the extended family culture in Africa. Someone who was exempted would appear accompanied by another person who was in need of treatment and say it was 'my mother's sister's grandchild' or something like that. Then some folk from Bopepe came and would claim free treatment on the grounds that, 'my house was burned down because of you' or, 'I was beaten because of you' or something similar. It was a very difficult situation, and one which needed a lot of prayer and much grace.

Our house-boy was the same Fidèle whom Mary and I had at Bopepe. He and his wife moved down to Banjwade and lived on the compound. About that time the government announced that anyone who had been employed up to and during the rebellion, but had lost their job due to enemy activity could claim back pay if they were taken back by their old employer. One day Fidèle turned up with his pay book and said he was claiming two years' worth of arrears. I could not possibly have paid him, but I looked at his book anyway, and there on the front page under 'Employer' was Mary Baker's name! I pointed this out to him and asked what had happened to Mary. 'She was killed by the rebels,' he replied. So as officially I had not been his employer, logically I did not owe him money. To my amazement he

Top:
Margaret revisits the site of the massacre at the landing stage at Banalia

Above:
The dispensary at Banjwade where Margaret worked during her final term in the Congo

accepted my argument, and that was the end of this episode, and Fidèle continued to work for both Jean and I.

We always kept a pretty hectic schedule at Banjwade. I tried to make Sundays a no-clinic day, but frequently had to work a seven-day week as illness and babies do not obey our time schedules. I would usually be on call at night for difficult cases, and frequently kept babies in the house if they were premature, frail, forceps delivery or simply needed extra care. I can well remember one exceptionally busy period when I had been called out thirteen nights in a row, and felt desperately tired. I was coming home at about 2.30am one morning, and there was a full moon, which bathed the village in its glow. Everything was quiet, but I was so weary, and as I walked along I begged the Lord with tears to let me have a night's rest. The next two nights were free from call-outs. How slow we are to ask for help! I wondered too if someone at home had been praying for me especially that night.

It was not always that easy to fit in a time alone with God at the beginning of a day with such a frantic lifestyle. Sometimes I would not get to bed until 4am, and then would have to get up two hours later to feed the sick babies if there were any, then make tea, tidy the place up and then settle down to a quiet time hoping that no-one would call. Sometimes I did get a call at this time, but then the house would usually be quiet until the end of the day. It is no surprise that one hears so many cries for prayer-partners. Missionaries especially need folk to uphold us in prayer daily. Sometimes the time for quiet is available, but sheer weariness makes concentration difficult, although God does wonderfully undertake in these situations. I have discussed this problem with fellow medical missionaries from other missions as well as my own, and have found many of them are in the same boat.

On one occasion we ran out of vaccines for the babies and children, and remained without any supplies for several months, until suddenly the government released a large supply, which was duly delivered to us. We set about telling the local villages by drum-messages, and to my consternation on the day the vaccines arrived almost 500 babies and toddlers turned up with their mothers. We hastily moved into the church to accommodate them all, but the noise was indescribable. We all needed earplugs that day!

Towards the end of my last term in Congo, I was helping in the dispensary with Leon, when a woman approached me asking if I was the 'Margarita of rebellion days'. When I said I was, she then told me she had come from a group of rebels on the other side of the river, in the charge of the major who had been responsible for me in those dark days. The major was ill and had asked if I would cross the river to treat him as he dare not come over to Banjwade for fear of being arrested. The woman had hardly finished speaking when I realised that Leon, his staff, my staff and my patients had all moved quickly to form a protective cordon around me. Leon challenged the woman who then ran out of the dispensary followed by about a dozen men. They all had canoes on hand at the river bank and quickly crossed to the other side. Their encampment was never found, but I was given a 'guard' whenever I left the house during the next two weeks, which turned out to be my last two weeks in Congo.

I had to come back to Britain to look after my mother. After my father's death she had eventually moved out to New Zealand, but had become frail and had decided to return home. She needed me to look after her, so I reluctantly resigned from UFM and flew home. With hindsight, I can see that all this was also part of God's plan for my life. As it says in Proverbs 3:6, 'In all thy ways acknowledge him, and he will direct thy paths.'

And finally

It felt strange to return to the UK without having a home to go to. My family were scattered all over the world; some were in New Zealand, one was in Malawi and the rest were in Britain. My mother was still in New Zealand waiting to come and live with me, but not only did I not have a home, but I had no job either. Initially I stayed with friends in Kent, and naturally we prayed about the situation and God gave me peace. I was soon to discover how he had my future all planned out for me.

During my first week back, I received a letter from a friend in my East London Church who was also a nurse. She mentioned a social work vacancy in West London, which included accommodation. I knew next to nothing about social work, but there was nothing to lose by applying and seeing if God would open this particular door. I received a telephone call within 24 hours inviting me to an interview, and two days later I had a job as assistant matron in an old people's home in West London complete with suitable furnished accomodation for two of us. This all happened within two weeks of my return to England. How gracious of God to have planned it all. I was enrolled for in-service training, and made a remarkably smooth transition from babies and obstetrics to the elderly and infirm, and I must admit I enjoyed it.

My mother came and moved in with me, and eventually I was promoted to the post of matron in another home in West London. While I was there I completed my social work training. God then led me on to yet another place in South-West London and we moved in there. About this time, I began to attend Hook Evangelical Church when my duties permitted. I had just signed a two-year contract when mother became ill and died seven weeks later in hospital. I had promised God that if Mother died before I retired I would go wherever he sent me, but now my hands were tied for the next two years.

By this time UFM had pulled out of Congo for various reasons, but yet again God had everything planned out. With the full backing of Hook Evangelical Church, I contacted SIM and was accepted for long-term service in Galmi Hospital again. On average it takes between a year and

'During my first week back, I received a letter from a friend in my East London Church who was also a nurse. She mentioned a social work vacancy in West London...'

eighteen months from the start of the application process to actually starting work overseas, as there are so many forms to be filled in, numerous medicals and interviews to attend, new equipment to be purchased and support to be raised, and so the two years flew by. Almost the very day my two-year contract expired, I was on my way to Galmi Hospital! In God's economy time is never wasted.

I arrived in Galmi in the hot season—and it really was hot with average daily temperatures of 45–50°c. The hospital was situated on the edge of the Sahara Desert in an Islamic country. It was a very different situation from Congo. In those days there was no air-conditioning or fans, and very little electricity except in the evening between 6.30pm and 10pm. We had water, but it was very cold and hard, which was not very helpful when we needed to do any washing.

My assignment was to develop an obstetric department. After the first month, I was on my own as the only midwife with one lady to help me with deliveries. There was also a communication problem at first, for while French is the official language of Niger, the village folk only spoke Hausa, which I could not speak and most women were unable to read or write. After a while I went to Kano in Nigeria for six months of language study. There was not a great deal of obstetric work initially as Moslem men did not want their wives to come to a Christian hospital, even though there was no other hospital anywhere nearby. If I had time on my hands, I would help out on the general side of the hospital.

Slowly the obstetric work grew from four beds to eight, then to twelve and eventually we needed a whole ward to ourselves of twenty eight beds and all our own facilities except the operating theatres. My staff also increased—firstly to three and then four midwives with eight trainee national assistant midwives. We taught them on a one-to-one basis, each according to her ability to learn and at her own pace.

My house was one half of a duplex, in other words semi-detached as we call it here in the UK. Just six weeks after I arrived at Galmi, a thief broke in while I was called to the hospital one evening and stole all my linen, cutlery, food, radio and cassette player. So for the rest of that term I had to borrow everything except food.

Niger has a very different climate from Congo. The dry season lasted nine months and even in the wet season rainfall was unpredictable. When it did rain, frogs, earwigs, crickets and flies appeared in profusion. There were sandstorms too, which covered everything in sand, unless it was covered up. The dry season had hot and cold phases. During the hot phase, as I have already mentioned, the temperature could reach 50°c, whereas in the cold phase temperatures would drop to 15°c at night, maybe rising to 22°c during the day. In the cold season the harmattan, a dust-laden cold wind would often blow for long periods, and the dust seemed to get in everywhere.

Market day was Wednesday, and if possible we would go and buy fresh meat, nearly always beef. The animal would have been killed only that morning, although by the time we bought it there were flies all over it. We could also buy onions, which were grown locally and apparently also exported to surrounding countries. Sometimes there were tomatoes, but they were rather tasteless. When we needed to stock up with any items that we could not buy at the market, someone would have to make the long 8–10 hour trip by road to the capital, Niamey. We would naturally buy in bulk, using large refrigerators that ran on kerosene and we cooked with butane gas.

Our work in the maternity ward increased weekly, and we found that 50% of our cases were very abnormal—usually seconded to us from government maternities, and our expertise in dealing with these cases developed. Many of the conditions I had to deal with are virtually unknown in our country, where we have adequate pre-natal clinics and health checks. It was not unusual to have to deal with over 100 women in one morning at the clinic, with only two midwives and maybe two assistant midwives. Outpatient departments were even more overworked, maybe 200–300 a morning. All the patients heard the gospel before the actual clinics began, and sometimes again half way through the morning as fresh faces appeared. Our working day, therefore, could be a long one—7am to 6pm or even later if a very abnormal case came in, and we were frequently on call at night.

On Sundays we tried to reduce the workload to absolute essentials only, leaving the minimum number of staff on duty so the rest of us could get to church. In the evening we had a time of fellowship on the compound in English which was always a very precious time.

My church at Hook was very faithful in writing letters, sending tapes and cards, so I was kept well informed of events there. As for our spiritual lives, we faced the same type of temptations as non-missionary Christians, but living in a small, almost closed, community, we had to learn to keep short accounts with one another. We learnt to say sorry much more quickly, and we also learnt how very much we need the constant cleansing of the blood of Christ. We held prayer meetings on the compound six days a week at 6.30am, lasting for half an hour, so we had to get up at 5am if we wanted a quiet time before the day began, as most of us were on duty by 7am or 7.15am.

In the national church, the standards were low compared to what we are used to in the West, but they did their best, which is all God requires of them. There was a lot of restlessness in the services, which is hardly surprising. Deep concentration is not always easy either in temperatures of 50°c or when a gale-force dusty wind is blowing through the glass-less windows. The music was often off-key and the singing could be raucous. Consequently, many of us found it hard not to weep during our first service at home when on home assignment.

My first furlough from Niger was in 1981. It was strange to be back in Britain without my parents or a home of my own, but Hook Evangelical Church very graciously rented a house for me, furnished it, and even provided me with a car for the whole year. When I first committed myself to God for full-time service, I received the promise, 'My God shall supply all your need according to his riches in glory by Christ Jesus.' (Phil 4:19) and not once has he ever failed. He has been so wonderful. To record all his faithfulness to me would require another book.

When I returned from my home assignment in 1981, conditions began to improve in Galmi. Electricity became available 24 hours a day, which enabled us to use air-conditioning and fans. A French drilling firm came and sunk a well, so deep that the water came out at 40°c all the time, and it was really soft and clean. Fresh vegetables were sold on the compound by men who brought them from farms in Nigeria. More staff came, and by the time my second term was over and I was due to retire, we had a compound of 32 houses, sometimes with as many as seven or eight different nationalities living in them.

Nationals began to take over the departments, with the missionaries working alongside or under them. The church in Niger has become stronger, and is still growing slowly. There have been problems, but God is still in control and is working out his purposes in his own time.

I was now coming to the end of my professional working life abroad, so where was I to live? God in his infinite love burdened Hook Evangelical Church to buy a small maisonette for me just four minutes from the church, and I was able to move in the same day I arrived home. My initial reaction was to cry; how good God is to supply every need! When I had dried my tears and returned my thanks to God, I investigated the flat, and found a tea-tray ready by the kettle, cupboards full of food, and even the bed was made! I felt very humbled. Such love and thoughtfulness had gone into all these preparations. A neighbour told me of the army of workers who had redecorated every room, while others followed unpacking my things and storing them in cupboards. Apparently another neighbour who had watched all this said, 'You'd think the Queen was coming!' I really felt like the Queen, though I wonder whether even she gets such a reception!

Much water has gone under the bridge since my final return to England. I was able to go back to the hospital and relieve a couple of missionaries who were on furlough, and afterwards I obtained a post locally in a high-dependency unit until I finally retired in 1997.

'There hath not failed one word of all his good promise.' (1 Kings 8:56) Every one has been fulfilled. It is with great awe that I look back on the events recorded in this book, and I just want to worship and praise the Lord for his leading and providential care. To him be all the glory!